Earning Their Wings

Earning Their

SARAH PARRY MYERS

Wings

THE WASPS OF WORLD WAR II

AND THE FIGHT FOR VETERAN

RECOGNITION

The University of North Carolina Press Chapel Hill

Set in Utopia and Klavika
by Jamie McKee, MacKey Composition
Manufactured in the United States of America

Cover photo courtesy of WASP Archive, the TWU Libraries'
Woman's Collection, Texas Woman's University, Denton, TX.

Library of Congress Cataloging-in-Publication Data
Names: Myers, Sarah Parry, author.
Title: Earning their wings : the WASPs of World War II and the fight
    for veteran recognition / Sarah Parry Myers.
Description: Chapel Hill : The University of North Carolina Press,
    [2023] | Includes bibliographical references and index.
Identifiers: LCCN 2023014323 | ISBN 9781469675022 (cloth) | ISBN
    9781469675039 (paperback) | ISBN 9781469675046 (ebook)
Subjects: LCSH: Women Airforce Service Pilots (U.S.)—History. |
    World War, 1939-1945—United States—Participation, Female. |
    Women air pilots—United States—History—20th century. |
    Women veterans—United States—History—20th century. |
    BISAC: HISTORY / Wars & Conflicts / World War II / General |
    HISTORY / Military / Veterans
Classification: LCC D790.5 .M94 2023 | DDC 940.54/4973—dc23/
    eng/20230403
LC record available at https://lccn.loc.gov/2023014323

For my dear friend

Jaime Sandhaus Rantanen

(1985–2013)

and to the WASPs and their families

who so generously welcomed me into

their homes and lives

Contents

Earning Their Wings

Introduction

Florence "Shutsy" Reynolds wanted to fly from the time she was seven years old. Her first introduction to the world of aviation was watching a pilot land a World War I–era Curtiss JN-4 "Jenny" plane in a local farmer's field near her family's home in Connellsville, Pennsylvania. Later, when an airport was built in Connellsville, her family spent Sundays watching the planes take off and land. In this era, flying was still a novelty for most Americans, many of whom had never seen an airplane. For those who were interested in aviation, flying was an expensive hobby or career pursuit. Paying for flying lessons or classes was outside the realm of possibility for many until a government program opened during the Great Depression.

After high school, Reynolds read in the newspaper that the government was opening a Civilian Pilot Training Program (CPTP), with free local ground-school classes to teach the basics of flying, including aircraft-operation procedures, navigation, and federal flying regulations, to civilians. Five students with the highest exam scores at the end of the course received scholarships for thirty-five flying hours. Remarking on her exam score in an interview, Reynolds proclaimed, "Was I surprised when I was one of the five? You better believe it!"[1] In order to receive the scholarship, she signed a statement that if the United States entered the war, she would join the military. Just a week later, she learned her scholarship was being revoked and given to a man, presumably because, in the words of one flight instructor, "Women don't go to war. Women don't fly."[2]

Reynolds received her scholarship at a time when the United States was still trying to catch up from years of isolation. The Axis powers were continually gaining ground and airspaces around the world. Still hopeful, Reynolds appealed to one of her Senate representatives for help, and he was able to get her scholarship reinstated. With the flying hours acquired, she wrote a letter to female aviator Jacqueline Cochran to ask about a recently advertised new women's pilot program within the Army Air Force (AAF) that would eventually be called the Women's Airforce Service Pilots (WASP).[3] Turned down because she was nineteen and the current minimum age requirement was twenty-one, Shutsy had to wait. Fortunately

1

for her, the age requirement of the program decreased from twenty-one to eighteen, and she reported for duty on December 7, 1943, the second anniversary of the bombing of Pearl Harbor, at the age of twenty. Her motivation for joining the WASP came from a desire to fly and a longing to serve her country. Raised in a self-described "patriotic family," Shutsy grew up learning about her uncle who died in combat during World War I, and her brother, Aloysius "A.J." Shutsy, was already serving in the US Merchant Marines at the time of her entrance into the WASP program.

As soon as war broke out in Europe in 1939, two famous female aviators, Jacqueline "Jackie" Cochran and Nancy Harkness Love, looked for ways to pursue aviation to aid the war effort. Separately, they actively petitioned their military and government personal connections to create women's pilot programs.[4] The AAF gave Cochran and Love authority to create two women's pilot programs that eventually merged to become the WASP. The purpose of these undertakings was to fulfill a need for pilots to perform work on the home front as increasing numbers of men served overseas. Love's program, the Women's Auxiliary Ferrying Squadron (WAFS), comprised twenty-eight highly skilled, seasoned pilots who had already flown over 500 hours. Assigned to the Air Transport Command, they ferried planes between factories and bases and only received brief military instruction. Cochran's initiative, the Women's Flying Training Detachment (WFTD), was for less experienced pilots with at least 200 flying hours. Except for combat maneuvers, they would take the same training as male pilots entering the AAF. Stationed at AAF bases within the continental United States, some members of the WFTD fulfilled assignments including ferrying planes, towing targets for male cadets to prepare for combat, and testing new wartime technologies or mechanics' repairs on planes.

At first, the AAF designated these programs "experiments," as there were stereotypes about women's capabilities as military aircraft pilots; these planes required physical strength, acumen, and specialized training to fly. This labeling of experimental aligns with the ways women's bodies have historically been used as an excuse to exclude them from specific military roles or combat.[5] Furthermore, since American women were flying military planes for the first time, the AAF emphasized that these pilot programs were a wartime necessity, as women were releasing men for combat. Other countries, including Germany, Great Britain, Romania, and the Soviet Union, also turned to female pilots due to wartime shortages of men. Women from all over the world volunteered to ferry aircraft in the British

Air Transport Auxiliary (ATA), and female Soviet pilots performed similar work and even served in combat. In Romania, women flew in an all-female unit for the Sanitary Squadron. While they did not fly in combat, their missions took them into combat zones where they flew soldiers wounded on the Eastern Front.[6] Germany's female pilots served as ferry pilots, test pilots, and glider instructors.[7] In the United States, a total of 1,102 women officially served as WASPs, not including 11 trainees who lost their lives during AAF training, out of the approximately 350,000 American women who served in the US military during the war.[8]

American female pilots could not fly in combat but could fly on dangerous missions. When she arrived at Merced Army Airfield in California, Shutsy Reynolds introduced herself to the commanding officer (CO), who informed her that he had not requested a WASP for his airfield and that she was "not welcome." She ended up stationed there for the duration of the war, and the CO's parting comments to her included a statement about how impressed he was with her work. At Merced, Reynolds flew personnel, materiel, and essential documents, but she also performed some of the dangerous work assigned to the WASPs, such as ferrying aircraft in need of significant repairs and transporting recently repaired planes. When flight-testing these aircraft, she identified repairs and ensured that no additional maintenance was needed before male pilots flew the planes on military bases or in combat.[9] Another dangerous mission flown by many WASPs was towing targets so male cadets could practice shooting live ammunition.

In general, military flying was risky—not just because of specific assignments but also due to the more extensive history of flight. New technologies consistently developed throughout the war, and much of the flying required physical strength rather than automation. For Shutsy Reynolds, her first sobering experience with the dangerous nature of military flying occurred less than a month after graduating from AAF training. One of her friends and classmates, Beverly Jean Moses, died while completing a cross-country flight due to an "aircraft malfunction."[10] After hearing about that accident and later witnessing a fatal airplane crash, Reynolds vowed never to visit another crash site. As a pilot, she wanted to retain her confidence and focus on flying rather than replaying fatal accidents in her mind.

During a memorial service for Moses, Reynolds learned from Beverly's mother that, as civilians, the WASPs were not entitled to military funeral honors. Their families could not display gold stars on the banners hung in windows to symbolize the loss of a family member in the armed forces.

Without military insurance, many of the families of the thirty-eight WASP casualties during the war received disturbing news that they were responsible for shipping their daughters' or wives' bodies back home. Fear of a public backlash to these wartime casualties and women's participation in the military led the AAF to limit female pilots' wartime assignments to the continental United States or immediate surrounding areas of Puerto Rico, Cuba, and Canada.[11]

In July 1943, the AAF affirmed the competence of the female pilots with their decision to merge the WAFS and the WFTD to form the WASP. Pilot training was a cost-intensive endeavor for the military. The armed forces' investment in women's training reveals their confidence that female pilots could be trusted to fly expensive government property. After the program's conclusion, the WASPs had piloted every type of aircraft used in the AAF and had flown over 60 million miles with equivalent "stamina and endurance" as male pilots, as well as a comparable "flying safety record."[12]

Despite its successes, the AAF shut down the WASP program on December 20, 1944—eight months before the end of the war. Before that point, Congress had already passed legislation to grant military status to all of the female units except the WASP: the Women's Army Corps (WAC), the navy's Women Accepted for Voluntary Emergency Service (WAVES), the Marine Corps Women's Reserve, and the United States Coast Guard Women's Reserve (SPARS, named for the coast guard's motto, *Semper Paratus*). As the WASP was the last female unit to go before Congress, the AAF assumed the bill would pass. Several theories explain the congressional rejection of the WASP militarization bill (as in, the legislation that brought military benefits via veteran status).[13] Sociologist Molly Merryman argues that the 1940s bill failed because of gendered fears surrounding women's military participation, since the WASPs performed highly skilled work in male-dominated spaces.[14] Additional considerations within the historical context also warrant consideration. Notably, Congress debated the bill just as the government shut down the CPTP and its male pilot instructors became eligible for the draft. As the smallest and only women's military unit that did not receive military status, the WASPs are largely absent from the historical memory of the war. After the program's conclusion, the WASPs waited over thirty years before finally receiving military status in 1977, during debates over definitions of the term "veteran."

During World War II, women filled men's positions in wartime work across industries previously inaccessible to female and minority employees. They served in the US military on military status for the first time on a large scale and in every branch.[15] The first American women officially designated veterans were the 223 US Army Signal Corps operators who served with the American Expeditionary Forces in France during World War I.[16] (Interestingly, they received veteran status in 1977, decades after the war, on the same bill as the WASPs.) Nurses who served during World War I also did not have rank or military status during the conflict.[17]

As in other industries and military branches, the stated purpose of women's newfound roles as pilots was to replace men for other duties, including combat. In her "My Day" column on September 1, 1942, Eleanor Roosevelt urged the American Civil Air Patrol and Ferry Command to use women pilots to help secure an Allied victory: "We are in a war and need to fight it with all our ability and every weapon possible. Women pilots, in this particular case, are a weapon waiting to be used."[18] She argued American women pilots could contribute to the war effort as British women were in the ATA in England. She also challenged the Civil Aeronautics Administration's (CAA's) conclusion that women were somehow psychologically unfit for flying military aircraft.[19] By the time Americans read Roosevelt's article, the AAF had already started planning the programs that eventually became the WASP,[20] but it did not yet see female pilots as a useful weapon. The Army Air Force viewed women as experimental temporary substitutes whose presence in the male-dominated military was a threat in need of regulation.[21] Any missteps, let alone slanderous rumors like the ones the WAC experienced, could lead to the disbandment of the program and tarnish the image of the AAF.[22]

Nevertheless, the WASPs saw themselves as *weapons waiting to be used* to avenge men's deaths overseas. Scholars have employed emotion as a historical lens, examining the ways that emotions like grief, hatred, and love fuel war efforts.[23] In the case of the WASPs, some channeled grief over lost family members, including those who died in military service, as well as hatred of the enemy and a desire to help the Allies win the war. Others experienced excitement and joy at the opportunity to fly advanced military aircraft at high altitudes for the first time. This sensory experience was a privilege reserved for military pilots and one that the WASPs enjoyed during the program's short duration.[24] They described the feel, sounds, sight, and smell of military aircraft and high-altitudinal flying. These emotions were a source of motivation on long days of AAF assignment, and the feeling of flying bombers, pursuits, and other aircraft shaped the women's experiences and the construction of meaning in their memories after the war.

The AAF used female pilots as gendered weapons and later cast them aside after the WASPs accomplished their mission of replacing male pilots serving overseas.[25] Amid private and public debates about the capabilities of their physicality, sexuality, and intellect, the WASPs threatened and upset definitions of military service, an emerging image of an elite male AAF, and what it meant to be a hero. Despite the nature of their work, promises of military status, and their identity as military pilots, these women's veteran status remained unfulfilled in the postwar period. Even though the WASPs fought to be taken seriously as skilled pilots, aviation was firmly established as a masculine field by the end of the war. Women pilots' military and aviation acumen and courage were trivialized as a novelty, which masked their dangerous roles and undermined their place as professionals in altitudinal spaces, a place that had seemed possible before the war.[26] Ultimately, *Earning Their Wings* argues that WASPs battled male resistance and denigration of their abilities within contested airspaces while creating a military sisterhood and an identity as pilots, which they harnessed in the 1970s to fight for their rights to the title "veteran."[27]

Sources, including over 200 untapped oral history interviews, military songs and folklore, scrapbooks, and other aspects of military culture such as classbooks and newsletters, provide a multidimensional study of these female pilots and their experiences.[28] Oral histories are one of the few sources that illuminate the women pilots' veteran identity, as well as the sensory experience of flying military aircraft, the phenomenon of female pilots of color passing as white, and aviators' opinions on women's liberation and accounts of dating. The insights gleaned from these interviews are woven into the text through observations of the ways women experienced wartime flight and viewed their service. While letters home and WASP newsletters also contain some of this information, oral histories allow for a more nuanced view. Most of the interviews used in this study are life-history interviews with an emphasis on the women's military service.[29] Oral historians discuss how memory is "socially, culturally, and psychically constructed," and the interviewing practice is less about gathering data for interpretation and more about engaging with "experience, subjectivity, and historical imagination."[30] Individual memories are often "rooted in places," as in the WASPs' shared identity from their AAF training experiences in Sweetwater, Texas, the primary site for their instruction.[31] Furthermore, while some interviews present a similar narrative that the WASPs constructed during their fight for militarization in the 1970s, the women's sensory and emotional experiences provide experiential insights.[32] In analyzing these oral histories, I intended to avoid romanticizing these aviators and perpetuating the "Greatest Generation" myth.[33]

This history of American female pilots fits within a larger narrative of military service and citizenship in US history, and the implications of definitions of "hero" and "veteran" in American society and culture. Often contemporary sources turn on the gendered portrayal of men during wartime as heroes fighting to protect women, their families, and the home front.[34] Historically, coverture laws, including the exclusion of women from the "obligations of citizenship" such as the draft and combat, rendered women "more vulnerable to other forms of public and private power."[35] Furthermore, serving in the US military was not just an *obligation of citizenship* for men; wartime service offered them a perceived opportunity to protect their homes from the enemy and experience the benefits of citizenship.[36] While military service is linked to citizenship in societies, servicewomen's and servicemen's participation in the armed forces can contribute to the militarization of individuals, groups, and societies.[37] Militarization is "the degree to which a society's institutions, policies, behaviors, thoughts, and values are devoted to military power and shaped by war."[38] The militarization of American culture during World War II resulted in a continued emphasis on conventional gender norms.[39] The WASPs are situated in this context of rising militarization during World War II, as they often served out of patriotic or nationalist motivations, including a desire to avenge men's deaths overseas.

Definitions of citizenship remained gendered and racialized during the war, as the ideal citizen-soldier in the public's mind remained a white man who served overseas, presumably in combat. To assert claims to citizenship, white women and military men and women of color and nonheterosexual orientations had to combat stereotypes, and they often worked to cultivate an image of respectability.[40] (However, decades after World War II, many women and men of color doubted military service as a path to citizenship.)[41] This wartime service was situated within the Double V Campaign for many Black Americans as they pressed for victory abroad for the Allies and for full equality and citizenship at home. Black men who served in the armed forces wanted to illuminate the "contradictions" of the Jim Crow military while proving their abilities.[42] Women and Black men's complete or partial exclusion from specific martial roles during World War II "excluded them from [the] band of brothers . . . where manhood and citizenship were defined."[43] This exclusion was due to "historical constructions of the military as a bastion of white male power."[44] There were also restrictive definitions of the term "hero" depending on the military occupation of servicemen and servicewomen.

Those who lost their lives in service for their country did not automatically receive heroic status in the American media or public, depending on the context of the death and nature of service. Often, lives lost overseas, particularly in combat, were considered more heroic in terms of media coverage, the memory of the war, and even conversations with Americans who lived or served during the war. The term "hero" was most often reserved for those who served in the military, as in the example of male conscientious objectors who performed essential work fighting forest fires on the home front yet were labeled cowards and draft dodgers.[45] While combat experience has historically been linked with definitions of masculinity and heroism, there are exceptions with regard to World War II male combat pilots. When these men experienced psychological trauma that rendered them unable to continue to fly, even they faced accusations of "cowardice."[46]

Although they served in the military, the thirty-eight WASPs who lost their lives in service to their country did not receive recognition of their wartime deeds. (The American public even today has largely forgotten its servicewomen, and there are few names of female veterans in the popular memory.) The US Merchant Marines, one of whom was Reynolds's brother, serve as an example of these narrow definitions of a hero. Serving in the navy on a civilian status, they shipped supplies and equipment to support US troops worldwide during the war. Despite their civilian status, the merchant marines followed navy rules and regulations and eventually received veteran status and benefits in the 1980s. Because of the dangerous nature of their wartime work, they suffered high casualties, but they were largely unrecognized in the American public and remained largely hidden in the memory of the war. For the WASPs, their civilian rather than veteran status kept them from the benefits of citizenship in the postwar period. Their heroism was masked, and the abrupt conclusion of the program was accentuated with a failed militarization bill. The majority of these women could not pursue the aviation careers they desired, and they left military spaces to return home, where they often felt unfulfilled.[47]

Situated within the recently emerging field of veterans studies, the WASP story illuminates debates around veterans benefits and homecoming transitions after war.[48] The term "veteran" is not easily defined or categorized but instead is contested. Furthermore, veteran struggles for social welfare provide insights into the intersections between civilian politics and the military.[49] These debates conjure questions of what a country owes its veterans, something Mark Boulton calls "putting a price on patriotism."[50] Since the origin of the United States, the federal government has concluded that service in the military is an obligation of citizenship, and therefore veterans are not automatically owed certain benefits. However, if veterans experience combat, particularly if they suffer a disability, they deserve compensation for their sacrifice.[51]

After the war, the WASPs missed the dynamic work culture of military life. They maintained a strong camaraderie during their annual reunions and efforts to keep in contact after the war. This reminiscing fulfills the emotional desires of veterans and their military sisterhood, and it shows the ways military men and women build a sense of community, regardless of their involvement in combat overseas.[52] When the WASPs fought for veteran status in the 1970s, some organizations constructed their representations of veterans in direct opposition to the female pilots. In the process, male veterans situated themselves as stakeholders of the title "veteran." For the WASPs, the fight for military benefits and recognition as veterans brought them closer to full citizenship and challenged the perceptions of the military as a hypermasculine space.

While their motivations for joining the military in World War II were varied and diverse, women were forced to confront societal ideas about military service and the citizen-soldier. Historians and scholars of gender and conflict have discussed people's reasons for fighting, but they have not explored the ways men and women negotiate claims to heroism. The public's memory of war has largely been gendered male, and the term "veteran" often conjures up images of men.[53] The media undermined women's roles and their status as professionals in the civilian and military sectors.[54] This inaccurate and displaced representation perpetuates the myth of men as protectors of women, often specifically white women, and as true heroes of war, regardless of the extent of their wartime service.[55] Other narratives illuminate this myth: men in the army spread inaccurate rumors about servicewomen in the WAC, and male civilian pilots propagated inaccuracies about female pilots in the WASP program. A wartime army investigation revealed that men within its ranks feared their draft into combat as WACs continued to fill noncombat assignments.[56] Male civilian pilots lost their draft deferment in 1944, and they argued that they deserved the assignments currently filled by the WASPs.

A love of flying, a hope for an aviation career, and a desire to help with the war effort motivated the women who became the WASPs.[57] While the scholarship on men's inducements for joining the military and fighting in combat is extensive and provides theoretical frameworks for this analysis of women pilots' motivations, works on women's motives in American wars primarily exclude their professional ones.[58] The media praised women who disguised themselves as men to fight in the Civil War due to patriotism or a desire to be with their men. In contrast, newspaper accounts demonized women who fought for a sense of adventure in society. Thus, women were required to portray gendered behavior even on the battlefield.[59] The WASPs also possessed a sense of adventure, and this was one way they constructed an identity as pilots.[60]

Women's reasons for joining the AAF offer insights into gendered debates within families about women in the field of aviation and the military and expectations for women in World War II–era America. Older generations of women in families, including great-aunts, grandmas, and even mothers, often disapproved of women flying. They believed aviation, now identified with the military, was not an appropriate career choice for women. Pilots who trained in the WASP program came from diverse social and class backgrounds, and they had to pass as white.[61] Most were able to accumulate the required hours needed for the program due to the free training offered through the government's CPTP.[62] The WASPs all shared a love of flying, and the majority decided to fly after their childhood experiences with early women aviators or barnstormers. Named for the farms that they landed their small aircraft in, barnstormers provided entertainment for people in rural America as they performed aerial stunts and took passengers on flights. For many, these pilots were their first encounter with aviation. Female barnstormers believed altitude was a *natural* space for women and would foster equality of the sexes in American society. The WASPs were also motivated by their professional desires to fly in the military. Regardless of their reasons for joining, they faced expectations and assumptions about their roles as women in the military.

In World War II, the American media, government, and military expected women to fill many varied and divergent roles in society. Asked to be faithful wives, mothers, or daughters by supporting the troops, they were encouraged to serve their country through their wartime work, and even to provide sexualized pinup images to men as motivation for fighting the enemy.[63] The media's message to women was self-sacrifice, serving to support men rather than pursue career goals, and this message emphasized that new work or roles were temporary, only for the duration of the war.[64] The same was true for women internationally, as they traded nationalism for long-term career advancement or watched as they fell short of full citizenship in the postwar era.[65] Popular graphic art depicting women serving their country both illuminated and calmed social anxieties about shifting gender roles, female masculinity, and definitions of the ideal woman.[66] There was even a cartoon strip, *Flyin' Jenny*, featuring a female pilot who competed with male pilots professionally but fit propaganda stereotypes with her blond hair, makeup, and pinup body type. Called a "lipstick pilot" in the strip, she helped Americans adjust to women's entrance into nontraditional work.[67] Wartime beauty standards emphasized femininity through dress, hairstyles, and makeup as a form of patriotism, asking women to "make themselves into something worth fighting for."[68]

There were similar expectations of attractiveness, femininity, and morality for other women in the military to detract from their nontraditional roles. Deemed "angels," nurses were viewed as performing safe, traditional work, and home front propaganda depicted them as sacrificial, caring, and feminine. In reality, many nurses served overseas in spaces near enemy fire, and those stationed in the Philippines were prisoners of war from the fall of Bataan in 1942 until early 1945.[69] There were debates about the extent of women's roles in the military and fears of women in military uniform within this wartime context. The American public and armed forces often viewed women's sexuality as deviant or dangerous.[70] For the WASP program, director Jacqueline Cochran created additional entrance and training requirements beyond those expected of male air force pilots to combat the gendered debates about women in the military and aviation.[71] She wanted an image of the WASPs that eased the American public's fears about the sexuality and morality of women in such a masculine environment.

The concept of altitude as contested space has been present in histories since the origin of flight, but it is one that historians have not fully articulated. In US history, pilots, commercial airlines, the military, politicians, and journalists have described high altitudes as spaces to enjoy, conquer, control, and occupy. Air traffic controllers monitor the spaces above airports, military bases, and aircraft carriers to ensure safety. Numerous historians have written on the sky as a battlefield or the space race of the Cold War, debating boundaries and "freedom of space" with the role of satellites in military intelligence.[72] President Franklin D. Roosevelt described altitude as space in a congratulatory letter he sent to Amelia Earhart after her historic flight from Hawaii to California in January 1935. He compared aviation pioneers to advocates of Manifest Destiny in the nineteenth century. As he explained, "And now, when air trails between our shores and those of our neighbors are being charted, you, as a woman, have preserved and carried forward this precious tradition."[73]

With the growth of the aviation industry and the importance of airplanes strategically in World War II, companies, militaries, and societies began envisioning their goals for the control or occupation of the skies. In April 1943, *Fortune* magazine argued that the world was no longer "divided by land and sea," declaring, "The air is a blue-water ocean to which every nation potentially has access for trade and high strategy in all directions."[74] Early pilots also described the sky as a physical space with experiences different from those on Earth or in society.

From the early decades of flying through World War II, female pilots described the realm of the air as a unique space filled with career opportunities and a means of women's liberation. Even though the US military excluded female pilots from the 1910s through the early 1940s, and civilian media coverage portrayed women as surprising novelties, these early aviators actively referenced the air as a site of future equality for all.[75] Those who flew in the 1920s embodied the modern women in their pursuit of adventure, liberation, and technology. While historians have discussed flappers, actors, and female drivers, they have ignored early women pilots.[76] Women pilots fit the adventurous archetype of the modern woman as they lived life recklessly, defied social constructs, and sought liberating experiences in the region of the air. Although historian Joseph Corn argues that, by the late 1930s, there were no additional aviation opportunities for women, the history of the WASP program illuminates the fact that World War II gendered flying a male-dominated field.[77]

World War II brought opportunities for women to fly at higher altitudes with more powerful aircraft. The WASPs described these bigger, sometimes faster aircraft as transporting them to a beautiful space that they could only access because of their assignments in the military. This concept of altitude as contested space pushes the boundaries of histories that explore the work culture of flight attendants and their struggles for rights within their work environment of airplanes.[78] Jenifer Van Vleck argues that the *empire of the air* was a domain of American imperialism and expansion in the decades after World War II.[79] She cites the geographic space of the air as a realm for American influence, similar to Michael S. Sherry's description of aviation as a "vertical frontier in American history."[80] This book argues that the air was also a space where fraught debates of gender roles and definitions of the ideal military veteran were contested and reimagined. The WASPs asserted their place as professionals within contested airspaces as they confronted male resistance and gendered debates about their abilities.[81]

The WASPs also operated within new military spaces, and their shared training experiences serve as a basis for understanding their work culture of camaraderie and their identity as pilots in a unique realm dedicated to training only women pilots.[82] They formed a military sisterhood in response to military life, flying the "army way" and situating themselves as weapons of war. Their identities were those of pilots, women, and military personnel within the hierarchy of AAF. Aaron O'Connell's interpretation of Benedict Anderson's imagined communities as including military brotherhood serves as a framework for this discussion.[83] As the WASPs transitioned from the predominantly female space of training to the male-dominated AAF bases, they intrusively threatened and upset notions of masculinity and heroism due to the dangerous work they performed, and the emerging image of an elite male air force.[84]

Female pilots' presence in the male-dominated space of the air force reflects trends similar to women's participation in technological fields and other professions previously deemed masculine.[85] While women in industrial jobs were also forced out of work in the postwar period, the WASPs presented a unique dynamic thanks to their presence in a masculine realm defined by courage, prowess, and rational intellect. The WASPs were intentionally placed in specific assignments due to male pilots' desire to risk their lives overseas, presumably more heroically, rather than on the home front. In addition, male pilots and AAF officials emphasized gendered assumptions about the WASPs instead of acknowledging their actual abilities, just as early twentieth-century male drivers dismissed women's technological skills as luck.[86] The WASPs developed strategies to confront this resistance while at the same time attempting to carve a space as professionals in a military and technological realm. They also worked in spaces literally made for men, as wartime cockpits and accessories fit average-sized men's bodies.[87] Ultimately, commercial and military aviation became male-dominated careers by the end of the war, and women could not fly military aircraft again until the 1970s.[88]

Although the government, media, and military described the WASP program as experimental, women were civilian pilots in the decades before World War II. Chapter 1, "'I Was Happiest in the Sky': From Air-Minded Barnstormers to Weapons of War," situates the WASP program within this larger historical context to argue that aviation offered opportunities for women and perceived equality. The chapter begins with a discussion of the broader history of flying, including opportunities for women in aviation and their work selling the safety of flight to the American public. Most of the WASPs were inspired by these early aviators and entertainers, although some worked in air shows before joining the WASP program. These women epitomized a 1920s modern or new woman for their pursuit of adventure, liberation, and technology. Furthermore, two of these early women pilots, Nancy Love and Jaqueline Cochran, started the programs that became the WASP.

Although women pilots in the 1920s and 1930s were from relatively wealthy families since paying for flying hours was expensive, many of them had families who could not financially support their flying. Instead, they earned their licenses and accumulated flying experience as they worked extra hours or through the CPTP. Overall, a love of flying and a desire for careers in aviation motivated and drove the women who arrived in Texas for AAF training. With the start of World War II, women were essential to filling rapidly expanding roles on the home front and overseas. Female pilots were eager to use their valuable aviation skills professionally and in a patriotic capacity, as many applied for the WASP program. They hoped their pilot training would allow them to serve their country as dangerous weapons in the war.

When entering the WASP program, women received instruction in a primarily female environment at airfields in Houston and Sweetwater, Texas. Chapter 2, "'We Live in the Wind and Sand, and Our Eyes are on the Stars': Identity and Camaraderie in Training," explores the ways that the WASP program fostered camaraderie and their identity as pilots in this unique military space dedicated to training only women aviators. However, this female space remained an oddity in the military, as the AAF was male dominated. Creating and maintaining traditions such as the "Our eyes are on the stars" motto, class songs, pilot rituals, and newsletters formed a military sisterhood that fostered trainees' successes while challenging definitions of military personnel.

Fear of military women's sexuality led the AAF to institute additional gendered rules and regulations for the WASPs to follow. Because of the threatening nature of military femininity explored by scholars of gender and war, these guidelines went beyond those given to male trainees.[89] The WASPs actively fought gendered assumptions about the limitations of their bodies, intelligence, and psychological abilities as they fought their way to graduation and demonstrated their flying skills. In an era when a woman in military uniform was considered controversial, the WASPs wore theirs proudly as a sign of their hard work. As WASP trainees donned their uniforms after graduation, they constructed an identity that denoted status, citizenship, and the language of the military. With the completion of training, the WASPs faced magnified gendered assumptions about their abilities as they left the all-female base in Sweetwater and entered male-dominated bases across the United States. Furthermore, the elite group of women who graduated from training had proved their ability to adeptly fly military aircraft and now had the opportunity to put their newly acquired skills to use.

After training, the WASPs moved into the male-dominated spaces of over 120 bases around the continental United States. They served in assignments including ferrying, towing targets, instructing, and test piloting. The third chapter, "'Looked upon as a Man's Game': Battling Contested Airspaces at Army Air Force Bases," argues that the WASPs maintained their identity as military pilots and fought to be taken seriously as professionals. Although they battled in this contested airspace of aviation, where courage, prowess, and rational intellect were essential, they remained anomalies to many AAF officials who deemed them an experiment for the duration of the war. Furthermore, female pilots' work in the AAF in dangerous home front assignments challenged definitions of what it means to be a hero. The categorization of their duties as women's work masked the dangers and skills essential to wartime flying behind a facade of novelty. These issues challenged the work culture and solidarity that the WASPs built during training. As the WASPs remained scattered at different AAF bases, they maintained networks with one another. They bonded as they developed strategies to prove their professionalism and rights to altitudinal spaces.

The fourth chapter, "'Not One of Congress's Cares': The 1944 Congressional Militarization Bill," analyzes the restrictions on women's citizenship through the debates surrounding the congressional militarization bill of the 1940s. Despite women's wartime successes piloting every type of aircraft available in the AAF with an aptitude similar to men's, congressmen viewed the WASP program as a threat to gender roles, and they chose to listen to falsified testimony rather than the testimony of top AAF officials. The 1944 militarization bill failed in Congress due to numerous factors, including the media's coverage, the conclusion of the War Training Service, which left male pilot instructors eligible for combat, and the actions of Jacqueline Cochran. The WASP program disbanded without military status or benefits, and women were excluded from military flying until the early 1970s. This disbandment left high altitudes as spaces literally for men, who now also dominated jet and space aviation.

The final chapter, "'I Never Flew an Airplane That Asked If I Were a Mr. or a Mrs. or a Ms.': Contesting Definitions of a Veteran and Receiving Veterans Status," tells the story of how in the 1970s, while the country was reacting to the women's liberation movement and the Vietnam War, veterans organizations fought against the WASPs to protect definitions of heroic military service and the title of "veteran." In this fight for veteran status, the WASPs organized and executed strategies to prove the military nature of the program. They contested notions of what it meant to be a veteran as they fought for their access to full citizenship and the title "veteran."

The story of the WASPs has ramifications for understanding today's issues of women's equality and citizenship in America's society and military.[90] The lifting of the Combat Exclusion Policy and the first female graduates from the US Army Ranger School illuminate the fact that military women still face the same stereotypical concerns over issues of protection, sexuality, and their ability to meet specific standards. While President Joe Biden signed an executive order that repealed the Trump-era ban on transgender people's enlistment in the US military, and the Pentagon issued new policies in 2021, cultural change in the armed forces takes time. As weapons of war, women and transgender individuals are still battling against gendered assumptions, sexual harassment, and discrimination, while their rights to military spaces, including combat, elite combat forces, and even burial at Arlington National Cemetery, are in a constant state of experimentation and negotiation.[91]

1 I Was Happiest in the Sky
From Air-Minded Barnstormers to Weapons of War

I was happiest in the sky—at dawn when the quietness of the air was like a caress, when the noon sun beat down, and at dusk when the sky was drenched with the fading light.
—Cornelia Fort, 1942

In the early decades of flying, female pilots viewed the field of aviation as a space filled with opportunities for women. As Fort's sentiment reflects, the realm of the air was a space of beauty and liberation for female aviators. The experience of flying or observing airplanes in the sky drew many Americans to become interested in flight in the decades before the United States' entrance into the Second World War in 1941. Fort's quote illuminates a love of flying that united women pilots from the early days of aviation to the women's pilot programs of World War II. A wealthy southerner from Nashville, Cornelia Fort was the first female flight instructor in Tennessee. Working as a flight instructor in Hawaii in 1941, she was in the air with one of her students when a plane with the red sun insignia flew below them. At first annoyed at the plane's violation of the traffic pattern, she soon noticed the "billowing black smoke" rising from the Japanese attack on Pearl Harbor. She later reflected on the experience in writing: "Most people wonder how they would react in a crisis; if the danger comes as suddenly as this did you don't have time to be frightened. I'm not brave, but I knew the air was not the place for our little baby airplane and I set about landing as quickly as I ever could."[1] After this safe landing, she later returned to the continental United States and joined the first women's pilot program in 1942. In that program, she met and befriended Teresa James.

Growing up in a family that loved aviation, Teresa James flew in stunting exhibitions in small towns in Pennsylvania. As a barnstormer she also took people up for flights, including her parents. James took these jobs because she earned what she felt was an enormous sum of money for each weekend's work. As she explained, "Some guy showed me how to do stunts in airplanes and I found out I could make fifty bucks on a weekend and that was big money.... You know, that was like gold. Gold, I'm telling you." James understood the risk of flying in this early era of aviation and said most of the time she did not think about the danger of it. Then she had a conversation with Walter Beech of Beechcraft Aviation Company. Beech told James that her stunt of flying up to 2,000 feet in altitude and then performing twenty-six "turns and a spin" was dangerous and that one day she "might go into a flat spin and not be able to come out of it." She said it "scared the hell out of [her]" and decided to stop performing that stunt.[2] Through this work, pilots like James carved spaces for women within aviation that inspired other women to fly. James's and Fort's early aviation career experiences also prepared them for the highly skilled ferrying work they would perform for the US military during the war.

The women who became the Women's Airforce Service Pilots cited early aviators and entertainers as a source of inspiration, while some of them, like James, were the entertainers themselves and flew in air shows or held other aviation jobs. The number of American women with their pilot's licenses increased during the 1930s. With their accomplishments, love of adventure, and embrace of technology, they embodied the modern girl or new woman of the 1920s. While politics, sports, and many industries were male dominated, in the minds of many female pilots and their communities, flying was not conclusively established as a masculine field for much of the first half of the twentieth century.

When war broke out in Europe in 1939, the US government created new opportunities for men *and* women to become pilots. That same year, a New Deal-era program, the Civilian Pilot Training Program (CPTP), was created to generate pilots if the United States entered the war. The CPTP made it possible for Americans to earn their pilot's licenses at a low financial cost, making aviation accessible to all classes.[3] In the fall of 1942, two women's pilot programs, the Women's Auxiliary Ferrying Squadron (WAFS) and the Women's Flying Training Detachment (WFTD), merged to become the WASP program. Experienced aviators Nancy Harkness Love and Jacqueline Cochran organized these endeavors, increasing women pilots' opportunities in aviation. For the first time, the US military saw women as weapons of war with multiple contexts—experimental weapons to bring an Allied victory.

Many female pilots retained their optimism about careers in aviation until the deactivation of the WASP program in 1944. It was only at the end of the war that they realized military, commercial, and private aviation were established as fields for men. Historian Joseph Corn argues that once women were no longer needed to sell the safety of aircraft to the American public around the start of World War II, there were no longer aviation jobs for women.[4] However, it is what happened during and at the end of the war that solidified aviation as a male-dominated field. In his study of postwar private aviation, historian Alan Meyer illuminates how male pilots "deliberately constructed, embraced, and perpetuated a masculine pilot identity."[5] Similarly, after World War II the military maintained a discriminatory practice of prohibiting servicewomen from flying military aircraft, and commercial airline companies relegated female pilots to the role of a flight attendant.

On December 17, 1903, Orville and Wilbur Wright took the first successful flight and made history as the inventors of the airplane. After this transformative flight, it took five years before airplanes gained popularity. Most people who heard about the 1903 flight believed it was fictitious. Historian Joseph Corn argues that the American public did not fully understand its significance until Orville Wright flew an airplane in Fort Myer, Virginia, in September 1908. The Wrights' demonstration was highly publicized and sparked an immediate interest in flight. That same year, the Wright brothers signed a contract with the US Army Signal Corps, and the army started training men as pilots in 1909. Civilian men and women pilots began to perform stunts and participate in flying competitions across the United States as the popularity of aviation grew.[6]

A few years after Orville Wright's 1908 flight, the first American women earned their pilot's licenses in 1911 and began to participate in exhibitions.[7] These women entertained the public, but they also set aviation records as they attempted to carve a space for women in the field. The number of female pilots increased from 34 in 1928 to 472 in 1932 to thousands by the early 1940s. Altogether, women accounted for roughly 2 to 3 percent of pilots in the United States during these decades. Importantly, it was during World War II that the number of female pilots doubled.[8]

At this time, female pilots viewed aviation as rife with opportunities for both genders, and they did not find high altitudes automatically defined as male spaces. Although there were many more male than female pilots, women still felt hopeful that equality in aviation was possible. Despite the reality of a minority of women pilots in aviation, it is early female aviators' perception of the field that was significant. Historians have revealed that perception matters in people's lived experiences and often influences a population's behavior and actions.[9] The small numbers of early aviators who viewed the sky as liberative and expansive inspired a generation of women who became the WASPs.

Regardless of their small numbers in comparison to male pilots, these early female aviators envisioned the sky as a place of career development and liberation for women. The first woman to fly across the English Channel, Harriet Quimby, hoped airplanes would "open up a fruitful occupation for women."[10] Journalist and pilot Margery Brown also believed in the promise of aviation as a career for women, asserting, "There is no question about the effect [flying] will have on [women's] characters. No longer will it be natural for them to take orders. . . . They will learn to be resourceful, to think rapidly and to act without shilly-shallying."[11] She argued that, in addition to developing skills of "perseverance, grit, and determination" through flying, female pilots would attain liberty: "Freedom as yet undreamed of awaits women—half way between the earth and the sky." Brown envisioned a future in which it was impossible for there to be a "sex distinction in the region of the air."[12]

Brown's comment about "the region of the air" illuminates how women pilots viewed altitude as natural airspace for women and men. Others used this exact terminology, as well as "the world of the air" and "highways of the air."[13] Some argued that flying would facilitate sexual equality for women in society, as it allowed them to become "confident, aggressive, and independent individuals who would soon demand and receive equal treatment."[14] These characteristics would have appealed to other women given the political climate of the United States on the eve of women's suffrage, even though the cost of flying was an obstacle for the majority of Americans until a government-sponsored training program began in 1939.[15]

Identifying aviation as an opportunity for equality was a part of the "winged gospel" that historian Joseph Corn discusses in his book of the same title.[16] This term, used by contemporaries of early women pilots, referenced the belief that airplanes were ushering in "a wondrous era of peace and harmony, of culture and prosperity."[17] Proponents believed that airplanes would first bring peace, as enemies would hesitate to attack. One day, planes would be so ubiquitous that everyone would own one, and then the airplane would finally advance equality and democracy for all.[18] Early female aviators bought into this gospel narrative, as did people of color.

Black pilots hoped that aviation would provide opportunities and further equality. Bessie Coleman, the first African American in the United States to earn a pilot's license, described "the air" as "the only place free from prejudices."[19] She offered this description even though she had to earn her pilot's license in France due to Jim Crow because no American flight school would admit her as a student in 1921. Nicknamed "Queen Bess," Coleman flew as a barnstormer during the 1920s but was only allowed to fly in shows with desegregated crowds. She hoped to use her earnings to open a flight school for Black students. Tragically, she died performing stunts in 1926 at the age of thirty-four.[20] Coleman's and other female pilots' perception of the air as a place of equality echoes the thoughts of soldiers of color throughout history and Black female activists during World War I.[21]

Like Bessie Coleman, African American pilot, engineer, and World War I veteran William J. Powell encountered rejection from flight schools in the United States because of his race but saw the sky as a place of opportunity for Black Americans. After acceptance at a flight school in Los Angeles, he eventually earned his pilot's license in 1932. Due to racial discrimination, the numbers of Black pilots were bleak in this era. In 1934, only 12 Black Americans held their pilot's license out of 18,041 individuals.[22] In the 1930s, Powell encouraged African Americans to believe in the winged gospel. He hoped that one day, when more Americans had airplanes than cars, Black pilots would fly white passengers. He envisioned Black-owned aviation companies that would circumvent the Jim Crow segregation in airlines. To make flying accessible to Black Americans, Powell created the Bessie Coleman Aero Club, sponsored the first all-Black air show in 1931, and published a monthly journal on Black aviators in the *Craftsmen Aero-News*.[23] Ultimately, he wanted Black pilots to convince white Americans of their professional skills and achieve "interracial harmony."[24] Powell believed that aviation was key to developing African Americans' potential: "There is a better job and a better future in aviation for Negroes than in any other industry, and the reason is this: *aviation is just beginning its period of growth, and if we get into it now, while it is still uncrowded, we can grow as aviation grows.*"[25]

Barnstormers perpetuated the gospel of air-mindedness, this belief that airplanes improved life.[26] They saw airplanes as providing a superior alternative to ground transportation and even improving relationships between countries worldwide. Air-minded people thought that airplanes would become a facet of everyday American life, just like the automobile, and they wanted to participate in the aviation industry's development, which included convincing the American public to fly. The most famous female pilot of all, Amelia Earhart, subscribed to this creed that all Americans would fly one day and that children in the 1930s were going to be a

"Flying Generation."[27] It is no wonder that so many women assumed flying was a pathway for liberation.

Numerous reasons drew women to pilot in the early years of flight. Some flew for the freedom that flying gave them or the feeling of "reckless abandon," presumably from gender constraints.[28] One pilot enjoyed flying open cockpit for "the freedom and the physical sensation of wind blowing strongly against her face" and described feeling "the power, the exultation."[29] Whether flying for an escape or to hone their abilities, a small number of women began earning their pilot's licenses throughout the 1910s, and some even employed their skills when the United States went to war in 1917.

Out of the few women that held pilot's licenses during World War I, at least three employed their piloting skills and knowledge of flying to aid the war effort, although not officially with the military. Ruth Law tried to become a combat pilot, but the army rejected her. Instead, she helped the Aviation Section of the US Army Signal Corps recruit male pilots and flew airplanes in Liberty bonds drives.[30] Katherine Stinson also wanted to fly in combat but became a flight instructor with her sister Marjorie Stinson, and they trained male pilots at their family's flying school in San Antonio, Texas. Katherine served as an ambulance driver in France toward the end of the war, and Marjorie worked as an aeronautical draftsman for the US Navy.[31] Amelia Earhart's flying instructor Neta Snook worked as an inspector of aircraft engines produced in factories.[32]

Flying exhibitions, including those by barnstormers, rapidly grew in popularity and success during the 1920s due to the availability of cheap surplus biplanes used to train male pilots during the war.[33] Many male veterans who had been pilots during World War I flew as barnstormers in this postwar period. Barnstormers performed aerial stunts, including barrel rolls and loop the loop, that incorporated spins and dives. They also parachuted out of planes, walked on the wings of airplanes, flew in flying circuses, and gave rides to passengers for around a dollar. Flying circuses were companies that hired barnstormers to perform these stunts for the public. Barnstormers and pilot performers toured the country, flying into even the smallest towns. They often wore costumes that contributed to the entertainment value of their shows. Harriet Quimby wore a sensational purple satin flying suit when she flew.[34] One man, pilot Roscoe Turner, waxed his mustache and wore a flying tunic.[35] The third woman to earn her pilot's license owned a namesake company, the Ruth Law Flying Circus, that toured the country entertaining audiences.[36]

Many of these early aviators earned a considerable amount of money, and some made a career out of flying, although exhibitionist flying came at significant personal risk. Injuries and death were prevalent among pilots who flew stunts.[37] Aviation was still in its fragile, precarious early stages. Pilots and wing walkers, people who performed stunts on the wings of the plane midflight, performed perilous maneuvers in the air. One wing walker danced the Charleston on the wing of a plane.[38] Katherine Stinson performed nighttime acrobatic stunts using strategically placed lights on the plane.[39]

Barnstorming fits within the more extensive history of other forms of entertainment in the 1920s and 1930s. Although Americans were first excited by simply watching airplanes take off and land, they soon wanted to see these daredevil acts. Carnivals, "freak shows," and circuses reached their peak at the same time as barnstorming.[40] Piloting stunts were also like the performances of Houdini, who captivated audiences with his death-defying magic shows. Unlike professional magic, a male preserve, aviation was still defined less rigidly by air-minded individuals.[41]

Women pilots were the epitome of the modern woman of the 1920s and 1930s, as they embodied adventure, new technology, and leisure. Typically identified by her appearance, including her makeup, bobbed hairstyle, and short dresses, the modern woman embraced her sexuality. Threatening social norms, she often smoked, drank alcohol, and gambled. A global phenomenon, she appeared in advertisements and was tied to consumer culture.[42] While historians have discussed flappers dancing, playing sports, acting in Hollywood films, or driving cars, they have ignored early women pilots. Airplanes symbolized modernity and national progress through technological development in the 1920s and 1930s.[43] Perhaps more than any other new women, female pilots were adventurous, and they often lived life recklessly, defied social constructs, mastered aircraft technology, and sought liberating experiences in the region of the air.[44]

These early pilots inspired the younger generation to see the sky as an opportunity and place for exploration, although this remained a dream primarily for white male Americans. Barnstormers inspired most women who later became the WASPs, as they performed feats at air shows and offered rides. One story that illustrates the dominant white culture of American society and aviation is that of WASP Pearl Brummett Judd. When she witnessed a publicity stunt in 1929, Judd felt that the airplane was "the most beautiful thing" she had ever seen. The stunt involved a World War I veteran flying a plane while carrying a Native American passenger who shot arrows at buffalo on the ground.[45] Judd was so impressed by the skill of the flight that her father bought her a plane ride for her eighteenth birthday, and she immediately quit college and got a job to pay for flying lessons. This racially insensitive performance is illustrative of the white-dominated culture in the field of aviation. Because of the nature of race relations in the United States, including the long-term economic and social repercussions of slavery, Reconstruction, and immigration laws, most Americans of color did not have the opportunity to make aviation a career or even learn how to fly. This reality reflects the social landscape of the United States in the early decades of aviation development.

Some of the women who flew during World War II, including Teresa James, were the barnstormers who inspired other women to fly, although this inspiration often came at significant personal risk. Female barnstormers flew in extremely hazardous situations, as the stunts were dangerous and airplane design was still in a "primitive state." According to historian Joseph Corn, some airplanes literally "fell apart in the sky" during the era of barnstorming.[46] Some female pilots embraced death as a part of women's contributions to early aviation's "pioneering effort." As pilot Louise Thaden explained, "There has never been nor will there ever be progress without sacrifice of human life."[47] Of ferrying aircraft in these early decades, Teresa James noted that it "was like the wagon train days of flying" due to its dangerous and rudimentary nature. For example, pilots had to calculate every so many minutes of flying as the equivalent of a certain number of miles and then hand mark checkpoints on a map to ensure they stayed on course to their final destination.[48] Nevertheless, by accepting these risks, female pilots earned decent pay and kept jobs in aviation.

With the growth of the aviation industry in the 1920s and 1930s, the American public needed convincing of aircraft safety, but this often undermined beliefs in women's skill and intellect.[49] A common misperception existed that if women could fly aircraft, the aircraft must be safe. Women participated in demonstrations through barnstorming and air races and sold planes as reliable and themselves as simpleminded. For example, one of the purposes of the annual National Women's Air Derby was to bring public attention to women pilots to encourage the "general acceptance of air transportation and travel."[50] Beginning in 1929, this competition played into the stereotype that if women, as the "weaker sex," fly successfully, it is "positive proof of the simplicity and universal practicality [of air travel]. It is the greatest sales argument that can be presented to that public."[51] The line of thinking was that the American public believes "anything outstanding that a woman can do or does do well is something that anyone can do."[52] Thus, stereotypes that considered women different from men not only physically but also intellectually influenced public thought. The American public categorized women pilots as entertainers rather than taking them seriously as professionals, let alone skilled aviators. Women successfully "made flying thinkable" to the public at a cost to their professional selves.[53]

These attitudes about women pilots are strikingly comparable to the ways male drivers have over the years dismissed women's technological skills as luck and assumed women are frail and incompetent with mechanics. In the first three decades of the twentieth century, car companies targeted male audiences for gas cars and female audiences for electric because electric cars were presumably smoother, simpler to operate, and more comfortable. As women were expected to possess less strength than men, advertisers focused on making the electric cars seem so simple that even a woman could drive them.[54] Male pilots in the late 1920s were similarly skeptical about women's abilities. Even if some found women "equals of men in courage and intelligence," they argued that women were physically weaker. They knew women had flown long distances and set records, but they questioned whether women could handle the kind of distances regularly required of commercial pilots.[55]

Other pilots who participated in air-mindedness were pilots who became celebrities in the American media and inspired a generation of youths to learn how to fly. From war heroes to record-breaking aviators like Amelia Earhart and Charles Lindbergh, pilots sparked an interest in flying for young girls who became pilots, especially the WASPs. Some read war stories about the Red Baron, a famous World War I German fighter pilot.[56] Others saw parades featuring Lindbergh after his famous 1927 transatlantic flight or watched Amelia Earhart at a public speaking engagement.[57] Pilot Margery Brown argued that Lindbergh inspired many women to fly not because of who he was as a person but rather because he was "an ideal." They wanted characteristics he represented, such as "courage, quiet confidence, modesty and spiritual freedom."[58] Future WASP Betty "Tack" Blake met Amelia Earhart in 1935, and after watching her take off, Blake knew she wanted to fly.[59] Interest in these aviators is evident in the WASPs' memories and the scrapbooks that they created and kept for decades after the war. Many of their scrapbooks contained poems written by Harriet Quimby or photos of Amelia Earhart from the media's coverage of her flights.[60] The fact that the WASPs kept these poems and photos in their scrapbooks also illustrates that early women pilots inspired them.

Amelia Earhart's influence on women in American society was pervasive and extended beyond inspiring them to fly. She was a National Women's Party member who fought for women's suffrage in the 1910s.[61] From the late 1920s until she died in 1937, she promoted aviation to American society to help the public feel comfortable with commercial flight. After Earhart achieved instant fame when she became the first woman to fly across the Atlantic Ocean in 1932, the media continuously compared her to pilot Charles Lindbergh, the first man to fly across the Atlantic. Unlike Lindbergh, she turned her achievements into accomplishments for her sex.

Earhart sought to prove that women could be as successful as men professionally, and she became a feminist role model. She and ninety-eight other female aviators created the Ninety-Nines (or 99s) in 1929 with the purpose of "forming the women pilots of this country into an organization for their mutual benefit."[62] They chose their name based on the number of women pilots who created the organization together. Any woman in the United States with a pilot's license could join the Ninety-Nines.[63] Historian Susan Ware argues that Earhart actively worked to advance feminism in the period after women's suffrage was achieved with the Nineteenth Amendment.[64] The Ninety-Nines wanted women pilots to be taken seriously as professionals, much as other women wanted professional equality after fighting for the right to vote.[65] Earhart saw flying as liberating for women because of the freedom that it allowed. Furthermore, if women succeeded in aviation, she believed prejudices against them in American society would disappear.[66] She was thus a "symbol of women's emancipation in the postsuffrage era."[67]

Earhart's status as a modern, liberated 1920s woman was also evident in her clothing. She wore pants, blouses, and sometimes leather jackets while flying. This attire was practical for her work, but it sparked media attention. Earhart even produced a clothing line consisting of outfits including loose pants and jackets for women who led "active lives."[68] Through these endeavors, she hoped to carve out a space for women in aviation and bring women closer to equality with men. Earhart's fatal crash in 1937 solidified her place in American memory, as the site of her accident and her body still have not been found.

A sense of adventure united male and female pilots, and it also united the women who became the WASPs. Driven by a pursuit of adventure, or even a desire to overcome their fears, they were often the first women that they knew in the field of aviation. Most of them learned how to fly among men in their communities, and it was not until the war that they met other female pilots. Just like the modern girl who came before them, the women who became the WASPs desired freedom, especially from the constraints of a conventional lifestyle. Joseph Corn argues that women were often drawn to aviation because it "symbolized freedom and power" and gave them "feelings of strength, mastery, and confidence."[69] Some WASPs actually wanted to learn to fly to overcome their fears.[70] Pilot Teresa James, who performed stunts in air shows, was first "terrified" of flying because its danger hit close to home when her brother broke his leg in a plane accident.[71] However, the desire to move past these experiences illustrates the thrill that women sought.

Women often possessed a sense of thrill seeking that drove their desire to fly, even though flying was still experimental and often unsafe. Many of those who became the WASPs described themselves as "adventurous."[72] They often believed that flying would fulfill their "search for adventure."[73] Some joined piloting clubs to stay connected with other pilots and to participate in flying competitions.[74] Whether through these prewar experiences or the WASP program, women constructed an identity as pilots by seeking adventure.

Their flying pursuits set them apart from their peers. While the modern girl with wings saw flying as the most promising space to find equality, not all Americans viewed aviation as a place for both the sexes. WAFS Florene Miller Watson revealed that segments of the American public believed flying was "not for girls" or women were not good pilots. Her 2006 recollection was probably the result of her retroactively pondering how things had changed throughout her lifetime, especially regarding the history of the WASP program. Women who learned how to fly and joined the WASPs, Watson said, "had that confidence in themselves that if I get a chance, I can do it. You may not have thought in those terms, but you were gutsy enough to give it a try." Watson mentioned that this ability and willingness to try was "definitely . . . part of [her] identity."[75] It was this determined nature that helped the WASPs successfully graduate from Army Air Force training.

Other WASPs considered themselves different from their female peers because they wanted to work in a male-dominated field, and they were often the first women in their families or communities to learn how to fly. In recent interviews, women described aviation through a retrospective lens as they recalled it becoming increasingly male due to the war. Catherine Vail Bridge commented that learning to fly was "something unusual that women ordinarily were not allowed to [do]." Yet it was also unusual for men, as only a small percentage of men and women learn how to fly.[76]

Other WASPs credited their family upbringing for their spirited pursuit of fields or hobbies associated with men. WASP Ethel Finley, who grew up on a farm in Minnesota, believed she "inherited" characteristics from her mother, "because she too was the kind of person who was one of the first to do things in her generation."[77] Finley's mother learned how to ride a bike when most children she knew who rode bikes were boys. She was also one of the first women in her community who learned how to drive a car. The women in WASP Bernice "Bee" Falk Haydu's working-class New Jersey family had a history of doing work typically reserved for men, including trading on the stock exchange and owning stores. Haydu was proud to be raised in a family that was "not constrained by the Victorian idea that women shouldn't work outside the home or that some occupations were available only to men."[78] While not all WASPs had these types of upbringings or even supportive families, they all shared a determination to pursue aviation as a career.

Born anywhere from 1907 to 1923, the women who became the WASPs had experience as pilots before they joined the program, and most received flying lessons during the Great Depression.[79] These women became aviators during a time when the number of female pilots was still small. Furthermore, flying during the economic depression meant that many had to be resourceful to figure out ways to pay for their lessons.

From various social and class backgrounds, including a broad spectrum of job and family experiences, WASP trainees often only shared a love of flying. Some women held aviation jobs, while others were in varied professions, working as dancers, models, child actors, or teachers.[80] While a few women, including Nancy Love, attended prestigious or expensive colleges like Vassar College; the University of California, Berkeley; or Sarah Lawrence College, others attended teachers colleges or local universities.[81] Several WASPs did not attend college or never graduated once they discovered flying.[82] The 1920s through the 1940s were decades when most women who had the opportunity to attend college majored in fields identified as female professions (i.e., teaching, nursing, or secretarial work).

Many women pilots acquired jobs that would provide enough funding for additional flying hours. WASP V. Scott Bradley Gough learned how to make parachute jumps to get a financial discount on her flying time. Making those jumps drew people to the airport. Since Gough was a young child when her mother died, her father raised her and her two brothers. Although the family had a very modest income, when Gough got a job at a bank, her father encouraged her to pursue her dream of flying and allowed her to spend a portion of her salary on flying lessons. He did not seem to assume that aviation was a male arena.[83] Other female pilots paid for lessons by teaching ground school at the local airport, which offered instruction in topics such as cross-country navigation, radio communications, and flying regulations.[84] One Nevada native worked as a schoolteacher and pooled her money with her brother to buy an airplane.[85] With a teacher's salary, some WASPs had to acquire a second job.[86] One unique story is that of a WASP who obtained her license via the Peruvian Air Corps. During her college study abroad in Peru, the Peruvian Air Corps offered free flying instruction if students paid for the gas.[87] Using a variety of methods and creatively juggling their finances, these women slowly increased their flying hours. The timing of acquiring these hours was ideal since the war would soon start, and the US government would turn to women for work.

While airplanes made no strategic military difference in World War I, technology had advanced rapidly in the interwar period, and airpower was vital to Allied victory in World War II. World War II marked a dramatic shift in the climate of the United States, as pilots turned from entertaining the public to seeking opportunities to risk their lives for their country. On September 1, 1939, Germany invaded Poland, and World War II started in Europe. Although the conflict had been building in Asia since Japan invaded Manchuria in 1931, the Japanese did not join the Axis powers in Europe until September 1940, when they signed the Tripartite Pact with Germany and Italy. The United States was technologically behind both Japan and Germany.[88] Although aviation experts and war veterans, notably Guilio Douhet and Billy Mitchell, had argued about the importance of airpower long before the war, their voices were ignored or stifled.[89] Therefore, the United States quickly compensated with pilots and technological advancements when Japan attacked Pearl Harbor on December 7, 1941.

Less than a year later, the AAF began using women pilots as weapons of war, just as they were employed in Great Britain, Romania, Germany, and the Soviet Union. In November 1939, just after the war began in Europe, women pilots began flying with the British Air Transport Auxiliary (ATA), a civilian organization responsible for ferrying aircraft separate from the Royal Air Force.[90] In Romania, female pilots in the Sanitary Squadron flew wounded men on the Eastern Front who needed surgery. Germany never created a women's pilot program, but a minimum of sixty-seven female pilots flew in a civilian capacity for the government during the war.[91] Unlike in Britain, Germany, and Romania, women in the Soviet Union fought in combat. The Soviet Union started incorporating female pilots into both all-female and predominantly male regiments in the fall of 1941. The Soviet air force held these women to the same standards and expectations imposed on male pilots.

The Soviet "Night Witches" were the first women to fly in combat. These pilots flew the same number of missions as their male counterparts, attained a similar flying record, and volunteered for both military service and combat. The only all-female regiment was the 588th Night Bomber Regiment. Its primary assignments were dropping bombs from Po-2 biplanes, open-cockpit planes made of wood and canvas, and fighting in combat when necessary. Members of the 587th Bomber Regiment flew the much sturdier Pe-2 bombers and participated in bombing missions. Those in the 586th Fighter Regiment flew the technologically advanced Yak fighters in combat. These units were the first in the world to include women in warfare.[92]

During the war in Europe, before America joined the fighting, the US government began preparing for battle by encouraging men to become pilots and offering free government pilot training to men and women. While flying in the 1920s and 1930s was primarily available to women from upper- and middle-class families or working-class women who worked extra jobs or chose flying over education, this situation changed in 1939, the year the war started in Europe. With the Great Depression still raging, the creation of a New Deal government training program, the Civilian Pilot Training Program (CPTP), made flying accessible to men and women of all social classes and ethnicities. One direct result of the CPTP was an increase in Black pilots from a "handful" in the 1920s to around 2,000 by the end of the 1930s.[93] Using classrooms on American college campuses, the government funded the training of pilots. Military service was not required, but it was the intended outcome, at least for male trainees.[94] Before joining the WASPs, women pilots needed to have a minimum of 200 flying hours, and although that number was reduced to 35 hours later in the war, the creation of the CPTP made their WASP experiences possible.[95]

A significant percentage of the WASPs received their private pilot's licenses via the CPTP, which created critical opportunities for women interested in aviation. There were some restrictions to women's admittance to CPT programs. Only one woman trainee was accepted for every ten men. In addition, women could no longer participate after the United States declared war in December 1941, since instruction was reserved for men the military hoped would fight in combat. Despite the narrow time frame and discriminatory acceptance practices, approximately 2,500 women received

CPTP training, which dramatically increased the number of female pilots in the United States. The Civil Aeronautics Administration (CAA) reported 4,211 women with private pilot's licenses in the United States as of January 1945, so the CPTP contributed greatly to this growth.[96]

As she would be in the creation of the women's pilot programs in 1942, Eleanor Roosevelt was a voice for women pilots when she protested their exclusion after 1941.[97] For WASPs who did not have financial access to aviation, the CPT programs offered the opportunity to learn how to fly. Raised on a small Iowa farm, WASP Marie Mountain Clark had been looking for opportunities to fly in the years before the war, and she saw the CPTP as her chance to learn. Hit particularly hard by the Great Depression, her family eventually recovered and helped Clark and her sister with their college expenses. Although at first rejected by one school's CPT program, since it had not yet incorporated female pilots, Clark soon found a school that accepted her application.[98] After completing the CPT program, she taught as a CPTP instructor until she joined the WASPs. For Maryland native and WASP Elaine Harmon, the CPTP is what sparked her interest in flying. When she found out about the program via a newspaper article, she immediately decided to apply. After receiving her acceptance, she felt as though it "was the most interesting thing that had ever come into [her] life."[99] Although it is unknown how many WASPs received training through the CPTP, since its records are scattered across the country, the majority likely earned their pilot's licenses through the program.[100] As the United States had not declared war yet and the CPTP did not have an explicit requirement to join the AAF, it is also unknown how many women planned on joining the war effort or anticipated the declaration of war in 1941.

In addition to offering this free training to adults, the US government emphasized getting children—boys *and* girls—interested in aviation. The Air Training Corps of America (ATCA) program, established in 1942, taught students how to build wooden airplane models of World War II aircraft. After constructing the models, students painted them black and sent them across the country for use in army and navy cadets' practice in aircraft identification. The ATCA also offered male-only classes on the basics of aviation to prepare students for pilot training if they chose to pursue that after graduation. Over 500,000 high school boys participated in this program in 1942.[101]

Another opportunity available for children and for women pilots, including some who eventually became WASPs, was the Civil Air Patrol (CAP).[102] In early 1942, the CAP stated that its purpose was to "weld civil airmen—and women—into a force for national defense by increasing knowledge and skill in every type of aviation activity."[103] Although women were not allowed to fly coastal patrols, the CAP allowed women and Black Americans to serve their country in aviation. Black women, including Lieutenant Willa Brown, the first African American woman to receive her pilot's license in the United States, were also allowed to serve in the CAP. As a lieutenant, Brown was the first Black female officer in the CAP.[104] Ahead of the US military, the CAP created the "first race- and gender-integrated, uniformed flying unit" in American history, the 111th Flight Squadron of the Illinois Wing of the CAP.[105]

However, there were limits to these opportunities for women and girls. Men were given preference in the CPTP, with more of them admitted than women, and once the United States officially declared war, women were no longer accepted into the program. Even in children's programs, boys were emphasized as pilots, while girls only learned to make models. With the creation of women's pilot programs during World War II, women had an opportunity to fly, but the story of the WASPs illustrates the solidification of the field of aviation as male.

As soon as the war started in Europe, Jackie Cochran and Nancy Love both looked for ways to pursue aviation when the number of women pilots and the opportunities for an aviation career were limited. Both pilots worked to create opportunities for women in the field of aviation. Cochran and Love had different childhood backgrounds, personalities, careers, and visions for the women's pilot programs. Nevertheless, they actively worked to get the US military to employ women as pilots during World War II. These attempts were not the first time female aviators had created organizations to serve their country in preparation for war or national emergency. Two women's organizations founded in 1931—the Betsy Ross Corps and the Women's Air Reserve—planned to use female pilots to free men for combat, although they did not collaborate with the US military.[106] In contrast, the successes of both Love and Cochran in the early 1940s provided work for female pilots within the US military, which provided a unique career opportunity for women at the time.

Although they came from different class backgrounds, Love and Cochran carved out spaces in the field of aviation in the late 1920s and 1930s, when female aviators were scarce. Love's upper-class family could afford her flying lessons, but they emphasized her need to find a job to support her flying. She found most jobs consisted of demonstrating planes to sell them to the American public or chartering passengers and cargo.[107] Jackie Cochran grew up in an impoverished family in Florida, and her interest in and funding for aviation came after meeting her husband, billionaire Floyd Odlum. While working in a prominent beauty salon in New York, she met Odlum, and he suggested that she earn her pilot's license to sell her potential cosmetics line.[108] After their marriage, Odlum provided Cochran the financial resources and political connections to achieve her aviation goals. She earned her pilot's license in less than three weeks and proceeded to win numerous air races and to break speed records.[109]

In addition to their different life experiences, Cochran and Love also had differing management styles and goals that created tension between them. Cochran was very driven and ambitious. Her access to political connections through her husband created opportunities for her and alienated people who disagreed with her methods. Her relationship with Love was fraught throughout the war. When proposing the women's pilot programs, Cochran and Love disagreed about what type of program to create. Love wanted a small group of women with a high level of experience, while Cochran wanted a large number of women pilots with fewer flying hours who received military training. During the war, there is evidence that Cochran and Love avoided each other. Love wrote to a fellow WASP and said of Cochran, "I haven't seen J.C. in months, and have assiduously avoided her. Our airplanes were both on Long Beach at the same time, but there's no use arguing with her—she only twists statements."[110] Cochran sought to be in the spotlight, while the more reserved Love conducted herself more diplomatically. Seemingly Cochran's opposite, Love was described by many pilots as being "pleasant" and having a "quiet voice."[111] Despite their conflicting personalities, the two women successfully persuaded the AAF to start women's pilot programs during a war that transformed flying into a male realm.

Love and Cochran each contacted the AAF months after the war started in Europe on September 1, 1939. Eleanor Roosevelt was also instrumental in persuading the AAF to employ women pilots, just as she advocated for the aviators' access to the CPTP. Less than a month after World War II started in Europe, Cochran wrote to Eleanor Roosevelt and asked that she consider supporting the use of women pilots for the war effort. Cochran hoped that the first lady would use her connections to encourage officials in Washington, including those in the army, navy, and coast guard, to discuss training women pilots for military service. Indicating that these women could engage in "all sorts of helpful back of the lines work," Cochran noted that male pilots would therefore be free "for [the] more important duty" of combat.[112] Furthermore, she tried to persuade Roosevelt by mentioning that women pilots were being used overseas, including in England, Russia, and Germany.[113] Upon her receipt of the letter, Eleanor Roosevelt forwarded it to the US Navy.[114] In November 1939, the first lady brought national attention to this issue, discussing the problems women pilots had in getting jobs in aviation in her "My Day" newspaper column. Roosevelt felt that women could be relied on during emergencies such as natural disasters to help fly people and supplies.[115] Nancy Love also started negotiations with the US military over the use of women pilots for the war effort in the spring of 1940.[116] She hoped that the AAF could make use of those with over 1,000 hours of flying experience.

AAF commanding general Henry "Hap" Arnold declined Love's and Cochran's requests. Later, in a 1946 report on the WASP program, the air force concluded that Arnold's rejections were due to the need for combat pilots (a role from which women were exempt), the AAF's "doubt as to the potentialities of women as pilots of military aircraft," and the lack of women pilots with a "considerable amount of flying experience."[117] The concern over women's flying abilities reflects responses the WASPs faced during their service in the AAF. Furthermore, the AAF considered the pilot programs that became the WASP experimental until women proved successful in flying military aircraft.

Eleanor Roosevelt again brought national attention to female pilots in the summer of 1941. At this time, Cochran traveled to England to observe women flying for the British ATA. After this trip, she met with Franklin D. and Eleanor Roosevelt to discuss women pilots' use in Britain. A few days after this meeting, at the behest of President Roosevelt, Cochran met with General Arnold and Colonel Robert Olds, head of the Ferrying Command. Arnold tasked Colonel Olds and Cochran with developing a plan. Despite the parties' "difference of opinion," Olds submitted a proposal to Arnold.[118] In the meantime, on August 5, 1941, Eleanor Roosevelt wrote an article about women pilots in her "My Day" column that was most likely a direct result of her meeting with Cochran. Revealing that she had recently learned about the work of female pilots in England, Roosevelt emphasized the fact that women flying for the ATA performed "neither combat duty nor dangerous service." Although ferrying involved the possibility of peril, this comment would reassure the public about the use of American women pilots. Roosevelt further argued, "[It would] be wise to give women pilots this opportunity, since we know they have been so useful in other countries."[119]

Relegating women to supposed "safe" roles also eventually undermined their place in aviation.

Despite pressure from both the president and the first lady, General Arnold rejected Olds and Cochran's proposal later in September 1941, but he left open the possibility to incorporate it later.[120] According to Arnold, since there were more male pilots than female pilots, the "obvious military advantage" was training men. When the British Air Commission contacted Cochran and asked her to recruit American women pilots for the ATA, she agreed, but she contacted Arnold first and asked that he wait to start a women's pilot program until she returned from England. Arnold agreed to her request, so Cochran recruited and brought twenty-five women pilots to Britain to fly in the ATA in early 1942.[121] These women signed twelve-to-eighteen-month contracts with Britain. After their contracts ended, several of these women would later join the WASPs.[122]

Although Arnold initially rejected plans for women's pilot programs, he changed his mind in 1942, and the work of the Roosevelts is again evident in this development. During the spring and fall of 1942, Nancy Love worked with the Ferrying Division to create a plan specifically for women pilots with over 500 hours of flying time. During these discussions, Arnold informed AAF officers that he wanted to tell President Roosevelt about a women's pilot program so that the president could announce it.[123] Just nine days after Eleanor Roosevelt brought attention to women pilots as "a weapon waiting to be used" in her "My Day" column on September 1, 1942, the media announced the formation of the WAFS.[124] The twenty-eight women who participated in this program had at least 500 hours of flying time. Unlike the WASPs, they would only receive training for thirty to forty days where they would learn military organization, including "technical orders on the planes they were to ferry, ferry routes, etc."[125] At the time Nancy Love started the WAFS, Cochran was still in England working with the ATA.

When Cochran returned to the United States in September 1942, after the announcement of the WAFS to the public, she was named director of a separate women's pilot program. Her program, the WFTD, accepted aviators with fewer flying hours and gave them five to seven and a half months of AAF training. The original plan was to train approximately 3,000 women pilots, although the program concluded when it had reached about a third of that number.[126]

When Secretary of War Henry Stimson announced the WAFS program to the press on September 10, 1942, a flood of attention followed via magazine and newspaper articles.[127] At the journalists' requests, female pilots posed for photographs that often showed them carrying suitcases, wearing flight suits, inspecting parachutes, and standing by airplanes. Article topics included the purpose of the WAFS and its experimental nature. Nancy Love received intense media attention, as she participated in countless interviews and spoke at numerous events around the country. Serving directly under Cochran, Love was responsible for the original WAFS program and women who flew in the Ferrying Division. A very reserved woman who did not like to draw attention to herself, Love opposed the media's intrusiveness for personal reasons and because it interfered with her work and that of the squadron. One journalist described her as follows: "[She is] quite reserved but like all pilots warms up to the topic of flying so eventually some of her past experiences come to light."[128] Nevertheless, Love still agreed to interviews, perhaps out of a sense of obligation, either due to societal pressures or a desire to help the fledgling WAFS program.[129]

The immense amount of publicity associated with the WAFS led Cochran to limit the media's exposure to the WASP program. Overall, she believed publicity for WAFS members "had done them more harm than good," although she did not justify her reasoning, and she requested that there be no publicity for the first 75 to 100 women trainees.[130] To monitor the amount of press coverage, she set specific rules and guidelines for the trainees and defined goals for women's portrayal in the media. Through these restrictions, she hoped to limit the public's knowledge of the program and prevent the AAF from shutting it down by providing an acceptable image of the women participants and hiding certain aspects of their work.

Cochran had three main goals for media restriction. First, she wanted to promote an image of the WASPs that would avoid the slander campaigns the Women's Army Corps (WAC) experienced; she wanted women pilots to be taken seriously as professionals in the field of aviation. Cochran also hoped that minimizing media coverage of WASP accidents and experimental work would minimize the possibility of a public backlash to the program.[131] Thus, she attempted to gain male acceptance of female pilots' abilities while presenting a chaste, moral image of the WASPs. However, it was just this conflicted image that eventually contributed to a trivial portrayal of program participants.

To advance Cochran's first goal, the WASPs followed rules and regulations about their interaction with national and local media sources to the extent that most Americans, even in the WASPs' own communities, did not know about women pilots. WASP trainees received instructions about the information they sent home to their parents or could release to their hometowns. Circulation of any information about the individual women required prior approval from the public relations officer on base. According to women pilots, the WFTD and WASP programs were invisible from their hometowns and the general public. Although the WASPs received media attention during the war, most of them realized when they returned home that most Americans did not know about the program even after the fighting ended.

Media coverage during World War II also differed from that during later US wars because the American media restricted the photographic images printed in newspapers. Unlike Vietnam War reportage, World War II journalism included very few photographs of deceased American servicemen's bodies. With those restrictions in mind, images of deceased women were even more taboo. In Cochran's second goal of media coverage, she hoped that by censoring images of WASP accidents and death, the AAF could avoid the public's concerns about the protection of women, specifically white women. If Americans learned of women's deaths from aircraft accidents, a public backlash to the program might result. As early as December 1943, Cochran and Taylor, through the War Department Bureau of Public Relations (WDBPR), worked to hide WASP experimental programs and accidents from the American public. To this end, the WDBPR required official clearance for articles printed about accidents. Cochran allowed the bureau to give the press information about WASP accidents as long as it reflected the WASPs' "good record" of flying, as in the example of how many miles they flew per fatal accident, and provided it refrain from giving a "defense of the accidents that have happened." She wanted the media to point out that the women pilots' "rate of fatalities" was equivalent to that of male pilots in noncombat service.[132] However, photographs of wrecks and accidents were "strictly prohibited."[133] If the American public saw these images of deceased white women in aircraft accidents, it could have, she believed, caused a public outcry.

The WDBPR and Cochran forbade publicity of WASP involvement in new experimental areas, including their work and training with the B-17 and other bombers. Their reasoning again revolved around the prevention of public disapproval: "[The WASP program] involves experimentation in training and utilization with attendant strong possibility of mistakes and losses, with resultant public criticism."[134] As this statement implies, it was essential to the program's success that the WASPs not upset the narrative of men as protectors and women as the protected.

Even from the origins of the WASP program, Cochran and the War Department outlined their decision to prevent a romanticized image of women pilots and focus on the WASPs' accomplishments. They prohibited journalists from publishing stories about the aviators that emphasized "glamour, hazards, and fatigue." Instead, they wanted articles to focus on the fact that the WASPs were "freeing men pilots for heroic duty."[135] As this quote suggests, the emphasis was on women performing work that, instead of being heroic, allowed men to attain heroism overseas. Numerous memos discussed the importance of emphasizing the "unglamorous" nature of flying for the AAF.[136]

This attitude of professionalism corresponded with Cochran's personal philosophy about aviation. Early in her flying career, she determined to set the most records and win the top air races. In these efforts, she continually stated her intentions to beat records held by men, not women. Cochran wanted to eliminate separate categories for the sexes in air races because she felt that only comparing female pilots against one another undermined them.[137] Furthermore, in her interviews with journalists, Cochran explained that she chose applicants to the WASP program who understood that AAF service is "hard work" with "little glamour."[138]

Once the media announced the formation of the two women's pilot programs to the public, the AAF received enough interest that it did not need to create a recruitment campaign like that for the other women's military programs during World War II. Some women pilots found out about the WFTD and WASP programs before the media's announcement, since the War Department sent out letters to see whether there were enough female pilots to proceed. The department sent letters to women in the Ninety-Nines organization, asking members who had at least 200 solo flying hours to fill out a questionnaire about their flying experiences and indicate whether they would consider serving as a ferry pilot for six months to one year.[139] Women, some of whom were not even pilots, wrote to the AAF asking for more information about the program and how they could participate. Over 25,000 women applied to the WASP program to receive military training, and 1,830 were accepted.[140] This extraordinary number of women expressing interest, compared with the small number of women the AAF trained, meant that there was never a shortage of pilots for the program. Of those accepted for training, 1,074 graduated, not including 11 trainees who died before graduation.[141] Numerous motivations, including professionalism and patriotism, drove the applicants to the WASP program. The lack of a need to recruit for the WASPs illuminates how the program appealed to women for several reasons, including the availability of a nontraditional job opportunity, the desire to help with the war effort, or the interest in flying due to the possibility of the air remaining a space for future career opportunities.

A love of flying, a hope for an aviation career, and a desire to help with the war effort were the top motivating factors for the women who became the WASPs. Historically, the same was true for other women who served in the US military, including those in the Army Nurse Corps during the Vietnam War, who wanted equal opportunity through benefits, pay, rank, and career advancements that were not available in the civilian world.[142] In a similar respect, the AAF offered the WASPs what many hoped would be a chance to advance their aviation careers, as they flew more cutting-edge aircraft in the military than they had flown as civilians. These female pilots were not motivated financially, as they could have made more money as civilian flight instructors.[143] Many of the WASPs describe flying as "second nature" to them, as they felt "at home" in the air.[144] Often, they wanted to use their aviation abilities in a way that would serve their country.

When the United States declared war in 1941, many American women were motivated to help out with the war effort for patriotic or personal reasons. Some were inspired to join the WASPs due to their love of flying and "the feeling [of] . . . making a useful contribution" to the Allied cause.[145] Others wanted to serve since there were no boys in their family, and they wanted to "represent" their family themselves.[146] Women pilots who had relatives join different military branches wanted to follow in their patriotic example.[147] Other aviators flew to avenge deaths in their families or to contribute to the war effort. A wealthy pilot from Nashville, Tennessee, WAFS Cornelia Fort, explained her reasoning in a *Woman's Home Companion* article in 1943: "As long as our planes fly overhead the skies of America are free and that's what all of us everywhere are fighting for. And that we, in a very small way, are being allowed to help keep that sky free is the most beautiful thing I have ever known. I, for one, am profoundly grateful that my one talent, my only knowledge, flying, happens to be of use to my country when it is needed. That's all the luck I ever hope to have."[148]

Fort, who was "happiest in the sky," was the first woman pilot killed while serving in the AAF. She tragically died while ferrying a plane in a flight formation with other male pilots, one of whom hit her BT-13 Valiant. Fort was unable to recover her aircraft, and it crashed.[149] She was twenty-four years old and the first female pilot to die during the war. Her description of flying for her country reflects the motivations of some of the WASPs. A theme of retribution was also present at the WASP training base in Sweetwater, Texas, which was called Avenger Field. The name of the field implies a desire to avenge the deaths of Americans fighting overseas. During training, the WASPs called themselves "the Avengers," and this language of retaliation also illuminates how the pilots wanted to be weapons of war.

Patriotism was in the figurative atmosphere of World War II. Women in other branches of the military, including the marines (Women Marines) and the navy (Women Accepted for Volunteer Emergency Service), also served due to patriotism or to avenge men's deaths since many men their age enlisted or were drafted.[150] Just as men and women served in other areas of the armed forces, the WASPs joined the AAF to pursue their careers and express patriotism. They were enthusiastic about the rare opportunity to simultaneously fly and help with the war effort.[151]

Despite its gradual shift toward a male pursuit, flying offered women more opportunities than they found on the ground, where their career choices were severely limited. Once several women discovered their love for aviation, they abandoned their college pursuits. When WAFS Barbara "BJ" Erickson London started flying, she lost interest in being a home economics schoolteacher and never finished college. Raised in Seattle, Washington, during the Great Depression, Erickson recalled that her parents had a "tough" time raising three kids. For example, she remembered rationing and how she could only have one pair of shoes a year. When she went to the University of Washington, she found that women only had two majors to choose from: physical education or home economics.[152] Disappointed with these options, Erickson soon turned to flying. Another WASP quit college after her first flight and then took a job to pay for flying lessons.[153]

Many of the WASPs felt disillusioned by their college experiences because they discovered that even if they had degrees in fields outside of teaching, nursing, or secretarial work, those were often the only careers they could enter. As they had for the previous generation, the skies offered these women liberating experiences. WASP Catherine "Cappy" Vail Bridge's campus counselor at the University of California, Berkeley, told her that most women who graduated from the university, regardless of their degrees, went on to secretarial school.[154] This frustrated Bridge, who worked hard on a degree in political science and wanted a government job when she graduated. Another WASP received a zoology degree but had difficulty finding a job, so she had to turn to work as a secretary.[155] Even within the US military, most of the positions that women held in the army, navy, marines, and coast guard were in traditional fields, including communications, health care, or secretarial work.[156] When WASP Mildred Ola Rexroat tried to decide which branch of the military to join, she chose the WASPs over the navy or marines because she "wanted to get out of an office and do something active."[157] The WASP program was the only women's military unit that offered solely nontraditional work.

Female pilots' reasons for joining the air force offer insights into families' gendered debates about women in the military and expectations for women in World War II America. Families often had mixed reactions to female relatives' earning their private pilot's licenses or joining the AAF. Often, older generations, including great-aunts, grandmas, and even mothers, disapproved of women flying and questioned these pilots' motivations, sexuality, and morality. Many men harbored the same doubts. Nevertheless, others supported women's decisions to pursue their career goals.

Some WASPs had parents who fully supported their desire to fly and even helped pay for lessons. WAFS Florene Miller Watson's father bought an airplane, and he, Watson, and her two brothers learned how to fly.[158] Watson's parents owned a jewelry store in Odessa, Texas. As a result of her upbringing, she said that "it never occurred to [her]" that she could not fly as well as a male pilot. Furthermore, her parents always allowed her to "do anything" that her brothers did, so when she learned how to fly, she had confidence. "If those boys could do it, heck yeah, I could do it," Watson recalled. It was not until later that she realized the American public believed that women could not fly or had stereotypical ideas about women pilots.[159]

There were women pilots whose parents disapproved of their decision to join the WASPs because they did not find aviation, now identified with the military, an appropriate career choice for women. Some kept their flying lessons a secret because they assumed their parents would disapprove.[160] When WASP Elaine Harmon decided to learn how to fly, she needed her parents' consent. She decided to get permission from her father: "I knew my mother would never approve and I was underage so I had to get parent's permission. And I needed forty dollars . . . so I sent the notice to my father's office and it came back right away with the money and his signature."[161] She kept joining the WASPs "a secret" from her mother, who "disapproved." Harmon's mother thought her daughter should have a career in a field defined as a women's profession, perhaps teaching in a public school, or perhaps staying home and working as a housewife or mother. Flying as an AAF pilot did not fit her mother's definition of being a "proper woman."[162]

WASP Marty Wyall grew up in a conservative home in Fort Wayne, Indiana, and faced similar attitudes. Her mother, who did not want her to wear pants, believed that the WASP program was "not ladylike." After gauging her mother's response, Wyall turned to her father, a World War I veteran. Supporting her decision, he told her, "There's nothing better than serving your country." When Wyall's father took her to the train station to leave for training in Sweetwater, her mother would not go with them. Wyall had mixed feelings about this: "[It] was kind of hard for me to understand why she was so negative, but I think that the way the older generation thought of women . . . that we shouldn't be doing this, and that was her attitude."[163] WASP Helen Wyatt Snapp's parents were in a state of "disbelief" when she told them about her decisions because "women weren't supposed to do that." She and her sister kept a secret from their parents that they were learning how to fly.[164] In these situations, the women in the families were clinging to traditional gendered roles, while the men were supportive of their daughters' decisions. These opinions also reflected the unease and anxiety surrounding women in the military and the war.

Others had parents who were concerned about the safety of flying once the war started. WASP Catherine Vail Bridge's mother was concerned for her well-being, but she eventually changed her mind because she knew Bridge loved flying and wanted it as a career. Before marrying and having a family, Bridge's mother had wanted to be a doctor, but she could not get a medical degree because she was a woman and her parents disapproved. So she decided that her daughter could fly because she wanted her to have a different life and work in her chosen profession.[165]

Some of the WASPs recalled that their parents fully supported them and wanted them to pursue their interests. Teresa James's mother wanted to learn how to fly, but when health conditions prevented her from doing so, she supported James's decision to do the same. James's mother and father went on numerous flights with her.[166] A number of the WASPs also had such supportive families that their parents or in-laws helped raise their children while they served in the WASP program. At least twenty-nine women pilots had children under the age of fourteen.[167] These women placed their roles as mothers on hold while they pursued their military and aviation careers. Like the WASPs who came from families where mothers worked in nontraditional roles, these women held attitudes reflecting their adventurous spirits, and they identified themselves as pilots rather than adhering to traditional gendered expectations of women.[168]

Knowing familial and societal reactions to women serving in the military during World War II, Cochran set stricter qualifications for women pilots' admittance to the WASP program than were required of male pilots. She wanted her program to be seen as rigorous so that participants would be taken seriously as professionals. Later, she would also set different rules for the female pilots to preempt any fears society might have about gender roles and women's military service. Given her experience, Cochran believed her program would offer women a chance to solidify aviation as a field of gender equality. Thus, she attempted to gain male acceptance of women aviators' abilities. At the beginning of the WFTD program, before it merged with the WAFS to become the WASP, General Arnold incorporated Cochran's role as special assistant and director of women pilots into the AAF. Since Cochran directed the WFTD, she decided qualifications for trainees' admittance to the program, and she worked with AAF officials to ensure training standards for graduation and completion were equivalent to those for male pilots.

Because of the WASP program's experimental nature, Cochran made the qualifications for female trainees' admittance higher than the standards for male pilots. She also wanted women to prove they were competent military aviators. The original WAFS program required women to be between twenty-one and thirty-five years of age and to possess a high school diploma, 500 hours of flying experience, a CAA commercial certificate, and a CAA 200 horsepower rating. In addition, they had to present two letters of recommendation. These criteria remained the same for later classes as the WFTD and WAFS merged to form the WASP, except for the reduction of flying hours from 500 to 200. On the other hand, male ferrying pilots needed 200 flying hours and did not need a high school diploma or letters of recommendation. There was also the additional requirement for women of an interview with Cochran or one of her administrative officers.

The initial hours of flying experience and horsepower ratings were lower for the WFTD and WASP programs since the AAF trained women before assigning them to official duties, such as ferrying aircraft from factories to AAF bases. The requirement of 200 hours of flying experience to qualify for the program was later reduced to just 35 hours. This lowered requirement resulted from a decrease in the number of available women pilots who had logged 200 or more hours of flying time. The age limit for the WASP program also changed from twenty-one to eighteen and a half.[169] Cochran hoped to prove women pilots' capabilities and suitability for use as weapons of war with higher levels of qualification.

The WASPs understood their role in the war effort and the broader history of aviation. Some trainees appreciated Cochran's work in forming the WASP program and her efforts to earn a place for women in aviation.[170] They encountered men who thought that women could not be proper pilots, and that those who could be aviators must be "rough and uncouth." Thus, Cochran had "convinced [AAF] air heads that women can fly."[171] The WASPs understood the significance of their wartime and aviation roles, as evidenced in their newsletters containing monthly columns on the history of women in aviation and updates from various theaters of the war, including the work of pilots overseas.

While Cochran wanted women to earn a place in aviation, she was not embracing of all women. She rejected program applicants who could not pass as white—namely, African Americans—to project an image of the WASPs as white. This projection would contribute to her creation of an image of military women that fit the media's ideal, much like the images propaganda posters designed for the WAC, the other women's military unit created under the umbrella of the army during the war. For the WAC, the army produced recruitment posters with images of middle-class white women. Propaganda posters featuring working-class white women or African American women were limited.[172] Cochran believed these Black women pilots would make the program controversial in the media.[173] This restriction existed although most of the other military women's groups, including the WAC (army), WAVES (navy), United States Coast Women's Reserve (SPARS), Army Nurse Corps, and Navy Nurse Corps, accepted African American women. In addition, while the AAF excluded Black women, it allowed African American male pilots to serve, although in segregated units.[174] The only other branch of the military that did not incorporate African American women was the Women Marines.[175] Two Chinese American women and two Native American women were admitted to the WASP program, although it is unclear whether any Hispanic or Chicana women served. Since there was no category of race or ethnicity on the paperwork women pilots filled out, it is almost impossible to know the race and ethnicities of the women in the WASPs.[176]

One of the requirements for the WASP program was an interview with Cochran or one of her administrative officers, and this part of the application procedure screened women based on their appearance, and likely on their perceived race.[177] In Cochran's final report on the WASPs, she outlined that part of the interview process emphasized applicants' looks. Interviewers selected "clean-cut, stable appearing young girls of the proper ages, educational background, and height, who could show the required number of flying hours properly noted and certified in a log book." Cochran or her administrative officers eliminated women who did not fit this description after the interview.

African Americans and other Americans of color, including Native Americans, Mexican Americans, Chinese Americans, Japanese Americans, and Jewish Americans, hoped to receive full citizenship after the war. The popular Double V Campaign for African Americans pushed an agenda of victory abroad and at home. According to historian Ronald Takaki, communities of color "went to war not only for victory over fascism abroad but also for victory over prejudice at home. In their struggle, they stirred a rising wind of diversity's discontent, unfurling a hopeful vision of America as a multicultural democracy."[178] Japanese American men and women wanted their military service to gain citizenship rights back in the context of Japanese American internment.[179] Segregation in the armed forces during World War II meant separate units for African Americans and segregated military buses, blood banks, and barracks.

In the AAF, African American men could become military aviators for the first time, and just under a thousand of them served as pilots in the Tuskegee Airmen.[180] African Americans did not serve as pilots ferrying in the Air Transport Command or in other units or branches during the war.[181] Like the WASPs, the Tuskegee Airmen were described as experimental, and they struggled for full citizenship in the US armed forces through their role as military pilots. Brigadier General Noel F. Parrish, commanding officer of Tuskegee Army Airfield, where the Tuskegee Airmen trained during the war, said that Americans had the "same fears" regarding Black and female pilots.[182] The African American women who applied for the WASP program were also looking to serve the country under the Double V Campaign of victory at home and abroad.

The records on African American women pilots who applied for the WASP program are very slim. There appears to be only one rejection letter from Cochran that remains in the archives.[183] In this letter, Cochran justified Sadie Lee Johnson's rejection from the WASP program by noting that there were "no provisions for the training of colored girls." Cochran suggested that Johnson look at the WAC, which was accepting African American women, or find a job near her home to contribute to the war effort.[184]

Although evidence of these applicants of color is scarce in the archives, recent news articles reveal that at least four other women, and possibly one additional pilot, applied to the WASP program and were rejected based on race. Pilots like Janet Harmon Bragg, Mildred Hemmons Carter, Rose Rolls Cousins, and Dorothy Lane McIntyre interviewed or published memoirs to tell their stories about being Black women aviators during the mid-twentieth century. In these interviews and memoirs, they each mentioned rejection from the WASP program. Bragg had an impressive background in flying, as she attended the Curtiss Wright Flying School and later, after being rejected from the WASPs, trained under Charles "Chief" Anderson at Tuskegee Institute's CPTP.[185] When Bragg went for her WASP interview, her interviewer, Ethel Sheehy, "gasped" and said, "I've never interviewed a colored girl." Sheehy also followed up her comment by suggesting that there would be no place for Bragg to stay in Sweetwater, Texas, because housing availability was for whites only because of Jim Crow laws.[186]

Another woman rejected from the program based on her race rather than her qualifications is Mildred Hemmons Carter. Like Bragg, Carter received pilot training from the Tuskegee Institute's CPTP.[187] Both Rose Rolls Cousins and Dorothy Lane McIntyre also attended the CPTP, although at different universities.[188] McIntyre ended up teaching aircraft mechanics during the war.[189] While Willa Beatrice Brown Chappell did not leave behind any evidence of applying to the WASP program, she made a career out of aviation during her lifetime, and she was instrumental in the inclusion of African Americans in the CPTP. This work brought her national attention, and she was even featured in an article for *Time* magazine in 1939 before the WASP program started.[190] Since Chappell was well known and had an extensive background in flying, it seems reasonable that she would have applied for the program.

Although there is evidence of these women's rejection from the WASP program, Cochran's description of African American applicants in her autobiography, published shortly after World War II, is extremely vague. Cochran detailed interviewing "several" African American women pilots who applied for service, but she insisted that most of them did not qualify for it. However, while she mentioned that they did not qualify, they made it to the interview part of the application process. Cochran described interviewing one African American woman who did meet the WASP standards. She took the applicant out to breakfast and revealed her more significant concerns: "I told her the manifold troubles I was having getting the program started and ended by stating that I had no prejudice whatever with respect to the color or race of my candidates but that the complication she had brought up for decision might, for one reason or another, prove the straw that would break the camel's back. [She] . . . recognized the force and honesty of my arguments, stated that first of all the women pilot's program should be stabilized and strengthened, and she withdrew her application."[191] Based on this exchange, it appears that Cochran was worried that African American pilots would be too controversial for the already experimental and unproven WASP program. Although Cochran commented that she had no racial prejudices, based on the time of this event, she might have questioned the abilities of African American women pilots, just as the AAF did with African American male pilots.[192]

WASP Vi Cowden offered another possible interpretation for Cochran's exclusion of African American women: "At the time we didn't even know any colored girls had applied, although we did wonder why there wasn't at least one who could be qualified. I felt Jackie Cochran did a fairly good job in dealing with the issue, saying it would have been extremely hard on the girl herself. Of course, that still doesn't make it any better."[193] Cowden's analysis of the situation insinuates that African American women pilots would have felt excluded by the white women pilots or discriminated against by the American public or both.

Another interpretation of the exclusion of African American women is that they were more associated with a political movement than other ethnicities, such as Chinese American or Native American women. However, it is still interesting that Chinese American women could join the military despite the solid anti-Asian sentiment during the war.[194] Though these attitudes toward Asian Americans existed, the WAC admitted Japanese American women into its units. According to sociologist Brenda Moore, a combination of the army's dire need for women and Nisei women's refusal to join segregated units resulted in their incorporation into "white" units instead of the segregated African American ones. Moore concludes that "the military services of both Nisei women and Nisei men helped to reduce the prejudice, stereotypes, and racial antagonism directed toward them in previous years."[195] While an analysis of Nisei women's experiences in the WAC does not provide a reason for the inclusion of Chinese American women in the WASPs, it does show that another women's military program considered Asian American women to be white. A further possible reason for including Chinese American women is that China was an American ally during the war.[196]

Two Chinese Americans, Hazel Ying Lee and Maggie Gee, and two Native Americans, Ola Mildred Rexroat and Margaret Chamberlain Tamplin, graduated from WASP training. Rexroat was an Oglala Lakota from

South Dakota, and Tamplin was Cherokee.[197] For their inclusion into the program, Cochran or her administration officer must have considered them white or able to pass for white.

There were also at least nine Jewish women in the WASP program.[198] Florence Elion Mascott was a trainee, and she said that she had "no problem" with admittance even though it was a "known fact" that she was Jewish. WASP Bernice Falk Haydu recalled that while she did not encounter antisemitism within the military, she did experience it during the war before entering the program.[199]

Despite their admittance to the WASP program, there is evidence of racial tension and discrimination in the stories of both Hazel Ying Lee and Maggie Gee. Lee was the first Chinese American to fly for the US military, and she was one of the thirty-eight WASPs who died during the war. Although relevant sources are limited, other WASPs indicated that Lee faced discrimination during her service. Some of her classmates worried about her training in Sweetwater, especially when she had to make a crash landing in a farmer's field one day. As WASP Madge Rutherford Minton told her parents in a letter home, "Incidentally our chief worry about Ah Ying was not that she'd crack up and kill herself but that some ignorant Texas farmer or rancher would shoot her for a Japanese spy."[200] Lee died as the result of burns from an airplane crash with another pilot. After her death, Lee's family faced discrimination when Riverview Cemetery in Portland, Oregon, refused to allow her parents to bury her in the "white" area of the graveyard. Eventually, the Lees won a legal case and buried their daughter in that section.[201] This event illustrates how "white" was a contested category for Chinese Americans during the war.

However, the other Chinese American WASP, Maggie Gee, offered a slightly different interpretation of Sweetwater and the places she visited during her cross-country training, including Atlanta, Georgia; Stuttgart, Arkansas; and Greenville, Mississippi. Thinking about these trips, she commented in an interview, "These small towns are very different than they are out here [Berkeley, California], at that time. I had no problems in these towns. If I were black, it would have been a different story." She also mentioned that she thought Cochran excluded African American women because of the discrimination and segregation in the South. Gee eventually met some African American women pilots who were rejected from the WASP program when she gave a lecture on "early minority women in flight" at the Berkeley City Club. However, during the war, Gee benefited from the "wages of whiteness." While she did not experience segregation, her brother did: "Since he's dark like I am, a little darker . . . he had to stay at all the black places."[202] She related this incident because of his public perception as Black or Hispanic, since neither Blacks nor Hispanics could share public spaces with whites.[203] Thus, Cochran selected candidates who would pass as white in American society. Pushing for gender equality did not extend to a desire to end racism.

Amid this discrimination and the segregated Jim Crow military, some of the WASPs trained with Tuskegee Airmen at Mather Field in California during the war. As at other bases, the Black pilots were not allowed to eat in the officers' mess hall despite being commissioned officers. Some of the approximately twenty WASPs stationed at Mather Field asked the commanding officer to change this policy. He relented and allowed the Black pilots into the mess hall, but only if they sat together in a specific section. When some of the WASPs sat with the Tuskegee Airmen at meals, this "really upset a lot of the white boys from Alabama and Georgia" who were also attending the B-25 transition school.[204]

Early pilots, particularly barnstormers, inspired the women who became the WASPs, the women who believed the sky was a space for freedom, opportunity, and adventure. Female barnstormers, the ultimate modern girls, inspired a generation of women to become pilots, many of whom sought liberation from the constraints of society. With the start of World War II, women were essential to filling expanding roles on the home front and overseas. The CPTP made flying accessible to thousands of American women during the Great Depression. Overcoming financial and sometimes familial constraints, they found an adventurous lifestyle through aviation. "Happiest in the sky," these women pilots were eager to use their valuable aviation skills professionally and in a patriotic capacity, as thousands of them applied for the WASP program. During training, the WASPs continued to develop their identity as aviators, and they established camaraderie in the predominantly female AAF training bases in Texas. They hoped their pilot training would allow them to serve their country as untapped weapons of war.

2 We Live in the Wind and Sand and Our Eyes Are on the Stars

Identity and Camaraderie in Training

When you take off, it's power. You push the throttle forward and it pushes you right back into the seat and you go on up. It's beautiful up there. It's a very special feeling.
–WASP Lillian Yonally

In 1943, Lillian Lorraine Yonally worked for Grumman Aircraft Engineering Corporation in Long Island after earning her private pilot's license while attending a secretarial school in New York City. At that time, there were nightly blackouts and flying restrictions on Long Island due to the war and fear of enemy attack. Excited about the WASP program, Yonally applied for admission as soon as she turned twenty-one years old on May 5 and quickly went to get a physical from a doctor at Mitchel Field. When relaying this story to an interviewer decades after the war, she laughed as she explained that the exam was conducted by "a male doctor who had never done a female [physical], which was interesting." Upon learning of her acceptance to the WASP program, her boss at Grumman loaned her money for the flight from Chicago, Illinois, to Dallas, Texas, and then for the train ride to Sweetwater for training. Arriving at Sweetwater, Yonally's immediate reaction was that it was "hot and dirty," as the dust of West Texas coated everything. She quickly discovered that the best way to wash her government issue (GI) coveralls was to wear them while standing in the shower and scrub them with a scrub brush and soap. They would air-dry overnight due to the arid conditions of West Texas.[1] The unique experience of adjusting from civilian to military life in this climate and learning to fly more powerful aircraft at higher altitudes served as a source of camaraderie for the women pilots.

"We live in the wind and sand . . . and our eyes are on the stars."[2] The WASP trainees adopted this quote, possibly penned by a French World

War II pilot, as the motto for their program when they began their schooling in Sweetwater, Texas, in 1942.[3] When entering the WASP program, women received training at the only all-female airfields in Houston and then in Sweetwater. The WASPs fostered a work culture of camaraderie and an identity as pilots in this unique military space dedicated to training only women pilots. This female space remained an oddity in the male-dominated armed forces, and it was a place where women were training for one of the most skilled positions. Creating and maintaining traditions such as mottoes, class songs, rituals, and newsletters formed a military sisterhood that fostered trainees' successes while challenging definitions of military personnel.

The military regarded female pilots as weapons of war whose sexuality was dangerous to the success of the program. Fear of women's sexuality led the AAF to institute additional gendered rules and regulations beyond those given male trainees for the WASPs to obey. When a woman in military uniform was considered controversial, if not a contradiction, the WASPs wore their official attire proudly and as a sign of their hard work and military prowess. These pilots actively fought gendered assumptions about the limitations of their bodies, intelligence, and psychological abilities as they fought their way to graduation and demonstrated their flying skills.

The media cast the WASPs as glamorous girls rather than skilled aviators. Fears of a slander campaign and public disapproval of the program drove AAF officials, WASP director Jacqueline Cochran, and the War Department Bureau of Public Relations (WDBPR) to project a sanitized image of the WASPs that was not too controversial given established gendered roles. These authorities restricted the media's access to information about the pilot training to combat the American public's fears about women in the military. The AAF was concerned that excessive media attention, particularly uncensored coverage of women's accidents or deaths, would alter the results of the experimental women's pilot programs. Thus the Army Air Force discouraged media outlets from discussing hazardous aspects of the women's work and the fatigue of long flying hours to accomplish this agenda. The result emphasized women's physical appearance, leisure time, and feminine characteristics rather than their actual performance. This focus undermined their work not just on a local military level, but on a national scale in the general public. At the end of 1944, when Congress voted against a bill that would militarize the WASPs, representatives were partially influenced by media coverage that relied on a rhetoric of glamour to describe the WASPs and accused women of unnecessarily taking jobs from male pilots. As one journalist put it, the WASPs were just a "Lipstick Squadron"—a romanticized image etched into the popular consciousness.[4]

Within the work culture of the AAF, the WASPs formed a sisterhood that negotiated military life and flying the "army way."[5] Their identities were those of pilots, women, and military personnel within the hierarchy of AAF military leaders, Jacqueline Cochran, and the American public.

During World War II, women pilots flew the same aircraft and received almost the same training as the men in the AAF, excluding advanced aerobatics required in combat.[6] Male pilots in the AAF were trained separately from nonpilots, and, just like the WASPs, they often received their pilot's licenses under the Civilian Pilot Training Program (CPTP). Male aviators experienced three different stages of training (primary, basic, and advanced). Initially set for four weeks, the instruction period was later increased to nine weeks in 1942 and ten weeks in 1944.[7] The WASP program was tailored after men's pilot programs since the AAF needed women to fly the same military aircraft.

During training, female pilots had a comparable performance record to that of their male counterparts. They had similar test scores, graduation rates, and even washout rates as male pilots.[8] Although officially considered civilians until militarization, the WASP trainees followed military rules and regulations during the war and saw themselves as military personnel. They performed the same duties as AAF officers in that they flew military aircraft, lived on military bases, worked with other military personnel, and obeyed AAF rules and regulations. WASP director Jacqueline Cochran organized the program intending to secure military status for women pilots. During the 1940s, each branch of the US armed forces obtained authorization from Congress before granting the women in their military units benefits (e.g., medical coverage).[9] Cochran hoped that, with women's similar AAF training and compliance with military regulations, Congress would grant them militarization quickly to afford them military benefits, including medical care, insurance, and a military funeral if they died during their service. It was no longer just about the right to fly—it was about women pilots' rights as military.

The first classes of women started training at Howard Hughes Airfield in Houston, Texas, while the rest of the classes received instruction at Avenger Field in Sweetwater, Texas.[10] The AAF selected Texas as the location for training because of the different weather conditions throughout the state. According to class 44-W-2, the AAF selected Texas because of the variety of

AAF bases in the state and the varied climates.[11] The first three classes of WASPs trained in Houston, but then the program moved to Sweetwater.[12] According to Cochran, the move took place because the base at Houston was "makeshift."[13] Sweetwater became available soon after the program got underway in Houston. In the spring of 1942, Sweetwater Municipal Airport expanded into Avenger Field to train military pilots. British and US pilots who volunteered to fly for the British Royal Air Force were the first to train at the field. Later that year, the army closed this training.[14] When Cochran heard that the male pilots who had been training at Sweetwater were leaving, she obtained permission to have the WASPs transferred to Sweetwater permanently.[15] She preferred the location at Avenger Field due to its "multiphase training possibilities, its maintenance facilities, its compactness and its location in a nice community."[16]

When training moved to Sweetwater, the WASPs were perceived as novelties, similar to early women flying entertainers. Indeed, male pilots descended on the field just to get a glimpse of female trainees. When male cadets heard about the all-female base, they made "emergency" forced landings or buzzed Sweetwater with their planes. Since more than 100 men made landings there within the first week of its transition to an all-female base, Cochran and the AAF had to place restrictions on the field. Male pilots were no longer allowed to land since "the field was barred both by gate and from the air except in real emergency." As a result, the female trainees started calling the base "Cochran's Convent."[17] This nickname is just one example of how the WASPs transformed military rules into a work culture that was more their own during their shared training experiences.

Women pilots received varying degrees of publicity throughout the war, as the AAF heavily censored information about the program to curtail any disparaging coverage of the WASPs. Government censorship of the media was not exclusive to the WASPs, as the US Office of War Information, the WDBPR, and other organizations monitored what the American public was allowed to know about the war.[18] After the original Women's Auxiliary Ferrying Squadron (WAFS) program's overexposure to the media in 1942, the WDBPR, AAF officials, and WASP director Cochran worked to control and censor media exposure for the duration of the war. They established specific goals for portraying the WASPs in public, restricting the amount of news released to the media. These efforts successfully controlled publicity, including coverage of the first WASP training classes, accidents, and experimental programs.

Since women's sexuality was considered dangerous, the AAF and Cochran worked to contain it throughout the development of the program, all while presenting an image of the WASPs that in many ways mimicked propagandized images of women in World War II. These limitations imposed on the WASPs played into previous constructions of the ideal American woman who upheld traditional values of morality and femininity. Like the women featured in propaganda posters, the WASPs appeared above all else as heterosexual, feminine, and nondisruptive to conventional gendered norms. There were private and public discussions about women's bodies, both literally, in terms of their physical abilities and potential limitations, and figuratively, concerning the representation of the military women in uniform. One of the primary purposes of these conversations and restrictions was to keep the program from appearing controversial to the American public, primarily in terms of gender roles, race, and sexuality. The WASPs responded to these restraints and debates through various tactics as they fought for acceptance as professional pilots.

Cochran set additional rules for the trainees to create and maintain an image of the WASPs that eased the American public's fears about the sexuality and morality of women in the military and traditionally masculine work. These were rules in addition to those given to male pilots in training. Women in the armed forces were expected to be attractive, feminine, and chaste while minimizing their nontraditional attributes. There were debates about the extent of women's roles in the military and fears of women in military uniform within this wartime context. Female sexuality was seen as deviant or dangerous, as mentioned in Eleanor Roosevelt's description of women pilots as weapons.[19] For the WASP program, director Jacqueline Cochran created additional entrance and training requirements beyond those expected of male air force pilots to combat the gendered debates about women in the military and aviation.

Cochran based her decisions on preconceived notions of sexual behavior and rumors that military women were either prostitutes or lesbians. During training, the WASPs were given "sex morality, personal hygiene and health lectures" from the venereal disease control officer.[20] While the WASPs were also required to follow the rules about their social conduct to curtail their sexuality, the only training men received in these areas was on sex hygiene, not "morality," to prevent contracting a venereal disease.[21] Historians have explored this double standard of expectations for men versus women. During the war, the US government framed its battle against venereal disease in descriptions of women as sexual transgressors. While men's desire for sex was considered acceptable, women were supposed to repress their desires. This rationale explains the military's decision to hand out prophylactic kits for men but not for women. Preventing the spread of venereal diseases was considered a primarily female responsibility. In addition, the creation of military regulations was to enforce and control sexuality. The armed forces defined homosexuality as a problem and actively restricted citizenship through military service to heterosexuals in the first half of the twentieth century.[22] These two slanderous extremes, women's promiscuous heterosexual activities and their supposed susceptibility to homosexuality based on their military experiences, were both fears of the American public and lies that came from men serving in the army who wanted to avoid the draft.[23]

Cochran was not alone in trying to regulate female sexuality and the image of uniformed military women. She sought to avoid a media slander campaign like the Women's Army Corps (WAC) experienced. The press accused WACs of serving as prostitutes for male soldiers and alleged that the women were lesbians. When surveyed, the American public found WAC uniforms unfeminine, so the army added skirts to WACs' dress uniforms and required them to wear skirts in specific theaters of war overseas. Colonel Oveta Culp Hobby tried to confront the aforementioned accusations by setting strict regulations on servicewomen's behavior, such as restrictions on going to bars. She also worked with the army to project a more respectable image in the media of a middle-class, educated WAC. The army tried to avoid accepting lesbians by asking applicants specific questions about their motivations for joining. Recruiters asked women whether part of the reason they wanted to join the WAC was to "be with other girls."[24] Historian Leisa Meyer argues that these actions resulted in an image of the WAC that "sometimes challenged and other times reinforced the very racial, sexual, and gender norms used to proscribe, as well as support, their participation in the armed forces."[25] To an extent, this also was true for the WASPs.

Like Colonel Hobby, Cochran also set rules and regulations meant to assuage fears of women's sexuality. There were rules regarding trainee conduct within the town of Sweetwater. For example, the WASPs could not eat at certain restaurants because of the establishments' association with drinking. Trainees could not stay overnight in hotel rooms unless they were with their husbands or parents.[26] The WASPs could not wear nail polish during training, and they could only wear a small amount of makeup.[27] Both the army and navy enforced this directive, and after training, women were to refrain from wearing bright shades of lipstick or nail polish.[28] These restrictions on cosmetics allowed the military to prevent a hypersexualized image of women pilots that would attract public fears of promiscuity. Feminist studies scholar Page Dougherty Delano argues that wearing makeup in the military during World War II was "a sign of female agency that included sexual power and citizenship and as such was disruptive of wartime's masculine codes of power."[29] Makeup highlighted what kept women from full citizenship, but it also empowered servicewomen as they confronted public perceptions of them as unfeminine and as they affirmed their own sexuality separate from masculine militarism.[30] Thus, in addition to ensuring a particular image of military women, makeup restrictions sought to prevent a disruption to the established masculine nature of the armed forces.

Other rules attempted to prevent women's encounters with men, including social engagements with military personnel and instructors both on and off the post.[31] The AAF closely monitored interactions between male and female pilots and personnel. During the first women's pilot program, the WAFS, the AAF did not allow women aviators to fly with a male pilot or copilot, including mixed flight or crew assignments. With the creation of the WASP program, this rule changed to allow mixed flights since the trainees would be receiving most of their instruction from men.[32] On the base at Sweetwater, the WASPs could not sit with their male instructors in the mess hall, and there was a separate lounge where the men could eat their meals.[33] Cochran hoped to prevent a slanderous media campaign against the WASPs by prohibiting interactions between the sexes.

The trainees were aware of the discussion surrounding military women. Some faced their parents' disproval of their decision to join the WASPs, which stemmed from concerns about the nontraditional work their daughters would be performing and fears about homosexuality and the public's perception of women in the armed forces. For example, WASP Elaine Danforth Harmon's mother did not approve of her decision to learn how to fly. When Harmon first received pilot training, she was underage and needed one parent's permission, so she asked her father. Of her life after joining the WASPs, she said, "Everything had to be kept a secret from my mother [who would disapprove]." Harmon's mother thought that being a "proper woman" meant being a housewife and mother or working as a schoolteacher.[34] Harmon also said that when the WASP militarization bill went to Congress in 1944, "the general opinion nationally was women were doing something that was unladylike . . . [and] dangerous."[35] During the war, some WASPs knew that some parents resisted their daughters' participation in the program due to fears over public rumors of homosexuality. It is unclear how many women engaged in same-sex intimacy or relationships due to social stigmas and the restrictions and policing of military women's sexuality during the war.[36]

A significant wave of national coverage of the WASPs occurred in the summer of 1943 when a *Life* magazine crew and a newsreel crew visited the base in Sweetwater. Their feature story was on WASP trainees.[37] The magazine's cover featured WASP Shirley Slade, wearing her hair in pigtails and sitting casually on the wing of a plane. Several references to women's femininity were in the article, including mentions of Slade's attractive appearance. Referencing three photographs of WASPs sitting in a cockpit, the journalist described the women's hairstyles rather than their work. One full-page image showed three WASPs sitting idly, "leaning against the corner of the primary hangar." Photographs of the WASPs performing calisthenics during physical training had captions describing the exercises as simply "fun." The article included other images of women writing letters, sleeping on benches between flights, and sunbathing in their swimsuits. While the WASPs had these moments of leisure, the *Life* article clearly emphasized these activities instead of AAF duties, portraying them as inconsequential feminine pilots.[38]

An army-navy newsreel crew on base simultaneously put together a film shown in movie theaters before the feature film and viewed by service members overseas. Allowing these two major national media sources access to the WASPs coincided with the AAF declaring the WASP "experiment" successful. Several of the trainees remembered the newsreel crew coming to Sweetwater to acquire footage. These camera crews filmed in 1943 and 1944, and the WASPs considered them an "eternal shadow" following them around due to the hours of video footage taken.[39] They filmed the trainees in various activities, including performing calisthenics during physical training, swimming, taking off in planes on the runway, and participating in graduation ceremonies. Other newsreels filmed in the spring of 1944 were of the WASPs sunbathing and riding in "cattle cars," their mode of transportation during training. In December 1944, an official Army Air Force cameraman took the last footage of the WASPs at Avenger Field.[40]

These activities also appeared in the army's short film shown to the American public in movie theaters.[41] Several WASPs saw the footage in theaters during the war or had family members and friends who saw it.[42] This

Army-Navy Screen Magazine motion picture, *WASP WWII News Report*, was supposed to represent the WASP experience to the American public. In addition to showing aspects of the pilots' training, it also showed women putting on makeup, swimming, sunbathing, reading magazines, and braiding hair. As with other forms of media, this motion picture reassured the American public that these women could remain feminine despite their military roles. Despite their work, the narrator reminded the audience, these pilots were "still [members of] the softer, fairer sex."[43]

No national advertisements portrayed the WASPs, as the program's "policy [did] not approve the use of WASP in commercial advertising" unless other servicewomen were featured as well. A wartime Tangee lipstick ad portrayed a model as a woman pilot. The caption reflected the gendered views of women workers during the war: "For the first time in history woman-power is a factor in war. . . . You have succeeded in keeping your femininity—even though you are doing man's work! . . . No lipstick—ours or anyone else's will win the war. But it symbolizes one of the reasons why we are fighting . . . the precious right of women to be feminine and lovely—under any circumstances."[44] A 1943 *McCall's* magazine featured an anonymous female pilot wearing bright red lipstick, gazing into a sky filled with wartime airplanes on its cover.[45]

Another wartime image featured different Cutex nail polish colors, each with a description reflecting the various aspects of women's aviation work throughout American history.[46] In a later advertisement, Cutex tried to publish an image of the WASPs alongside women from each of the other military branches, but the AAF did not grant permission.[47] While the proposed advertisement featured women in the WAC, Women Accepted for Voluntary Service (WAVES), US Marines, United States Coast Guard Women's Reserve, and WASP, Cutex substituted a woman from the Navy Nurse Corps for the WASP image.[48] These and other images reinforced the stereotype expected of American women in the armed forces. They also followed the trend of most American propaganda posters, which consistently portrayed women wearing makeup, seemingly to affirm the status quo. Similarly, the army and navy only allowed women to wear "light" makeup, not bright shades of lipstick or nail polish seen on posters. In so doing, they hoped to minimize public fears that military women were promiscuous. It was perhaps out of these fears that the AAF prohibited advertisements from portraying female pilots. The AAF also took measures to ensure a specific image of the WASPs at the all-female training base in Sweetwater, Texas, as women learned to fly the "army way."

Military training for the WASPs was organized and developed to militarize women pilots into the AAF, although aspects of the program remained civilian until women could be declared members of the armed forces. The WASPs were subject to military discipline but were not subject to court-martial jurisdiction. They performed military drills, lived in military barracks, wore military uniforms, received the same military training as men except for combat, and served in military assignments while stationed at AAF bases.[49] When the WASPs were directed to report to Texas for training, some received a telegram explicitly stating this intention to incorporate them into the military: "It is probable WASPs will be militarized. If you are not prepared to follow through in this event, do not report at Sweetwater on 6 Sept."[50]

In November 1942, WASP trainees went to Texas for training at their own expense since they were civilians.[51] They also paid for their own transportation home if they washed out.[52] In addition, women pilots were required to pay for other aspects of training. They received $150 a month during instruction, and they used this salary to pay $30 for physical training clothes, $1.65 a day for room and board, $1 for mess hall meals, and fees for transportation to the training field.[53] Male trainees, on the other hand, received $75 a month until graduation. This amount is half the women's salary, but male pilots did not have to pay for lodging, clothing, food, or insurance that provided full medical and dental health coverage. After covering these expenses, women pilots had much less than $75 a month, depending on the amount spent on mess hall meals. This discrepancy was a result of the WASPs' civilian status. Furthermore, male pilots received comprehensive insurance with medical and dental services.[54] If the WASPs wanted such coverage, they were required to purchase it independently through a civilian company.[55] Finally, the WASPs also had to pay for a part of the cost of their uniforms.

The WASPs had several different uniforms during training, including coveralls, a dress uniform, and a physical training (PT) uniform. Trainees were also issued men's GI mechanics coveralls to wear during flights and ground-school classes; the WASPs called them "zoot suits" because they were baggy with so much extra fabric. The women would often belt the coveralls at the waist, rolling up the sleeves and pant legs. "Zoot suits" referenced the suits African American and Chicano men wore during the 1940s as they challenged middle-class expectations and formed an ethnic identity.[56] The excessive material used to make these outfits was controversial and considered unpatriotic due to wartime shortages and rationing.

WASPs' name for their coveralls coincided with the famous Zoot Suit Riots. Bonding over the awkwardness of these uniforms, they nicknamed them and took playful pictures of themselves wearing them. There are numerous mentions in WASPs' letters, diaries, and memoirs of the term "zoot suits," minus a reference to the riots. In addition to coveralls, the trainees wore hairnets or turbans when flying to prevent their hair from getting in the way midflight.[57] If they did not want to wear hairnets or turbans, they could wear their hair in braids, which many women found "the most sensible method" of dealing with their hair.[58] As evidenced in their slang use of "zoot suits," women bonded over this aspect of military life, reminiscing about it years after the war and talking about their coveralls in their newsletters.[59]

The AAF decided that even though the WASPs were civilians, for "military security," they needed to wear dress uniforms like the other women in the army, the WAC. Early classes of the WASPs had dress uniforms comprised of tan khaki pants, white button-up shirts, brown shoes, and a tan flight cap.[00] Although members of the original WAFS had matching uniforms designed by a tailor whom Nancy Love hired, new official attire was needed when the two women's pilot groups merged to form the WASP.[61] In the fall of 1943, a research and development branch of the AAF and over thirty companies developed an official WASP dress uniform.[62] As Cochran explained in an interview years after the war, Bergdorf Goodman was one of the designers.[63] These official WASP dress uniforms were Santiago blue, similar to the color of the AAF men's uniforms, and they consisted of summer and winter skirts, pants, jackets, and berets.[64] While the AAF paid for the skirts, pants, jackets, and berets, the WASPs were required to pay for the remaining items that made up their dress uniforms, including blouses, ties, purses, shoes, undergarments, and gloves.[65]

There were specific AAF regulations about when and how WASPs could wear their uniforms. For example, they could not wear their PT shorts in downtown Sweetwater, they could not wear "loud colored socks," and they could only wear coveralls on the flight line.[66] These regulations reflect a desire to make the WASPs look uniform and military, but the rules about not wearing shorts in town in Sweetwater align with previously mentioned rules about maintaining women's propriety. For the era, shorts equated to immodesty when worn in public, let alone by women in the military.

There was also a public discussion of military women's and even non-military women workers' uniforms in the media, and it offered women ways to attract a man by appearing a bit flirtatious without crossing the line into promiscuity.[67] The editors of *Good Housekeeping* created a list of "rules" for "How a Woman Should Wear a Uniform" in order to lure men, noting that "most" men "don't like a woman in uniform."[68] Editors told their readers not to wear their uniforms when on a date, off duty, at night, or while smoking or drinking. Furthermore, they advised women not have a short, "mannish" hairstyle or walk in a masculine "swagger." In essence, this article was trying to ensure women looked feminine. Another wartime article specifically addressed nonmilitary uniformed women to make sure they only wore their official attire at work. The article stated, "Army and Navy men . . . live in a uniformed world of men," so "when they have any time off they want to see girls and women looking thoroughly and appealingly feminine."[69] This essay ignored the fact that military women also wore uniforms, and it implied that a woman in uniform disrupted visual distinctions between men and women.

Although civilian, the WASP trainees constructed an identity as military pilots through the wearing of their uniforms. Other wartime servicewomen also formed new identities as they "assumed and embodied newly available subject positions of the female soldier."[70] Similar to military men, women were also proud of their branch of service. In one class song, the WASPs compared themselves to WACs and WAVES. Instead of wearing olive green or navy blue, the women pilots took pride in their Santiago blue uniforms, whose colors, the song's lyrics told other women in service, "[were] never meant for you." After all, the WASPs asked, "who would want to be confined to earth?"[71]

They even gave one another advice on how to properly wear those Santiago blue uniforms, noting that this "should be a matter of personal pride."[72] The author of this newsletter article argued that trainees should not have to be reminded of the AAF regulations "on the proper wear and care of . . . Santiago blues." Thus, she included excerpts from the regulation book. For example, when wearing their uniforms, the trainees could not wear any other civilian clothing, and they should keep their official attire "cleaned and pressed, with . . . insignia bright and free from tarnish." Most importantly, the trainees were supposed to "at all times conduct themselves in a manner befitting the dignity of the uniform."[73] Several wrote letters home to their families expressing their excitement and pride over receiving and wearing their dress uniforms.[74]

Along with their uniforms, the WASPs wore military-issued dog tags for identification in the event of their death. One WASP explained the significance of receiving her dog tags in a letter home to her sister: "It gives me a peculiar feeling to be wearing an official identification tag around my neck; somehow it intensifies the significance of the whole thing. Now I think I really am a part of this war."[75] The act of donning dog tags and military uniforms caused the WASPs to construct an identity that denoted status, citizenship, and the language of the military.

In addition to requiring uniforms, WASP training kept women on a strict, regimented military schedule to indoctrinate them into the army way of life. Training lasted from five to seven and a half months and included ground school, cross-country flying, night flying, instrument flying, and daily calisthenics. Ground-school courses included physics, navigation, math, meteorology, radio procedure, and Morse code. There were three different phases of training—primary, basic, and advanced. A typical day could include a 6:00 a.m. taps for wake-up, 6:15 a.m. breakfast in the mess hall, 7:00 a.m. instrument flying, 8:00 a.m. PT, 9:00 a.m. ground school, noon lunch in the mess hall, 1:15 p.m. flight line for instruction or check rides, 8:00 p.m. dinner in the mess hall, 8:30 p.m. meeting, and 10:00 p.m. taps, which signaled for everyone to be in their beds.[76] This transition from civilian to military life led many female pilots to assume an identity as pilots and military.

A critical aspect of training that would save many lives in the dangerous space of wartime aviation was instrument flying. This type of flying, also known as blind flying, required the pilot to only use the instrument panel inside the aircraft without seeing outside the plane. Instrument flying was necessary for specific AAF assignments, and in case female pilots flew into a fog, clouds, or other conditions. In order to teach instrument flying to pilots, the AAF used contraptions known as Link Trainers. These were stationary blue boxes that faintly resembled airplanes with mini wings and had a small area inside that replicated a cockpit instrument panel. Trainees would be shut inside these un-air-conditioned boxes and would listen to their instructor give instructions through headphones. They experienced simulated flight situations, and the Link Trainer recorded the trainees' use of the instruments. A grade was assigned based on performance. WASP trainees often stressed about the hours spent inside these Link Trainers because of the challenging nature of responding quickly and accurately to instructions.[77] Some even considered it the "most difficult" aspect of their training.[78] As many were aware of the importance of Link Trainers, there was a phrase passed around during the war: "Link training is a pilot's Life Insurance."[79]

During each of the three phases of their instruction, the WASPs flew more complicated aircraft as they moved from primary to basic and then to advanced training. These aircraft were increasingly more advanced in terms of their size and the skill required to fly them. The WASPs' continued progression through this training solidified their military sisterhood, and they would reminisce about the sensory experience of flight—the feel, sounds, sight, and smell of military aircraft—decades after the war.

The women's introduction to planes on their training base began as soon as they arrived, and before taking to the air they knew they would have an entirely different experience from flying civilian aircraft that were less powerful and traveled at lower altitudes. When one WASP arrived at Avenger Field, she noticed "the roar of the engines and the, maybe a little scent of gas over here." She further recalled, "But I could see, barely see the exhaust . . . of some of those engines. . . . It was so exciting. . . . The roar of those engines!"[80] Some WASPs simply loved "the sound of air."[81] Another WASP said that her "heart simply started to pound" when she saw the "tremendous air fields, the huge hangers, and the beautiful planes in the air." The primary trainer plane (PT-19) that she flew was "so different" from planes she flew at home, as it was faster, had twice the horsepower, and had more instruments.[82] Trainees described the open-cockpit PT-19 as a "neat little airplane" that was "lots of fun." The basic trainer, the BT-13, was infamous for the way that it vibrated down the runway. One of the difficulties in flying the BT-13 was that it was hard to get out of a spin.[83] The advanced trainer, the AT-6, was one of the women pilots' favorite planes, as it felt "natural to fly" and responded "instantly and smoothly" at the controls.[84]

In the same vein as the early female aviators, the WASPs described military flying as freedom, and they observed the beauty of the skies from high altitudes. One WASP commented, "To me, you're free [while flying]. You're free of everything. You're up there all by yourself, and you're just free. I like that feeling. The only place you can get it is up there in the air all by yourself."[85] Many felt that the air was a "comfortable" place that offered a sense of belonging. As one WASP observed, "I always say the worst thing about flying is coming back to Earth. That's the hardest thing for me. I would stay up there, I would."[86] Some female pilots described the beauty of the sky during night flying: "[There were] falling stars and you could see them so clearly in contrast to the blackness of night." Others noted the clouds: "[You could] play a little game, run around the clouds, you know, to see if you could get through here."[87] The WASPs enjoyed flying at high altitudinal spaces in aircrafts that were heavier and faster than those available in the civilian world. Through this flying, they also asserted their rights to these spaces as professional pilots.

WASPs were given check rides by Army Air Force officers and civilian pilots during each phase of training. A trainee's first check ride was with a civilian pilot. If she passed, she would then have an AAF check ride. If a WASP received an "unsatisfactory" grade for the civilian check ride, she would take a few more hours of training and then take another civilian check ride. If this second attempt also proved "unsatisfactory," she would then take an AAF check ride and most likely "wash out" of training, meaning she failed training and would have to go back home.[88] When a trainee washed out, it reminded the other women pilots about the intensity of their education. When one WASP's baymate washed out of training, she wrote a letter home to her sister, saying, "It gave us all a mighty queer feeling to look at that empty bed in the corner. However, I'm beginning to see that it isn't a disgrace to fail in this business; this Army technique damn sure isn't easy."[89] Overcoming these intense moments and fear of failure allowed female pilots to solidify their military sisterhood, as those who passed made it through obstacles together.

Trainees also learned how to perform marching drills, prepare for weekly barracks inspections, wear uniforms properly, and carry out military courtesies such as saluting. In addition, they familiarized themselves with the basics of chemical warfare.[90] WASPs marched to each aspect of training, including ground-school classes, the flight line, and the mess hall. They saluted and stood at attention when an officer entered a room.[91] Following these rules and regulations helped the WASPs learn the "army way," as they frequently called it.

The WASPs solidified their bonds as women and military personnel through their shared experiences transitioning from civilian to military life. WASP trainees received demerits in the same manner as male cadets. For regular army inspections, they needed to keep a clean bay in the barracks, which meant having polished shoes under the bed, clothes hanging neatly in lockers, blankets neatly tucked in, and pillows aligned with the right side of the bed, among other things.[92] For example, they could receive demerits for having a bucket of ice water in the bathroom unemptied before the barracks inspection.[93] Trainees could also get demerits for taking food out of the mess hall "at any time." However, according to WASP Eleanor "Gundy" Gunderson, this rule was often violated, as the women who got back from night flights were hungry. At a WASP reunion in 2011, Gunderson told a humorous story about how she and some other trainees stole milk and other snacks out of the fridge one night when they returned from flying.[94] Over these shared moments, the WASPs grew closer together and formed an identity as military pilots.

Women trainees also forged ties over their fierce pride in service to their country, firmly placing themselves alongside men fighting overseas as weapons of war. The WASPs manipulated this analogy in terms of avenging men's deaths: "We are out to avenge . . . our men who have made last landings in Africa, Bataan, Pearl Harbor, [and] Kiska."[95] On numerous occasions, the trainees called themselves "the Avengers," a reference to their role in World War II and the airfield's name where they trained in Sweetwater. They openly proclaimed their role in helping "win the war" and "make men free."[96] One trainee reminded her classmates that they should not complain, because "somewhere a Marine was lowered into an unnamed grave under the only insignia—Old Glory."[97] In several newsletters, WASP trainees included excerpts from an AAF Blue Network Broadcast entitled *Wings to Victory*, thereby illuminating the women's identification with male pilots. One broadcast reminded listeners about the prisoners of war tortured and mistreated by the Japanese. It also provided imagery of a deceased POW whose eyes reflected "torment unspeakable," and it encouraged listeners to make full use of "our [the United States'] avenging planes." While the audience of this broadcast was male pilots, female trainees' inclusion of this excerpt in their publications shows they identified with the imagery of "avenging planes."[98] Furthermore, they interpreted themselves as weapons in the war.

During their training experiences, the WASPs created traditions and pilot rituals that reaffirmed their military status. These activities serve as a basis for understanding their evolving work culture. In addition to adopting the "wind and sand" motto referenced earlier, the WASPs also wrote songs, published newsletters,[99] and took the Walt Disney character Fifinella as their mascot. Thus, during rare moments of leisure, female pilots developed a camaraderie in this unique military space.

Beginning with the first class, the WASPs developed and maintained a newsletter tradition. The earliest pilots in training started the *Fifinella Gazette*, named for the Walt Disney cartoon character that the WASPs had adopted as their mascot.[100] Later classes continued the newsletter tradition, calling their paper *The Avenger* after the airfield in Sweetwater, Texas, where they trained.[101] These newsletters were published and distributed among WASP trainees.[102] Presumably, the WASPs could print their own opinions about their training experiences since the WASPs, not the AAF, published the circular.[103] Although the newsletter was not sanctioned by the AAF, it was distributed to Cochran, General Arnold, and Major General B. K. Yount, commanding general of the AAF Training Command. AAF officials could request copies of the publication or even subscribe to it.[104] Although air force officials and Cochran read or at least received their newsletters, the WASPs felt secure enough to publish complaints about issues ranging from the army way of training and calisthenics to the difficulty of understanding their instructors.[105]

Another tradition of the WASP trainees was that each class created song lyrics, just as male pilots did in the AAF. The WASPs sang these songs during their instruction, and each class chose one song to sing at the graduation ceremony.[106] Almost all of these lyrics rhymed, and they also corresponded to the musical scores of popular songs. Therefore, despite their upbeat tone and simplistic words, the songs offer insights into the ways WASP trainees encouraged one another and experienced their training. Essentially, the lyrics represent how the women wanted to remember their pilot instruction. Male aviators in World War I also wrote their own lyrics to the tunes of popular songs. These melodies revealed "dreams, disappointments, fears, humor, loneliness, loves, [and] frustrations," just as the WASP song lyrics did.[107]

Like male pilots, the WASPs received classbooks, akin to modern-day yearbooks, upon graduation. Classbooks for both male pilots and the WASPs contained pictures of General Arnold and other superior officers, class photos of each individual pilot, cartoons, and anecdotal stories.[108] These volumes felt like "a morale builder" for the trainees, especially for the last group that graduated.[109] In addition, classbooks contained words of inspiration such as the following quote: "May we have the courage, the perseverance, and the same single-mindedness of purpose to maintain the principles for which we fight now and without which no peace can be lasting."[110] The WASPs also signed their classmates' classbooks, just as high school and college students signed yearbooks.[111]

These WASP traditions of newsletters, songs, and classbooks show the camaraderie and military sisterhood the women shared. The trainees advised one another, bonded over life in West Texas, shared mistakes to ease the hard work of flying, and even grieved over the death of classmates. In direct contrast to the media's interpretations of the program, the WASPs provided evidence of the unglamorous nature of military training. An analysis of these issues illustrates the methods the WASPs used to cope with the rigors of their education. Overall, the WASPs all shared a love of flying that transcended any experiences or hardships they endured.

Like their male counterparts, some of the WASPs bonded over their shared living spaces, as they experienced the same "sense perceptions and bodily events" during training in West Texas.[112] In Sweetwater, there were barracks where six women lived in a bay, or room in the barracks, with six army cots. There were eight bays in a barrack.[113] Like the rest of their training, sharing a room with six women was an adjustment for some WASPs. Ann Chisholm Dessert Oliver said that she was the "prude" in her bay because the other women were more comfortable with this situation since they had lived in college dorms or were married. Oliver recalled yelling when one of the trainees started to take off her clothes to get in the shower: "[I shouted,] 'Stop! One of the rules of our bay is that nobody can go lower than their bra and pants and then they go in and take their shower.' And all of the girls just looked at me in utter amazement."[114] The trainees also adjusted their sleeping arrangements during sweltering nights in Sweetwater, Texas. Since the barracks did not have air-conditioning or fans, the women would pull their cots outside and sleep there. When they woke up the following day, they would be "covered with sand," yet another reason behind the WASP "We live in the wind and sand" motto.

Working-class men also fostered a sense of brotherhood amid common dangerous work experiences like coal mining, and their environment was an integral part of their work culture.[115] Military men, too, formed bonds across class or regional backgrounds as a result of their shared spaces. In World War I, soldiers who fought alongside one another in trenches formed tight friendships.[116] Infantrymen in Vietnam spent most of their time isolated with their unit, and they went weeks without seeing other units. As a result, the men developed close ties, a concept known as unit cohesion.[117] The WASPs, in a similar sense, bonded over the heat, wind, and aridity of West Texas.

Although some WASPs were from Texas, the majority were not. Female pilots came from every state in America, and only 92 of the 1,074 of those who graduated from training were from Texas. Trainees mocked or mimicked Texan accents.[118] They even bonded with Sweetwater residents who invited the WASPs into their homes for meals or to their ranches to ride horses.[119] The WASPs frequently described the wind, dust storms, and fluctuating weather patterns.[120] In a reoccurring column in *The Avenger*, one trainee concisely summarized these conditions: "Hot but humorous—that's how we are most of the time here in Texas."[121] A cartoon of a trainee with a distraught face and spiky hair provided a visual representation of the weather. The caption read, "Windy on the flight line today??!"[122] The

WASPs complained that the winds and open-cockpit flying made their skin extremely dry, as evidenced in an exaggerated story about a trainee who used saddle soap, a leather-care product, on her face.[123] Laughing about Texas provided another experience for the WASPs to bond over, as women found yet another commonality and another topic to brighten their conversations.

WASPs developed a camaraderie as they "worked together toward a common goal" of completing training and felt the constant pressure from check rides and tests. Through these experiences, they became "lifelong comrades." As training advanced, the trainees "grew closer" together, and they "exchanged funny anecdotes and tales of close calls on . . . flights."[124] Sharing a sense of humor helped them bond.[125]

The trainees often approached their duties with a sense of humor. Anecdotes, cartoons, fictional stories, and photographs of the train-ees in entertaining poses occur throughout WASP publications and in women's private collections. Examples of humorous photographs include women "modeling" baggy GI "zoot suit" coveralls or hugging a sign reading "Women trainees only in this area."[126] In another instance, the trainees wore several layers of clothing because the red and green flags at the field were accidentally raised together. A red flag meant the WASPs were to wear civilian clothes, while a green flag meant they were to wear coveralls.[127] So some of the WASPs wore their dress clothes over their coveralls.[128] Male soldiers also relied on jokes and humor to dispel tense situations. During the Civil War, servicemen told jokes to lighten the atmosphere after fighting in combat.[129] Like the WASPs, male military personnel in World War II created newsletters with cartoons, funny photos, and jokes with the mission statement of "indoctrination, training, [and] morale."[130]

The trainees used humor to discuss flying mistakes or difficulties, par-ticularly in the early stages of their education. One cartoon depicted a WASP making the mistake of sitting on her parachute and then having it open while she was carrying it.[131] A recurring newsletter column entitled "Sky Happy" contained brief anecdotal stories of trainee errors. In one story, a pilot yelled at her instructor that the aircraft was on fire. It was then that she realized it was only the blue flame of the exhaust.[132] When joking about military life, one WASP warned, "Beware when you get back to civilian life," because she had performed her mess hall chore of stacking her dishes and pouring the coffee from her saucer back into her cup at a local restaurant in Sweetwater. This comment subtly reflects the trainee's understanding that being in the military stood in sharp contrast to her life before and after the AAF.[133]

Sometimes aviators blamed mistakes or aircraft malfunctions on the Walt Disney character Fifinella, a character that was called a female "gremlin."[134] Author Roald Dahl wrote a popular children's story about fictional gremlins who sabotaged aircraft while he was serving as a flight lieutenant in the Royal Air Force in Britain during World War II. Walt Disney Studios soon received the copyright for the story, published in 1943, and it quickly gained popularity among pilots in the United States.[135]

The image of Fifinella was another source of bonding for the WASP trainees, just as gremlins and other cartoon characters were for male pilots. Fifinella appeared on WASP stationery and patches on the sleeve of the women's uniforms. Furthermore, several WASP songs mentioned Fifinellas, and a column in the *Fifinella Gazette* featured imaginary stories about the character.[136] Trainees also used the imagery of the character to their benefit, calling her a "kind hearted gremlin who rides with students, helping them out of tight spots."[137] The fact that the WASPs adopted Fifinella illuminates their creativity and sense of humor, as well as their adoption of a superstition, similar to how male pilots would perform the same ritual before a combat flight.[138]

Another superstition that women pilots adopted was dropping a quarter into the wishing well at Avenger Field for good luck before a flight.[139] The well was built by Lieutenant General Barton Yount and General Arnold and dedicated to the WASPs.[140] Some trainees also engaged in the pilot ritual of throwing a trainee into the wishing well at Avenger Field once she completed her first solo flight, although this was more of a bonding celebration than an expression of hope for good luck.[141]

As a result of the reality of the WASPs' dangerous work, newsletters also provided a forum for trainees to share serious advice, including ways to remember specific ground-school lessons or how to make a proper emergency landing.[142] Some WASPs felt that their sense of humor helped them get through the rigors of ground school.[143] Newsletters offered mnemonic devices to help trainees recall aircraft specifics or flying techniques.[144] Each issue of the *Fifinella Gazette* provided hand-drawn pictures and specifications for various military airplanes.[145] Other articles offered humor to relieve stressful situations. One WASP offered suggestions on how to have successful and enjoyable cross-country trips. Even if they got off course and missed checkpoints, she suggested that trainees lie to their instructor and say they had reached each checkpoint. Furthermore, if forced to land in a "West Texas town," trainees should find a location that either offered "good food or a cadet flying school!"[146] Although WASP instructors and the AAF would not condone them, these suggestions offered a way for the women pilots to feel more relaxed about their first cross-country flights.

The WASPs also encountered sobering reminders of the dangerous nature of their work, such as the death of a classmate. Although the WASPs thought of themselves as military, death was a reminder that they were still officially considered civilians. During the program's existence, eleven of the thirty-eight WASP casualties were trainees who died before graduation.[147] Since these pilots were civilians, in the event of their deaths during the war, their families or friends sometimes had to pay to have their bodies shipped back home, and they also paid for the funerals.[148] According to accident reports, at least some WASPs had their bodies shipped at the government's expense. As one accident report stated, "The U.S. Employee Compensation Commission will allow for burial expenses up to $200.00 and remains will be shipped at government expense."[149] While the WASPs were not entitled to receive a military funeral, there were some exceptions. The pilots closest to the deceased would often escort the remains home and attend the funeral. Since the AAF did not pay for WASP escorts, Jacqueline Cochran often paid these women's travel expenses out of her personal bank account.[150]

In some cases, WASPs could receive a semi-military funeral or memorial service, and all WASP casualties received small recognition in the form of letters. General Arnold and Jacqueline Cochran wrote to the families of the deceased women, including their husbands, if they were married, and their parents or closest relative.[151] In most letters, Cochran told families that she hoped they could "find comfort in the fact that when [their loved one] was called upon to make the supreme sacrifice she was serving her country in the highest capacity permitted women today."[152] These letters comforted some family members, including WASP Mabel Rawlinson's mother, Nora, who wrote a letter back to Cochran. Nora Rawlinson explained how much her daughter enjoyed flying as a WASP and expressed hope that Mabel's life had not been "sacrificed in vain." She brought the letter to a powerful conclusion: "[Mabel] has proved that girls may also give the 'last full measure of devotion' to their country."[153] By quoting President Abraham Lincoln's Gettysburg Address, Nora Rawlinson aligned her late daughter with men who died in battle.

Although female pilots were not considered military during the war, Mabel Rawlinson received a military funeral. A local newspaper article detailed that her service was "the first military funeral for a woman in Kalamazoo and, possibly, in Michigan." The Kalamazoo Civil Air Patrol placed an American flag on Rawlinson's casket, held a gun salute, and had buglers play during the service. There were also airplane flyovers in the former WASP's honor.[154] Thirty-four years after Ms. Rawlinson's death, when the WASPs received militarization in the late 1970s, her mother, Nora Rawlinson, was still alive to see her daughter receive recognition for her wartime service.[155]

Two other WASPs also received military funerals. Dorothy Mae Nichols received "military rites," according to her hometown newspaper. She had a fatal accident while serving with the Sixth Ferrying Group at Long Beach, and the other WASPs from the group served as the pallbearers at her funeral. WASP Betty Stine also had a military funeral, according to a Santa Barbara, California, newspaper. Stine, who fatally crashed during her last flight right before graduation, was granted "full military rites," and her parents, who were at Avenger Field for her graduation, received her "wings and uniform posthumously."[156]

Understandably, the loss of a classmate also affected the WASPs psychologically.[157] When Kathryn "Kay" Lawrence died in an accident during primary training in Sweetwater, WASP Adaline Blank wrote a letter home to her sister describing how it was such a "terrible blow" to lose someone "so close" to them, especially a trainee in their flight class. Blank said that she realized accidents are "inevitable" in a pilot's life, but she still felt "jittery." "It took real nerve to do my first solo spin that [next] morning," she admitted.[158] WASP classes also donated their classbooks in memory of deceased classmates and instructors.[159] Years later, in the 1990s, one WASP said of Mabel Rawlinson's death, "It was a very traumatic time for all of us there. . . . This was the first time that I had seen a friend die. So it was a trauma for me and I think for all of us."[160]

The WASPs communicated their grief over these trainee deaths in memorial services and practices. There was an "In Memoriam" segment in their newsletters for the deceased, and these publications also posted memorial service announcements for the women.[161] Some of the WASP trainees were friends with Betty Stine, one of the thirty-eight women pilots who died during the war. Before her death, they had taken a fun trip to Juarez, Mexico, during one of their weekends off, and while they were there, Betty had purchased a bottle of tequila and a big straw hat. They collectively decided to share the bottle after graduation in her memory. Later, Betty's friends gave the hat to her parents when they came to the base. One of the WASPs said of the Stines' visit, "I'm afraid I was chicken. I couldn't talk to her parents.... I don't think I could have handled [that]."[162] In the case of Kathryn Lawrence, there was a memorial service held at the Methodist church in Sweetwater.[163]

Some WASPs even kept or carried published prayers (e.g., "The Prayer before Combat") and poems about the dangers of flying.[164] They described feeling nervous to take their next flight, especially after witnessing the death of a classmate.[165] Instructors had trainees go up for a flight soon afterward to help them push past their fears.[166] Recent interviews show that the WASPs were deeply affected by these losses. Although women pilots only experienced a few months of training together, they described how they quickly grew close to their classmates, particularly their "baymates," the six women they shared a room with in the barracks.[167]

In addition to helping one another through grief, the WASPs also developed close bonds through their interactions with instructors. Trainees' interactions with their male instructors were often the result of gendered assumptions that many men in the AAF and American society had about women. These men believed that women were incapable of becoming successful pilots due to a lack of intellectual, physical, and emotional capabilities. One male aviator remarked that he "turned pale at the mere thought of entering the traffic pattern with 'all those women.'"[168]

Men believed women could not handle military aircraft or even flying because of the stereotype that women were physically weaker. Unlike modern planes, 1940s aircraft required physical strength, rather than automation, to fly. Some dismissed the abilities and successes of the WASPs as "luck" to further preconceived notions about masculinity in the AAF; this behavior was similar to the ways contemporary male doctors dismissed nurses as nonprofessionals.[169] These reactions existed even though the WASPs passed the same AAF physical examination for flying that men did.[170] One officer accused women of being "too weak" to fly heavy aircraft, and he supported his argument by claiming that women could not do more than ten push-ups.[171] However, as early as June 1943, *Time* reported, "Already discarded by military airmen is the notion that women airmen are good only for flying light craft like piper cubs."[172]

As the WASP program continued thanks to their successes, women pilots were assigned to ferry heavier and faster aircraft after graduation, proving their abilities throughout the war. Heavier aircraft were multiengine, such as the B-17 or B-29 bombers that dropped bombs overseas. The faster aircraft that the WASPs flew were typically pursuit planes (e.g., P-38 or P-51).

These were used overseas for fast combat fighting, and they protected the bulkier, slower bombers. Heavier aircraft were more challenging to fly in terms of the required strength and skill set than the lighter ones the WASPs piloted during training. Some instructors provided the WASPs with instructions on handling heavy aircraft to prepare them for these more advanced planes. For example, one instructor taught women to perfect their flying techniques because the more precise their flying, the less physical strength required. He also had WASPs do exercises to build up their arm, wrist, and hand strength.[173] The WASPs heard about AAF officers questioning the women's physical strength when discussing the militarization of the program, as one WASP mentioned in a letter home to her family. Even though flying was tiring and required a "great deal of physical stamina," she believed it was "worth it."[174]

The WASPs also quickly overcame the aircraft restraints of cockpit design as they used their upper-body strength to maneuver large aircraft. Scholar Rachel Weber addresses the gendered motivations behind military and civilian construction of cockpits initially built for average-sized men. These spaces did not suit women's or smaller men's body sizes.[175] Two of the problems with cockpit design included the weight accommodation of ejection seats and the location of controls on the flight deck in relation to the seats. Since many women are "shorter, [and] have smaller limbs, and less upper-body strength" than men, the WASPs often could not reach all controls on the flight deck from their seats. Furthermore, ejection seats were designed for heavier people, and they needed to be altered.[176] Some WASPs sat on pillows to reach the controls, while others put blocks on the pedals to comfortably access them.[177] There were height limitations for male and female pilots, and sixty-four inches was the minimum height for women. The AAF raised this height requirement from the original minimum of sixty-two and a half inches as the WASPs flew increasingly larger and heavier aircraft.[178]

In addition to concerns about female strength, there were also questions about other aspects of women's bodies. However, the WASPs learned to adapt like any good soldier or airman. Women pilots faced the restrictions of an aircraft built for men when using the relief tube midflight. WASP Virginia Dulaney Campbell shared a story about the lack of a pilot relief tube for women in the plane she was flying on a cross-country trip during training. On the flight from Sweetwater to El Paso, she realized she needed to go to the bathroom, but she was hesitant to land because she knew there would probably not be a women's bathroom on any airfields. So Campbell decided to use the pilot relief tube. Before doing so, she needed to take off her jacket and zoot suit. After removing them, she realized she was wearing a "one-piece red flannel underwear." She carefully removed it while still trying to keep the airplane on course. By this point, she explained, "I'm sitting there in my bra and I . . . look for the pilot relief tube. It was there. I finally find it, and it's this big around. [Laughter]." Campbell recalled what happened when she decided to use it regardless: "Needless to say, I don't think anything went in the pilot relief tube. But where it went was all on the floor—all around my clothes. Everything is sopped! Now I gotta get the whole lot back on."

Before putting all her clothes back on, Campbell reached the airfield in El Paso, and the tower operator at the field asked whether she was ready to land. She replied that she would "call back" when she was ready, and she continued to get dressed. In the meantime, the tower operators asked whether she was "in trouble" or needed them to "send someone up" to help her land. After finally landing, the other women pilots asked Campbell whether she needed to use the bathroom, and she said, "Forget the damned ladies room!! I don't need it." She laughed about the story years later as she told it in an interview to a fellow WASP, but she also said it was "so embarrassing" at the time. Furthermore, Campbell learned from her mistake and "never" had that problem again.[179]

A wartime AAF medical study of the WASP program concluded that more research on relief tubes was needed, including to determine whether the current design was "adequate." The findings also noted the need for a "clothing design to provide more ready access" for women. The study's authors mentioned that one company had designed a "special suit" that was still untested in a "large scale trial."[180] However, these problems went unresolved during the WASP program, and they are an issue that still plagues twenty-first-century female military pilots.[181]

The WASPs also faced medical expertise designed to undermine their military capabilities.[182] Until the mid-1940s, some doctors and medical experts believed that the physical strain caused by airplane aerobatics would damage a woman's reproductive organs or that women would be emotionally unfit to fly during their menstrual cycles.[183] Anthropologist Mary Douglas provides a framework for understanding these medical concerns through her arguments about the body's orifices.[184] These inaccurate medical conclusions were reached in spite of the fact that women had flown as pilots for years before World War II.[185] There was also the belief that menstrual cycles hurt women's flying abilities; women pilots would need to be "off duty for a few days each month" and would therefore be rendered "undependable" compared with male pilots.[186]

However, the WASPs resisted by refusing to report their cycles or claiming they were "irregular."[187] During the war, women pilots proved they could "safely, efficiently, and regularly" fly all types of military aircraft despite physical restraints.[188] Furthermore, at the end of the WASP program, Cochran concluded that the women's health had "not interfered with their service."[189] Part of Cochran's conclusion came from a medical study conducted on the WASPs during their service. The purpose of this study was not just to assess the women's performance but also to consider the future incorporation of female pilots into the US military. Various flight surgeons and medical officers collected data from 430 reported cases of women's menstrual cycles.[190] This was the number after some cases were "thrown out" because the WASPs gave "replies that they thought . . . would enhance the percentage[of responses] in favor of women pilots"! Therefore, in addition to inconsistently reporting their menstrual cycles, the WASPs also altered their responses to questions about them.

When asked, none of the trainees said cramps would interfere with their flying. The medical officers noted no changes in "visual acuity and depth perception" during flights when considering the performance of female pilots who had their period. Finally, there was no correlation between a woman's period and her elimination from training, and "of the 11 fatal accidents, 112 major, non-fatal accidents, there were no demonstrable contributing menstrual factors." The conclusion of the study was as follows: "Menstruation is not a handicap in selected candidates to prevent a woman from fulfilling her job as a pilot of military aircraft."[191] Histories from AAF bases where the WASPs served also concluded that the WASPs did not lose flying time due to their menstrual cycles. While one base reported that some of the pilots needed one to two days off for their period each month and were "more easily upset [and] tired more quickly" when they had their period, this type of report was scarce in AAF base histories.[192] These studies and reports made women's bodies a source of debate among medical professionals.

There were also doubts about women's psychological aptitudes and their potential impact on women's flying abilities. Cochran and the AAF had a series of medical studies conducted on the WASPs, including aptitude and psychological tests. In the end, these medical reports showed that women pilots "had as much endurance and were no more subject to fatigue and flew as regularly and for as long hours as the male pilots in similar work."[193] Furthermore, WASP test scores were comparable to those of the male pilots. Female trainees' washout and graduation rates were comparable to the male pilots' rates because primary instructors eliminated pilots who were not of the highest caliber.[194]

The trainees' dating lives were also strictly monitored while at Sweetwater, and although they were forbidden to date instructors, the lines between students and teachers were blurred. During training, there were at least 100 male personnel at Avenger Field, including civilian and military flight and ground-school instructors, guards, and other staff.[195] There were around 100 women trainees in each WASP class and around three classes training at Avenger Field at one time, for a ratio of one man for every three women.[196] Some women dated AAF pilots and personnel, even though doing so was forbidden.[197] These WASPs justified this behavior by saying it was inevitable for women pilots and AAF men to marry because they shared a love of flying and had close contact during training and afterward on AAF bases.[198] Female trainees would also sneak off to a cabin whenever they had the occasional day off, and they would hang out with several of the instructors. The men and women only "talked and laughed," and there was no kissing because trainees caught with an instructor would be "expelled."[199] Years after the war, when a group of five WASPs reminisced about training, they laughed about the ways that the pilots and their teachers found opportunities to meet.[200] Although most were careful not to push the boundaries too far and be dismissed from the program, the women bonded over these secret excursions.

The WASPs employed different strategies for meeting up with male instructors to avoid washing out of training. Many WASPs dated civilian— not army—instructors, according to WASP Maggie Gee, because the majority of army men were married and had less interaction with the trainees. On the topic of sex, one scarcely discussed in archival sources about the WASPs, Gee said that she did not think any trainees slept with their instructors in order to pass training. Nor did she remember any trainees getting pregnant during the program.[201] While it appears many WASPs hid their dates with instructors, one trainee washed out of the program for dating a flight-line civilian instructor.[202]

Not all WASPs were interested in dating instructors. Out of respect for maintaining a professional military image, some did not consider it acceptable to transcend the boundaries of the rules and regulations. These women approached their relations with the opposite sex in what they saw as a strictly professional manner by refusing to date pilots while in the service.[203] There was also a WASP song that warned against relationships with male officers. "Zoot-Suits and Parachutes" told a fictional story of a WASP who slept with a pilot: "The moral of this story, as you can plainly see, / Is never trust a pilot an inch above the knee. / He'll kiss you and caress you, and promise to be true, / And have a girl at every field as all the pilots do."[204] This song alludes to the stereotype about male pilots sleeping around that at least some of the WASPs must have found to be true. The WASPs also spent time with male or female instructors and their families in a platonic capacity in their homes and apartments.[205] Many instructors invited the trainees to eat Christmas dinner or spend holidays with their family.[206] Regardless of their interactions with instructors, the trainees bonded with one another through their shared experiences and the memories they created.

Of course there was an element of risk in experiences with male instructors who held the power to keep women out of the skies and the military. Instructors exercised a certain degree of control over whether women pilots passed or failed check rides during training. On occasion, male aviators treated the WASPs according to their gendered assumptions about them, as evidenced by WASPs' interactions with their teachers. In instances of intimidation and harassment, the WASPs ignored or resisted their instructors or sought to prove their flying abilities. Not all encounters with male instructors and check pilots were adverse. Many WASPs observed that male pilots' acceptance came after the men flew with female pilots.[207] Negotiating their interactions with male instructors prepared the WASPs to transition into the predominantly male AAF bases, serving in various assignments.

Some male instructors who carried gendered assumptions tried to prevent the WASPs from passing training, perhaps because women challenged their military identity. WASP establishment officer Leoti Deaton said at the conclusion of the program, "Previously, many of the officers, particularly the check pilots, were openly disparaging and openly resentful toward the training of women pilots."[208] Deaton's analysis from her years of working with the WASPs at Sweetwater illuminates a distinction that sometimes existed between AAF pilots and civilian pilots. Female aviators frequently found check rides with civilian pilots to be preferable, as AAF pilots "were very unhappy being associated with a women's field" and articulated their intention to fail as many women as possible.[209] An AAF check pilot told one WASP, "I came here . . . to see how many of you women I could wash out."[210] Such experiences were frequent enough that trainees would warn upcoming classes about the current instructors.[211] Whether intended for intimidation or a teaching method, these threats often encouraged the WASPs to work even more rigorously. Furthermore, female pilots had the same washout and graduation rates as male pilots, so regardless of their interactions with instructors, there were still a comparable number of women graduating.[212]

There were WASPs who believed these AAF men were even embarrassed that their work involved teaching women. Perhaps this embarrassment derived from the belief that teaching women was insignificant compared to teaching male students who would fight in combat. The WASPs who encountered these instructors hesitated to report them for fear of being washed out of training, as they could also receive demerits for "improper or disrespectful" behavior toward officers or instructors.[213] One WASP had an encounter with an instructor who "flipped the plane into a maneuver that was so violent that [she] was knocked unconscious," and blood came out of her nose and eyes. She chose not to report the man, even though he did not apologize, because she was worried about graduation.[214] Another WASP described the abuses of her instructor who screamed, cussed, hit the stick against her knees until they bruised, and held his earphones out the cockpit so the loud noise of the wind would come through her earphones.[215]

Many WASPs talked about their instructors hitting the stick against their knees midflight, and they even compared bruises with one another. One woman revealed that when a trainee made a mistake during a flight, her instructor would "slam the stick back and forth banging [her] knees." This WASP felt that it was an "effective" tactic that made the trainees feel a "lack of respect."[216] Another told her parents during training that although she had teachers who cussed her out and pounded her with the stick during flights, she would "rather have a rugged instructor who makes flying hell than one who barely or perhaps doesn't get you through the civilian and Army checks."[217] To these female pilots, graduation meant more than any hardships suffered during training. Other WASPs encountered sexual harassment from instructors. One confided in her parents that Captain Rose had become a "problem," as he had touched her hand, telling her that he was "looking forward to having her in AT-6 training." Her solution was to "avoid him as much" as possible.[218]

Because of this physical or sexual harassment, trainees chose to resist their instructors through various methods. It was possible to request different trainers, and some WASPs had their requests fulfilled.[219] When WASP Kay Herman's instructor kept taking the controls over, she forcefully asked him to remove his hands from "her" controls.[220] Others made light of the tense interactions between WASPs and male instructors by writing articles, poems, and cartoons in their newsletters. In one article, a trainee posed a fictional interaction between an instructor and student in which the former yelled, "Can't you do anything right?"[221]

Not all interactions with male instructors and check pilots were combative or antagonistic. Some WASPs noticed male behavior patterns and determined that male pilots eventually accepted women pilots, even as comrades. After an initial period of "rudeness," "complete acceptance and admiration" followed once the male pilots interacted with the female pilots.[222] WASPs worked to overcome resistance from male aviators who were initially "skeptical" of women's abilities, but after flying with the women, the men "almost always accepted" them.[223] These reactions were also evident in WASPs' encounters with male pilots on AAF bases during their assignments after training. Negotiating their way through these experiences with instructors, trainees achieved a sense of accomplishment as they drew closer to graduation, and they believed themselves prepared for their AAF assignments when they would leave their all-female space to work alongside primarily male pilots.

Graduation ceremonies and celebrations reinforced women's embrace of a military sisterhood. Throughout their training, many of the WASPs had experienced "not really aggression, [but a] competitiveness, a real push, a desire to get through and do it."[224] So, when they did complete training, the WASPs celebrated, publishing news of their graduation in hometown newspapers and sending invitations to their family members to join them in their class's graduation ceremony.

The WASPs threw parties to celebrate the completion of their final army check rides. Members of class 43-W-8 called their celebration a "To Hell with Army Check Rides' Party," and a skull-and-crossbones image adorned the top of the invitation card. This unsanctioned, candlelit night party was held to allow the women to "drown [their] fear of Capt. Miller in good company and good food"—and likely in illicit alcohol, given with this reference to drowning their troubles.[225] At their final army check-ride parties, some WASPs smuggled in bottles of alcohol that they sometimes buried between the barracks at Sweetwater.[226] There were also official army parties for the WASP graduates, and local papers published news of the women's graduations.[227] The civilian company that ran the airfield, Aviation Enterprises, gave each WASP an "Award of Graduation" and sent each woman's parents invitations to the graduation ceremony.[228]

Despite training difficulties, the WASPs longed for graduation day and subsequent assignments allowing them to fly military aircraft at an AAF base officially.[229] Most of the WASP class songs described their elation at finishing pilot training and how they would always "treasure" their pilot wings.[230] One WASP said the program graduation ceremony was "100 times more thrilling than college graduations."[231] Articles in the program newsletter assumed a reminiscent tone when mentioning training at Avenger Field.

The new graduates often passed advice or words of encouragement to the new incoming class. Class 43-W-3 issued a warning: "You'll be deglamorized speedily. You'll acquire sore muscles . . . [and] a farmer's leathery neck. . . . You'll gripe and you'll love it."[232] One of the class songs of 44-W-8 offered this guidance: "Now before we go, / There's a thing or two . . . that we'll say to you. . . . / There are tears and heartaches and checks to go. / You will keep yer heads up and win we know."[233] Numerous song lyrics and newsletter stories provided a forum to describe daily struggles. By venting about these issues, the trainees collectively acknowledged their similar feelings. Class 44-W-7 sang, "You've earned your wings the long hard way, with lots of work and little play." A later class hailed upcoming WASPs as follows: "You left your lovelife, your night life and all such good things; / To get those silver wings."[234] These lyrics reassured the trainees that their work and sacrifices serving their country were worthwhile and ultimately rewarding.

The shared experience of training was something that fostered women's sense of camaraderie and identity as pilots. The WASPs formed a support network to help trainees through their education and the loss of a classmate, providing advice and encouragement along the way. By joking about daily struggles, women pilots used humor to release their frustrations. Like their male counterparts, they created or maintained traditions in rare moments of leisure, wrote class songs, performed pilot rituals, took humorous photographs together, and published a monthly newsletter. WASPs dedicated precious, limited time to these activities, evidence of the bonds they formed as a military sisterhood.

As Cochran and the AAF worked to promote an image of the program that would appease the American public, the trainees responded in their own ways, whether by bending the rules about dating or giving distorted answers to medical officers about their menstrual cycles. Some even scoffed at parental concerns about their sexuality and expected gender roles. The WASPs actively fought gendered assumptions about the limitations of their bodies, intelligence, and psychological abilities as they fought their way to graduation and demonstrated their flying skills and military prowess. They even adjusted to the physical constraints within cockpit design in their struggle to prove that airspaces were not just for male pilots. When a woman in military uniform was considered controversial, the WASPs wore their uniforms proudly and as a sign of their expertise as military pilots.

As WASP trainees donned their uniforms after graduation, they constructed an identity that denoted status, citizenship, and the language of the military. With the completion of training, the WASPs faced magnified gendered assumptions about their abilities as they left the all-female base in Sweetwater and entered male-dominated bases across the United States. In these spaces, their work culture would be contested and solidified. Furthermore, the elite group of women who graduated from WASP training had proved their ability to adeptly fly military aircraft and now had the opportunity to use their newly acquired skills as weapons of war.

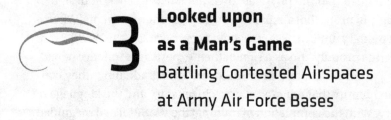

3

Looked upon as a Man's Game
Battling Contested Airspaces at Army Air Force Bases

The P-51 was the love of my life. It was so well engineered that when you were flying, and once you had it trimmed, if you leaned forward, it would go forward. If you leaned back, it would go, it would go up. You could turn it, just— you didn't have to touch it. —WASP Vi Cowden

After she graduated from WASP training, Virginia Dulaney Campbell went to Merced Army Airfield in California, where male officers only gave her one assignment during her tenure on the base because, they claimed, other WASPs stationed there had performed poorly.[1] Each morning, she would wait in the operations room for orders. One day, Campbell was assigned to ferry a male Army Air Force general to San Francisco. After the flight, she recalled, "You should have seen the look on [his] face. He said, 'You made it.' Just like it was a big surprise." After that, Campbell requested a transfer to Stockton Army Air Base. When she arrived at Stockton, the man at the gate asked her why she was there. When she told him she had orders, he remarked, "What do you mean orders? You're a woman." His surprise at a female pilot on base was not unique. After some back-and-forth, he called the commanding officer, who confirmed Campbell's orders. At Stockton, she worked as a test pilot and encountered gender discrimination from male mechanics. Campbell argued that she worked to prove her professionalism to men in the AAF in each of her assignments.[2]

Although women pilots had been in aviation in the decades before World War II, AAF men considered the WASPs above all else "novelties" when they arrived at AAF bases after training.[3] In calling these pilots "novelties," the Central Flying Training Command, a regional section of the Army Air Force, referenced male attitudes toward women flyers and the introduction of women into the male-dominated AAF. During the war, many WASPs encountered numerous male pilots who did not even know women were flying for the AAF. As the Central Flying Training Command stated, "War and Army flying in particular had been looked upon as a man's game. It was no wonder that male pilots as well as others looked askance at the possibility of using women as pilots in numerous and sundry activities vital to the war effort."[4] These men and often the American public believed that both war and military flying were "a man's game," and it is no surprise that the WASPs encountered hostility during their service. Once the women proved their abilities to top AAF officials, they progressed closer to militarization as they attended officer candidate school. The WASPs served in assignments across the United States, but they still relied on their military sisterhood despite isolation from other women. On AAF bases, the WASPs maintained their identity as military pilots with even more vigor and fought to be taken seriously as professionals, but they faced resistance.

Although they battled in this contested airspace of aviation, where courage, prowess, and rational intellect were essential, they remained oddities to the AAF officials who saw them at best as an experiment for the duration of the war. Categorizing WASPs' assignments as women's work masked the dangers and skills essential to wartime flying behind a facade of anomaly. These issues challenged the work culture and solidarity that the WASPs built during training. As the women remained scattered at different AAF bases, they maintained networks with one another as they developed strategies to assert their military skill, expertise, and rights in often-dangerous altitudinal spaces. In so doing, the WASPs challenged what it meant to be a wartime hero. While wartime flying was challenging work that was physically uncomfortable and exhausting, female pilots found flying at high altitudinal spaces in heavier, faster aircraft than were available in the civilian world rewarding. Through this flying, they asserted their rights to these spaces as professional pilots.

After training, the WASPs worked in various assignments on over 120 AAF bases in the continental United States during the World War II. These assignments were ones that male pilots also performed, and they included ferrying, target towing, tracking and searchlight missions, radio control flying, basic and instrument instruction, engineering test-flying, and administrative and utility flying.[5] Women pilots were assigned to different categories of jobs as they proved their abilities. When members of the original Women's Auxiliary Ferrying Squadron (WAFS) ferried light aircraft successfully, they began to receive assignments for ferrying heavier multiengine aircraft.

After these initial successes, WASP director Jacqueline Cochran petitioned the AAF to allow the WASPs to fly in increasingly treacherous and
more experimental work. Since the WASP program was a test of women
pilots' capabilities, Cochran wanted women to serve in as many AAF roles
as possible. After ferrying, the second assignment given the WASPs was
target towing, and then the aviators progressed to the other types of work.
The purpose of expanding WASP assignments into different areas was to
determine, experimentally, whether female pilots could complete those
aspects of military flying successfully. If the trial rendered positive results,
the AAF planned to employ women pilots permanently in the future or
during another war. After the program concluded, the AAF wanted a record
of all WASP activities in the event another women's pilot program was
created.[6]

Ferrying was the first assignment for women pilots in the AAF, and they
needed to prove their success in this formative stage of the women's pilot
program. While all AAF assignments involved an element of danger, ferrying was deemed less controversial for the Army Air Force and the American
public. Perhaps this was because women were not placed near the line of
fire, as they were in towing targets. Ferrying also required the most significant number of women pilots during the war. This duty demanded that
WASPs prove their competency as pilots to ensure the program's success
and allow women to earn a position as military professionals. As they
ferried planes, women pilots maintained a loose network to support and
encourage one another. They continued the friendships formed during
training and further developed their identity as military pilots.

Although the first group of women pilots, the WAFS, did not experience AAF training, they still connected over their mutual love of aviation,
despite the often-isolating work of ferrying aircraft. Cross-country flights
were physically exhausting and uncomfortable. Women often had to
dehydrate themselves since there was no female relief tube in any aircraft,
and it was often difficult to find a women's bathroom on bases. As the
work required quick turnarounds, pilots often had no time to shower, eat
regular meals, or do laundry. In September 1942, the original WAFS were
the first women placed in ferrying jobs.[7] Initially, women pilots were only
allowed to ferry primary and liaison aircraft. Nancy Love, head of the
WAFS, requested that the women transition to more advanced aircraft,
but this did not occur until the spring of 1943. The program was declared
a success, and women pilots transitioned to additional types of planes,
such as multiengine aircraft.[8]

Although these women had civilian status, they differed from male civilian pilots in that they collectively could fly every type of plane in the AAF. Male civilian pilots only knew how to fly a limited number of types of planes.[9] Ferrying was challenging work that required flexibility from male military pilots and the WASPs as they had to adjust to different types of aircraft depending on the trip. For example, there was no room for an instructor in the P-47, a wartime pursuit aircraft, so a pilot's first flight in the plane was alone. One WASP who picked up P-47s from the factory to take them to military bases for male pilot training remarked that the plane was "cumbersome" to fly, adding, "[It landed] faster than you would expect because it was so heavy."[10] Ferry pilots had to remember these details about planes and adjust to the feel of flying them. Early ferrying successes were vital to continuing the women's pilot programs, and the women's excellent flying record itself was an act of resistance that silenced questions about their abilities. This work ensured the continuation of women's ferrying duties for the AAF.[11]

Despite these successes, WASPs who ferried planes and nonflying officers faced resistance from AAF men. Sometimes the AAF would assign a woman pilot several back-to-back trips without letting her know in advance. Thus these aviators would find themselves away from their assigned base for a week or more without any packed luggage. WAFS Teresa James said that other women pilots taught her tricks for refreshing her clothes each night since there was no time to wash them. James would take her pants and put them in between the mattresses she was sleeping on so that they would get pressed during the night. Her lengthiest trip was thirty days with one set of clothes![12] Some women aviators played tricks on one another while still at their assigned ferrying base. Several WAFS pilots placed a bucket of water on their friend Betty Gillies's door and then left the door ajar four to five inches. When Gillies opened the door, the water landed on her head. In return, she sewed the sleeves of her friends' uniforms shut![13] These rare moments of camaraderie and leisure contributed to the work culture of the pilot program, as women struggled in the male world of the AAF, where they continually were perceived as trivial.

Several WASPs who ferried planes encountered complications on overnight flights due to contemporary mores about women traveling alone. These aviators often stayed in nurses' quarters, but if there were no facilities for women, they would have to stay in a hotel room.[14] Since single women traveling alone were associated with prostitution, many hotels would not allow women pilots to stay overnight. Even some dining rooms and restaurants refused to serve women who ate alone.[15] One WASP had a hotel incident involving gender protocol while visiting her fiancé in Tennessee. She needed her fiancé to pretend to be her brother and make reservations for a hotel room. Southern hotels would not allow single women to stay overnight without a chaperone.[16]

When trying to land at AAF bases and airfields, the WASPs often met with surprised personnel. Since the WASP program was experimental, some AAF men and control tower operators had not heard of it. WASP Florine Maloney remembered her encounter with ignorant air force personnel: "When we were flying, of course, actually the group was not well-known. . . . I can remember calling into the tower for landing instructions and the tower came back and wanted to talk to the pilot. . . . And I said, 'You ARE talking to the pilot.'"[17] When the WASPs landed on an AAF base, men were "curious" about women pilots and watched them land at the field.[18] When WASP Joanne Wallace Orr landed at an airfield late one night after ferrying a plane, the man at the flight desk handed her a prophylactic kit. Not realizing what it was at first, she took it and then went to get some sleep. She said that when she saw the man again later, he was embarrassed and apologized: "He said 'We've never had a woman in here before, and it didn't occur to me we'd ever have a woman. . . . Next time will you please speak?'"[19] As in this example, the WASPs were a novel disruption to the male military culture on AAF bases.

Sometimes men perceived female pilots as less of a novelty and more of a threat. In a reversal of traditional gender roles, the WASPs protected male passengers when they ferried them across the United States. Nonflying AAF officers expressed hostility or hesitancy at flying with women pilots, as in WASP Virginia Dulaney Campbell's experience at Merced Army Airfield. Other WASPs encountered men who were not just resentful but fearful of flying with them. Stationed at Foster Field, Dorothy Allen ferried nonflying male officers to different bases in Texas. In an interview decades after the war, she remembered resistance from some of the officers. For example, one protested that he did not want to "fly with a woman," but the major at the base told him that he did not have a choice since Allen was the only pilot available. Later, after the flight, the officer apologized and told her that because he had "never flown with a woman before," he was hesitant. He then stated, "I would be willing to fly with you anywhere any time."[20] Allen's experience represents a pattern of behavior among male pilots whose skepticism often turned to acceptance.

The need to constantly prove their abilities proved tiresome for some WASPs in the male-dominated atmosphere. As Alyce Stevens Rohrer told her parents in a letter home, "The men around here like to look down their noses at a women test pilot anyway. If everything goes allright according to them it was just luck and if I do something wrong it's just what they expected. You know what I mean. I really don't like to carry to extreme the 'women can do anything men can do' attitude, but I do think it's silly for them to always have to be shown." She continued by saying that while men who flew with her would believe she was a good pilot, it would take "forever" for her to take them all up.[21] Rohrer's comments reflect the frustrating struggle of becoming accepted as competent professionals with whom it was safe to fly. Her comment about the dismissal of women's abilities as "luck" reflects a similar trend among women drivers of the previous decades.[22] Rohrer distanced herself from an "extreme" stance, perhaps referring to political arguments about women's equality with men. Regardless, her frustration at not being taken seriously as a pilot is evident and demonstrates the contested status of the WASPs as military professionals in this hypermasculine space, despite their proven successes.

The same was true of WASPs assigned to tow targets, in that they were often able to overcome popular assumptions about women pilots. In this assignment, the WASPs took on much more treacherous roles as they towed targets for male Army Air Force cadets to practice shooting live ammunition. The intentional placement of women in this dangerous type of work was to protect men's lives at home so they could carry out a more crucial assignment—combat overseas. Such work was far from an ideal pilot's duty. In August 1943, shortly after women were allowed to ferry increasingly more advanced aircraft, the AAF decided to place the WASPs in another "experimental assignment" to "ascertain their adaptability for duties as other than ferry pilots."[23] The WASPs' work of towing targets was kept a secret for over three months, as Cochran and AAF officials were concerned about the public's reaction to women doing something so dangerous.[24] Even after WASP successes, the AAF restricted the publication of certain aspects of target-towing assignments.

Although the work was dangerous, male pilots described target towing as routine and mundane because of its repetitive nature. The WASPs towed targets at fifteen airfields in the United States during the war.[25] This assignment consisted of flying the same pattern in the air so that male cadets could practice shooting ammunition by aiming at the sheet target attached to the end of a cable on the plane. There was a circle in the middle of the sheet, and since the ammunition was colored, it left behind a mark when it hit the target. AAF officials thus could know who hit closest to the target. As one WASP described the experience, "It was the only flying I did where I flew . . . by the seat of my pants." Furthermore, pilots who towed targets often would convince mechanics at the base to put longer cables on the plane so that the sheet could be a little farther away from the plane.[26] Of course, male pilots also agreed that this work was "uncomfortable and scary," since the targets were so close to the back of the aircraft.[27]

Although the WASPs replaced some men who towed targets to free them for combat, male pilots who remained and continued towing duties often resented women serving alongside them. The first AAF base where the WASPs towed targets was Camp Davis in North Carolina. Twenty-five WASPs were assigned there in July 1943.[28] While the WASPs performed dangerous work here, this base was infamous for its disdain for women pilots. Some of the officers at Camp Davis required that the WASPs prove their flying abilities before being allowed to tow targets. Even though the women pilots had graduated from AAF training, these officers took them up for check rides. According to WASP Betty Budde, "We thought we were through training, but the men just don't believe we can do anything till they check us out." She said that she and several other women were required to do check rides in the AT-17, even though most of the WASPs had over fifty hours of flying time in this aircraft.[29] Furthermore, many of the men stationed at Camp Davis blatantly objected to the women's presence, and they refused to ride with the WASPs.[30] These reactions stemmed from male responses to women disrupting masculine stereotypes about dangerous work and from servicemen's desire to claim the field of military aviation as masculine.[31]

Pilot William "Bill" Bauer, the communications officer at Camp Davis when the WASPs towed targets, witnessed some of these problems at the base. Although some of the male pilots had "chauvinistic attitudes" toward the WASPs, Bauer noticed that the women were "capable pilots."[32] He also identified two types of WASPs: some were "hardened war horses that had been flying for years," and others were less experienced, younger pilots.[33] His description of "hardened war horses" seems to imply that they were seasoned aviators who could adapt to wartime flying. While it is unclear which WASPs were not as proficient, perhaps Bauer referred to recent graduates or to WASPs whom he witnessed exhibiting less skill than others.

Target towing was risky, not only because of the possibility that the cadets could miss the targets and hit the planes but also because the planes used were heavily damaged or old.[34] As a result of this damage, male and female pilots towing targets flew war-weary aircraft unfit for combat. The mechanics on base had trouble keeping up with the amount of work and often ran out of replacement parts. WASP Mabel Rawlinson died in a crash because of an unfixed faulty hatch. Angered by these working conditions, several of the WASPs contacted Cochran to discuss them. However, Cochran refused to change the Camp Davis situation because it was the first time she assigned WASPs to duties other than ferrying. Cochran depended on women's success in this endeavor before placing the WASPs in other experimental roles. In interviews years later, the WASPs said they believed Cochran refused to take action because she thought it would damage the WASP program.[35]

Thus the WASPs at Camp Davis learned to adapt to the circumstances. One of the women called her duty at the camp "grim" with "few carefree interludes." A journalist summed up her observations of target towing with the description that there was "no glamour . . . just hard sober work."[36] Despite these circumstances, other WASPs enjoyed this duty, especially when they would "zoom down over [male pilots] and maneuver around so [the men would] have to work fast to keep up in their sights."[37] Based on AAF generals' reports, Cochran and Arnold judged the WASPs more successful in target towing than male pilots.[38] Once the WASPs were deemed "successful" in this new form of work, the AAF sent them to other fields to tow targets, and they transitioned into other forms of dangerous work.

Media coverage of the WASPs engaged in target towing masked the danger of this task.[39] One journalist called target towing a "complicated game of hide and seek" that required "monotonous" duties.[40] By using the word "game," the reporter implied that the WASPs were not performing perilous work. Other articles used domestic rhetoric to differentiate target-towing assignments. For example, much like wartime propaganda, a report comparing the plane's instrument panels to a washing machine panel compared factory work to housework. That same journalist described WASPs who were off duty as waiting around "hoping to get an extra chore that pops up."[41] Another journalist added that while men found towing targets "sheer boredom," women pilots considered it "another adventure."[42] This description trivializes the work and makes it sound like the WASPs were less skilled and therefore more easily thrilled with a level of routine duties that men considered boring.

Flying spotlight-tracking missions was another type of assignment for the WASPs that involved potentially life-threatening consequences and

released male pilots for combat, the perceived ultimate and more honorable goal.[43] Thus, while propaganda portrayed men protecting women
through their military roles and service overseas, the WASPs served in
roles that seemed to be the reverse of protecting them from hazardous
situations or work. With just a few women on these bases, women were
targets literally and figuratively.

Spotlight-tracking missions involved flying the same pattern at different
altitudes while men on the ground pointed searchlights at the plane. Instrument flying, which the WASPs learned via the Link Trainer, was necessary
for this task because looking outside the plane caused temporary blindness
to the point that the women could not see their instruments.[44] During
training in Sweetwater, the WASPs sat in Link Trainers, the stationary blue
boxes with replicated cockpit instrument panels, and instructors took them
through simulated flight situations. Like towing targets, spotlight tracking
intentionally placed women in potentially fatal situations on the home front.

In October 1943, the AAF trained WASPs in additional types of aircraft,
including B-17s, B-26s, and then B-25s, but the AAF prioritized training
male pilots in these planes to prepare them for overseas service.[45] This preference often led to conflicts between Jacqueline Cochran, who was trying
to place the WASPs in more varied roles, and AAF officials, who wanted
to focus on male pilots. In one telephone conversation between Cochran
and General K. P. McNaughton of the AAF Flying Training Command,
McNaughton said that he did not want the WASPs to "hog all the time"
on B-17s because the air force needed to keep training men. He argued,
"Any minute that we spend checking off girls on four-engine equipment,
regardless of whether it's for engineering or anything else, we're just spin-
ning our wheels."[46] This quote implies that he thought any work that the
WASPs performed using B-17s was supplementary and worthless compared
with training male pilots.

The WASPs often tested aircraft, planes either returned from the war
overseas or heavily used. These "war-weary" planes were often too damaged to be repaired or safely flown, mainly because the instruments
malfunctioned or overtaxed mechanics had not had time to repair them
properly.[47] Often, the mechanics repairing aircraft on AAF bases were
"overworked, underpaid, and underappreciated" because of wartime
demand for their services and the increasing numbers of them sent for
overseas service.[48] As a result, planes were placed on the flight line for
testing before they were ready to be flown. The WASPs flew the aircraft
and then performed a "write-up" of continuing problems with them and

the likelihood of their continued use in the AAF.[49] The WASPs who worked as test pilots learned methods of resistance to protect themselves from unnecessary hazardous situations.

Test-piloting work was also stressful, as the WASPs bore the burden of ensuring the aircraft's safety for other AAF pilots. In this work, they flew planes to determine their continued use in the air force. This duty placed pressure on the WASPs because they were responsible for future accidents. Male pilots could be injured or possibly even killed because of problems WASPs should have detected before signing off on an airplane.[50]

The WASPs asked crew chiefs to fly with them in the damaged aircraft to protect themselves, and they confronted mechanics when they failed to fix the aircraft properly. Women pilots quickly learned that if a crew chief was unwilling to copilot a plane with them, it must not be fully repaired. WASP Virginia Dulaney Campbell used this tactic each time she tested a plane. When she tested airplanes that had been cleared for flight but did not have the necessary fixes, she went directly to the mechanics to discuss the problem. For example, while flying a plane one day, Campbell noticed that it was on fire, and after landing, she realized the oil line had broken because the mechanic had not fixed it. When she and her WASP copilot, Doris J. Elkington Hamaker, got out of the plane, the crew chief argued with her about fixing the oil line. Outraged, Campbell "reached across on the wing . . . [and] took a whole handful of [oil] and . . . wiped it all across his face." She then asked, "What's that?" This act must have surprised the mechanic, who likely remained speechless.[51]

Other WASPs positioned themselves as courageous and decided to prove that they could fly any plane, no matter how "war-weary." For example, when flying a plane that had returned from the European theater, one WASP recalled, "Three men turned [it] down because the gear was not functioning. And my creed was I'll take anything. I'll show them. I think all of us women felt that way."[52]

However, many WASPs also believed that the AAF viewed them as disposable in their test-piloting work. At AAF bases, the WASPs flew on days when male pilots were grounded due to the weather. Some of the WASPs concluded this was because they were considered "expendable," and the work of testing was crucial to the war effort.[53] In other words, the AAF desperately needed the planes to be fixed on an expedited timetable so that they could send them back overseas as quickly as possible.

Men's hostility toward women pilots' presence on bases originated in women's occupancy of a role that would have previously been considered a space for men. In these masculine military spaces in the highly technical field of aviation, the WASPs often risked their lives to allow men to stay safe on the home front. When male pilots at Fairfax Field in Kansas City, Missouri, heard about WASPs assigned to their base, they acted, in the WASPs' opinion, like "the world had come to an end because women were coming."[54]

WASP Virginia Dulaney Campbell remembered an instance when a male control tower operator let her know what he thought about female pilots as she came in for an emergency landing. She offered this example in an oral history interview years after the war, and she cited it as representative of other similar occurrences during that time. While stationed at Stockton Army Air Base, a major was grounded after breaking his back bailing out of a plane. Since he could not fly until he fully recovered, he tried to convince Campbell and another WASP at the field to take him up on their next flight. Finally, they agreed to let him ride along on a UC-78 flight. As soon as they started the flight, Campbell said they had several problems:

> The first thing that happens is we get a distance from the field, and the flaps get stuck in full down position. And the major is sitting back there, and he says, "Oh, my god." I said, "Relax, major, this happens to us all the time. No big sweat"—which it wasn't. We could handle a plane with the flaps down. Next thing that happens, the engine goes out. . . . By now, we're in real trouble. We've got full flaps down, one engine. Stockton was a whole congested area—buildings everywhere around the field. We didn't have a cross runway with this particular wind and we had a hell of a crosswind.[55]

So Campbell called the base and asked for the emergency landing procedures. The control tower operators told her to "hold on" while they requested permission. At this point, the major asked Hamaker to let him sit in the copilot seat. She agreed because she was getting "restless," and Campbell told him that it was still her plane, so he agreed not to "interfere." Finally, the tower told them to bail out. But there was no parachute for the major, who was not supposed to be on the plane, so Campbell refused to bail out and insisted she was going to land. The man in the tower gave orders for the base to bring out the fire trucks and ambulance. Then the radio went silent to wait for the landing. Campbell recalled waiting for the plane to land: "[It was] dead quiet over the air and then this voice comes over the microphone and announces, 'A woman's place is in the home.'"

At the time of this interview, Campbell was laughing at that remark, but she recalled that it was far from funny at the time. Instead, this comment indicates the type of reprimand directed at women and the way in which men resented women's new and ever-expanding wartime roles in this now defiantly male space. While she was still trying to land, the major asked Campbell whether he could land the plane, and after some arguing, she agreed. He made a "perfect landing" and then sneaked out of the plane during "all the confusion." He hung on to the side of the aircraft and then jumped off once it came to a complete stop. No one found out that the major had been there. Furthermore, Campbell said, "For weeks I got all these compliments on that perfect landing. [Laughter] I hadn't made the damned thing, but I couldn't say I hadn't, could I?" Although she eventually relinquished control of the plane, Campbell's insistence on flying as a pilot throughout the rest of the flight exemplifies how the WASPs asserted their place as skilled military pilots in the predominantly male space of the air.

If the WASPs could fly aircraft effectively, male pilots assumed those aircraft were safe and easy to fly, even if they had previously deemed them perilous or challenging to pilot. These assumptions continued from the 1920s and 1930s, when, with the growth of the aviation industry, female aviators helped prove the safety of airplanes to the American public. These early demonstrations often undermined women pilots' professional skills and role in aviation. According to historian Joseph Corn, the typical contemporary belief that planes women could fly must be secure and easy to handle reinforced the notion that women were "frail, timid, unathletic and unmechanical."[56]

Ironically, in this wartime context, instead of demonstrating a plane's safety to the American public, the AAF needed women to sell the safety of certain airplanes to military men. During World War II, as new types of aircraft were developed and flown, a number of them were viewed as more treacherous than others. As a result, male AAF pilots often dubbed these planes "widow maker," "flying coffin," or "flying prostitutes."[57] The last term, "flying prostitutes," was a sexualized reference to the plane's lack of support, since the B-26 had short wings for its size, making it appear less stable.[58] Although humorous, these names lowered morale among pilots who were supposed to be flying the B-26.[59] However, once men saw women pilots flying these aircraft, they often changed their minds. For example, when the WASPs flew the B-26 Martin Marauder with no accidents, the *Martin Star* reported that the B-26 was "gentle as a lamb . . . in the hands of" the female pilots.[60] When WASPs flew demonstrations of the B-26 to male pilots who called the planes "pilot killers," it had "a very favorable effect on male pilot training."[61] The WASPs also flew P-39s, P-47s, and B-29s when male pilots refused to fly them.[62] By reassuring men about the safety of these aircraft, the WASPs participated in gendered work similar to women's efforts in the early days of aviation and to later generations of female flight attendants selling the safety of aviation to the American public.[63]

General Paul Tibbets taught two WASPs, Dora Dougherty Strother and Dorothea Johnson Moorman, to fly the B-29 Superfortress, and they demonstrated its safety to male pilots at various AAF bases. After each demonstration, the WASPs would take crews up to teach them how to fly the B-29. Male pilots initially considered this bomber unsafe because its early iterations developed engine fires, but male opinion again changed after the women's demonstrations.[64] (Ironically, while performing a check ride during her training on the B-29, one of the engines of the plane Strother was flying caught fire!)[65] One AAF officer, Patrick Timberlake, described the effect of WASPs flying into an AAF base: "The first one came in, and the people were out there to watch the airplane come in, and the door opened, and this dainty little WASP gets out. . . . She's . . . the command pilot. Then the copilot gets out, and another WASP, the whole crew was WASP. It's funny, this didn't go on for long, because there wasn't enough of them, but it was a hell of a morale feature."[66] This tactic not only worked like propaganda to demonstrate the safety of the aircraft to these AAF men, but it also perpetuated the image of women pilots assumed in previous decades.[67]

In addition to flying into AAF bases, some WASPs flew demonstrations for the men in advanced aircraft schools. For example, the WASPs who had recently graduated from B-26 school flew the plane in front of male pilots who complained that it was a "flying coffin."[68] The purpose of this demonstration was "to shame the men" into piloting it, and it proved effective.[69]

One of the more controversial assignments—at least at first—was that of WASPs teaching male pilots, since women were placed in a role of authority over men. Here, they were more than men's equals, as their skills exceeded their male students. In March 1944, Jackie Cochran asked General Henry Arnold about WASP assignments as instructors. When Arnold asked the Eastern and Western Flying Training Commands to use more instructors, they were reluctant to accept women pilots. The Eastern Command responded that it had "a large surplus of men."[70] The Western Command reported that its commanding officers and other officials believed that women pilots should not instruct men. As one officer reported, "Unfortunately, in most circles, women pilots are considered inferior to men pilots, which is not the case, but the general attitude would require a considerably better job of a woman instructor to obtain the same results and maintain a harmonious atmosphere than is required of a man in the same situation." Another officer offered this perspective: "The psychological aspect of a woman instructor would probably be a great morale blow to the aviation cadet. He prides himself on being a member of the Air Corps and having been instructed by an Air Corps Graduate." Even General Barton Yount expressed his opinion to AAF Headquarters that WASPs should not be instrument instructors.[71]

Regardless of these negative responses, Arnold still allowed the placement of WASPs as instrument instructors in the summer of 1944, and by the conclusion of the WASP program, the Eastern Command had concluded that the women were successful in the role.[72] Before teaching other pilots, many of the WASPs attended a six-week-long flight instructors' school. These women pilots received additional training in acrobatics and formation flying to instruct men serving in combat.[73]

In addition to training men in the AAF, there is some limited evidence that the WASPs trained some of the male pilots in the 201st Mexican Fighter Squadron of the Mexican Air Force at Foster Army Airfield in Victoria, Texas.[74] Nonacademic sources state that the WASPs also trained men in the 201st at Pocatello Army Air Base in Idaho, but it is more likely that some of the female pilots ferried P-47 planes to that base.[75] Predominantly white female pilots training men of color from a different cultural background presents interesting dynamics in addition to those of gender. While they did not train male aviators in the Black segregated units at Tuskegee Army Airfield, it is unclear whether the WASPs trained American men of color at US airfields during the war.

Although at first resistant to women's instruction, male pilots often changed their minds after flying with the WASPs, much as nonflying officers who rode with the WASPs on ferrying flights had done. As the Eastern Flying Training Command reported, "The students did not resent being assigned to a WASP instructor as soon as she demonstrated her flying and instrument proficiency."[76] When Elizabeth Strofus took up a male pilot to teach him instrument flying, he was reluctant to even ride in the plane with her. Strohfus said this man was a "good friend," so she was surprised at his attitude. As they got ready to get in the plane, she noticed he was "really dragging." When Strofus asked him why, he replied that he was "afraid to fly" with her, so she let him fly the plane on takeoff, but she took control of it when they got in the air. She performed some acrobatics, and after flying for over thirty minutes, she landed the plane. When Strofus got out, she asked her friend, "Do you think you could trust me if this aircraft went into any kind of an unusual position?" He answered yes, and from that day forward, she "never had any more trouble flying instruments with the men" at that base.[77]

In a letter to her parents, WASP Marie Mountain Clark said the male pilots were resentful at first, although this changed after they worked with female instructors. George Stewart, one of Clark's students, took her for a flight (off the record) after he passed his check ride. He asked her to fly on instruments and jokingly "shouted" at her as she did during his training. Other WASPs justified situations where they faced resistance; women pilots were "first in a new venture," so they expected discrimination and other issues.[78]

Other WASPs found that some male students' eagerness to fly in combat superseded their disdain for women instructors. WASP Ethel Finley was one of the first female instructors at Shaw Field in South Carolina during the war. Her role was experimental, and AAF officials "wanted to see if women could instruct men in flying." Men that Finley trained concentrated on heading to combat "so that anybody who wanted to do that job [of instructing] would be just fine with them." On the first day with each round of new students, she started by telling them, "This is the first time it has been tried in the military to have women instruct men. And if you prefer not to be part of this or have me as the instructor you may ask for a change." She insisted that she never had any students ask for a new instructor. Furthermore, while none of the men at the base were antagonistic toward her, Finley also argued that WASPs should tell "negative aspects of the program or how men treated women" to interviewers or the media, because she did not want the WASPs to earn a "reputation at the expense of men." She eventually admitted, "I think that there were a few incidents say like of jealousy or where men felt threatened, [but] it's the same way today [for female instructors]."[79] Other WASPs did not remember any specific instances of hostility, but they knew that other WASPs experienced it.[80]

Besides flying instructors, the WASPs also checked out pilots returning from combat duty to ensure they could still fly well after their overseas experience. This assignment was particularly problematic for the AAF atmosphere that was rife with gendered disruptions. Male pilots resented women pilots judging their abilities, and they often swore at the women or refused to let them take the controls. It was so bad for one WASP that a sergeant gave her a monkey wrench to hit the men with if they would not let go of the controls![81] Gendered assumptions influenced these men's belief that women were inferior pilots and should not be allowed to critique male pilots, especially those who had served overseas, presumably a more honorable role in a man's world.

Another nasty, albeit less common, side of male resistance was the possibility of sabotage. These sabotage acts are examples of the misogyny of male mechanics who resisted and directly confronted women pilots' presence in the AAF. In the years after the war, Cochran and some of the WASPs discussed a few instances of sabotage, none of them well documented. These acts went unprosecuted because of the perceived delicate nature of the WASP program and fears that public exposure of these misdeeds might lead to a backlash against the women pilots.

According to Cochran, one WASP died because of sabotage at Camp Davis, and there were other instances of "petty sabotage," which she defined as "not organized" and not on a large scale.[82] One WASP found her rudder cable cut, and other pilots viewed this as an act of sabotage.[83] Another woman flew a plane with an unscrewed flight control unit, and she contended that "nobody could be so careless as to leave the whole throttle quadrant unscrewed from the airplane."[84] A similar incident occurred at Napier Army Air Base in Dothan, Alabama. A WASP "cracked up on the landing" of her aircraft and hit her head in the process. She was hospitalized from her injuries, and she later learned that the base personnel concluded her aircraft had been sabotaged. Staff discovered that bolts had been removed from several parts of the pilot's plane, making them loose. They checked the planes more thoroughly after this incident. No one was held accountable for these incidents, but base personnel suspected civilians who had been on the base packing parachutes, particularly German prisoners of war working there.[85] Some of these occurrences might have been mechanics' errors, but the WASPs who experienced them were supported in their assumptions by other pilots and base personnel. Encountering sabotage was a direct and violent result of male resistance and an attempt to undermine WASPs' roles as legitimate aviators and professionals, whether as women or as members of Allied forces.

Bringing female pilots a step closer to professionalization and militarization was the AAF's decision to send some of the WASPs to officer candidate school (OCS), where male pilots also received officer training. Although they were never promoted to officers or stationed overseas due to the failure of the 1944 militarization bill, many of the WASPs attended

OCS at the AAF School of Applied Tactics in Orlando, Florida. Unlike the WASPs, male pilots who graduated from this training received promotions to second lieutenant. OCS training lasted three to four weeks, and the goal was to eventually send all the WASPs through it. After the AAF decided to disband the WASP program, no additional women attended OCS.[86] If they had received military status, the female aviators who passed OCS training would have been commissioned as second lieutenants, affording them the same status as male pilots with comparable flying experience.

During OCS, women pilots took courses on subjects including "Air Force Emergency Equipment," "medical aspects of high altitude flying," "sanitation and disease prevention," wilderness survival training, first aid, and weather theory. Even though the WASPs did not fly in combat, they also took classes on identifying different poisonous gases in the field, and they had training to use a .45-caliber automatic pistol.[87] There is no explanation for why the last two types of knowledge would have been relevant to women pilots, but several possible theories exist. Perhaps the AAF wanted to see how women performed in these courses for future reference if women ever served overseas in specific capacities. Alternatively, the AAF might have wanted to keep the training for male and female officers consistent, or perhaps no adaptations were made to the OCS even though the students were women. If the WASPs had received military status, their training in OCS would have placed them on an equal rank as male pilots, bringing them closer to full citizenship as military personnel.

The WASPs, however, remained second-class citizens, as they received lower pay and lacked most medical benefits from the AAF. The difference in pay was not unusual since men and women often received different salaries for the same positions during the 1940s. Most of the WASPs who discussed this discrepancy asserted that they focused on the opportunity to fly military aircraft rather than on their pay scale.[88] After graduating from WASP training, female pilots received $250 a month, which they used to pay for their uniforms. They received $176.82 worth of uniforms, usually consisting of either summer or winter dress attire. After that, WASPs received a discount of 50 percent off any other uniforms or supplies they needed.[89] After men graduated, they received $250 worth of uniforms and $380 a month in pay.[90] The per diem rates for ferry pilots were $7 for men and $6 for the WAFS and WASPs.[91] On top of these pay differences, male pilots received special income tax deductions not given to the WASPs.[92]

As civilians, the WASPs received different medical benefits than male military pilots did. One medical service provided was dental appointments with a medical officer.[93] The AAF also offered the WASPs insurance packages they could purchase.[94] However, the women had to pay for hospitalization when ill or injured because they did not receive compensation for these services, even for service-related accidents. For example, one WASP got a fungal infection in her eyes from passengers she ferried while on duty. She had to pay for four operations and go without pay during the procedures and recovery.[95] As initially planned, if the WASPs had received militarization, she would have been covered financially for this job-related incident. While these differences in pay and medical benefits resulted from the women's civilian rather than military status, they are also evidence of women's status as second-class citizens.[96]

Furthermore, the AAF prohibited women pilots from flying in combat and restricted them to the continental United States, except for a few limited places outside the country's borders, including Canada, Puerto Rico, and Cuba. Officially, the WASPs never received the combat training of aerial gunnery and advanced aerobatics because the American public assumed women should not participate in battles, or could not conceive of them doing so. For the same reason, the majority of the WASPs flew within the continental United States. This restriction stemmed from the expectations of Americans, including politicians and military officers, who were not comfortable with women dying in combat or overseas.[97] This belief extended almost worldwide, as the only country that allowed female pilots to serve in combat during World War II was the Soviet Union.[98] Gendered understandings of war placed men as the fighters while women supported them.

Unknown to the American public, a select number of the WASPs received assignments to fly outside the continental United States. Although the official US Army Air Force (USAAF) historical study of the WASP program and wartime congressional records state that they flew only within the continental United States, a few of the WASPs ferried planes outside US borders.[99] Three of them transported aircraft from Grand Island Army Air Base in Nebraska to Texas, then to Batista Field in Cuba, and then to Borinquen Field in Puerto Rico.[100] Another WASP received an assignment at Batista Field in Cuba.[101] Others ferried planes to Canada.[102]

These outside assignments to Canada, Cuba, and Puerto Rico were the exception, although there is one other example of a female pilot flying outside the borders of the United States during the war. In January 1945, after the deactivation of the WASP program, Nancy Love flew in a war zone when she piloted a C-54 over the Hump, the eastern end of the Himalayan

Mountains in the China-Burma-India theater. Other American women were already serving in this theater during World War II, including nurses, WACs, and women in the Office of Strategic Services, but they were not serving as pilots. General C. R. Smith requested that Love make these wartime flights, and they were hidden from the public but off the record, as General Arnold had already given orders that no women would fly for the AAF as of December 20, 1944. While these journeys are recorded in Love's logbook, her trip report, and the special orders from the Ferrying Division Headquarters, she did not discuss them in interviews or any personal written accounts.[103]

Perhaps since Canada, Cuba, and Puerto Rico were so close to the United States geographically and relatively far from the major theaters of the war, the AAF made exceptions in assigning the WASPs to these locations. In General Henry Arnold's final speech to the WASPs, given to the media via a press release, he only mentioned assignments "within the continental United States." He told the WASPs, "That was what you were called upon to do—continental flying."[104] With this emphasis, Arnold spoke to his much larger audience in newspapers across the country. He wanted to clarify that women pilots served in a "safe" zone on the home front.

The absence of these international assignments in the congressional record, wartime reports, US wartime media sources, and the official USAAF history of the WASP program was an intentional, glaring omission.[105] By performing dangerous work, the WASPs disrupted gendered ideas about men as protectors of women. American propaganda during the war perpetuated this image. Many publications called for women to participate in the war effort so that their men could return home faster.[106] The WASPs stood in contrast to these messages in the American public. Their overseas assignments, particularly those that took them to Puerto Rico and Cuba, would have disrupted the public's conception that only male pilots flew overseas to fight the enemy. These notions also influenced the gendered division of labor during the war.

The experiences of WASPs in the male-dominated space of the Army Air Force were similar to those of women in technological fields and other professions previously deemed masculine.[107] Women's presence impacted the ways the military defined and limited their roles as skilled workers. In the AAF, women served in some of the more dangerous assignments on the home front, including towing targets. In addition, male pilots labeled jobs that the WASPs were now performing with gendered language that set them apart as women's work. Once these tasks were reframed as women's duties, male pilots expressed hostility at receiving the same assignments as the WASPs. This typing of military jobs by sex was different from what occurred in home-front industrial environments because of the added dimension of danger. Thus, through this division of labor, male pilots were more likely to be perceived as heroes. The WASPs were intentionally placed in potentially fatal situations, as AAF men preferred to die overseas rather than in assignments on the home front.

Both the roles assigned to the WASPs and their interactions with AAF pilots and personnel illuminate how male pilots claimed definitions of "hero." While historians and scholars of gender and conflict have discussed people's motivations for fighting, men's reluctance to engage in combat, the ways that the memory of war is most often gendered male, and the ideal images of women's heroism as self-sacrificial, they have not made arguments about the ways that men and women negotiate claims to heroism.[108] For women who serve in the military, from those in early American wars who cross-dressed and fought in combat to those inspiring the contemporary media's image of military women in the twenty-first century, the idealized heroic woman is an image of self-sacrifice in supporting roles.

Portraying women as self-sacrificial and supporting men undermines their roles in wars and their place in US society and the military. Propaganda during World War II portrayed women's wartime work as temporary, domestic, and feminine, duties that put their country above the pursuit of a military career.[109] This description is similar to twenty-first-century stories of female servicewomen.[110] These inaccurate and displaced representations perpetuate the myth of men as protectors of white women and as the true heroes of war, regardless of the extent of their wartime service.

Much of the work the WASPs accomplished was dangerous, and their roles in carrying it out contradicted traditional notions of femininity. WASPs often assumed jobs men preferred not to perform during the war, such as towing targets. Male pilots viewed it as more masculine and worthwhile to die in combat than on the home front. The WASPs performed other risky assignments, including testing heavily used aircraft, flying spotlight-tracking missions, and ferrying planes from factories to military bases. The planes coming out of the factories had never been flown before, and many had mechanical defects. Lastly, WASPs sometimes transported confidential military equipment. All these duties involved some element of danger, causing the WASPs to disrupt traditional gendered notions about femininity and ideas about heroic military service.

When women pilots performed these dangerous assignments, there was a shift in how male pilots described the work.[111] In the AAF, male pilots attempted to classify by gender the jobs that women were now performing. The media and male pilots referred to WASP assignments in the AAF as "chores" even though male pilots also performed the same duties.[112] For instance, men claimed the work of towing targets was "sheer boredom" because the process involved flying the same pattern repeatedly. One veteran pilot of World War II, Jimmy Blaine, believed women pilots were better in some ways than men. Blaine said, "[Women by nature are] more sensitive to the technical aspects of flying than men are . . . [and] have more coordination."[113] The WASPs themselves called some of these tasks "dirty little routine jobs that AAF pilots do not like to do." These reactions reinforced stereotypes that women were better suited for tedious, repetitive work. While male pilots also performed several of these perilous assignments, women pilots stretched traditional gender boundaries by risking their lives in a male-dominated field. Men justified women's wartime roles as feminine to protect their heroic, elite military image of the AAF.[114]

This image of the Army Air Force was one of servicemen performing highly skilled, courageous service in dangerous assignments. When the WASPs performed on the same level as men on the home front, it disrupted this trope. Despite their treacherous assignments, the WASPs had the same fatality and accident rates as male pilots "in similar work." The total of thirty-eight WASP fatalities averages to one WASP fatality per 16,000 hours of flying.[115] The fact that the WASPs performed at the same level as male pilots also undermined the masculine AAF image.

As male pilots showed their preference to risk their lives in what they perceived as more honorable overseas duty rather than at home, they minimized women's roles in military service. General Arnold praised the WASPs for taking the tasks that "hot-shot young men headed toward combat or just back from an overseas tour" did not want.[116] In a base history of the WASP program, one AAF official gave a similar justification: "Duties being performed by the WASPs are of a continuing nature, and do not lend themselves to piecemeal performance by combat pilots awaiting assignment to combat duties."[117] This conclusion supports the premise that pilots viewed combat as something beyond female capabilities. It also indicates that the WASP assignments were significant enough to require dedicated and trained pilots to perform them. When male pilots received assignments for jobs that the WASPs were either currently working or previously had been working, it led to "resentment," according to several AAF bases. According to one AAF official, "The substitution of male for female pilots . . . [led to] a resultant resentment by the former sex."[118] This reaction also came from men who identified those duties as simply women's work.

This gender division of labor was pushed to the extreme in the postwar period when flying became a career exclusively for men. This push was similar to the ways women had been forced out of engineering in the previous century, according to historian Ruth Oldenziel.[119] Commercial aviation and military aviation via the air force, which became a separate branch of the military after World War II, were established as male-only occupations. Women were excluded from flying military aircraft for over two decades after the war, and commercial airlines refused to hire women pilots in the postwar years.

Male AAF officials wrote histories of the WASP program to provide conclusions about WASP performance for reference if the air force employed women in the future.[120] Some base histories mention complaints that the WASPs went to officer candidate school in Orlando or to advanced aircraft school because these additional forms of training, coupled with the small numbers of WASPs assigned to each base, disrupted the "continuity" of the ongoing work on AAF bases.[121] These histories offer varying opinions and sometimes results concerning the quality of WASP performance, but they all agree that the WASPs should have received military status. Furthermore, these histories offer an analysis of male responses to female pilots' presence in the military.

AAF officials concluded that women pilots' civilian status hindered both the WASPs and the Army Air Force. Overall, WASPs' civilian standing kept them from a "complete adaptation to a military atmosphere."[122] Part of this conclusion might have resulted from Cochran's decisions about the disciplinary procedure. In addition, the WASPs did not always "observe ordinary military channels" when requesting transfers to other bases.[123] While female pilots could request a transfer after six months in an assignment, they sometimes went directly to Cochran instead of following the chain of command.[124] This circumventing of procedure also applied to WASPs who wanted to resign from the program.

As civilians, the WASPs (and male civilian pilots) could resign, unlike male AAF pilots. According to Cochran's final report on the program, a total of 150 WASPs resigned. Cochran attributed this "high rate of resignation" to their lack of military status. Since the WASPs were civilians, they could give notice "at any time."[125] Some of the 150 resigned as soon as they heard about the program's disbandment in the fall of 1944.[126] Others left to get married or spend time with their husbands when they received overseas assignments.[127] Still others resigned because of family reasons, including sick parents, pregnancy, or lack of childcare back home.[128] A final reason for resignation was problems with commanding officers (COs) giving the WASPs assignments on AAF bases while also refusing to transfer them to other bases when problems arose.[129] Not all WASPs who had this problem resigned from the AAF.[130] When the CO at Mercer Army Airfield refused to give women assignments because some of the previous WASPs had made mistakes (e.g., accidents involving wrecked planes), one WASP resisted by showing up at the flight line daily regardless. She was only given one assignment while on that base and then transferred to another base.[131] Whatever their motivations, these resignations represented problems with women pilots' civilian status.

Some officials also took issue with Jacqueline Cochran's leadership style. More than anyone else, the WASP director challenged the image of a military hero, as she served in direct contrast to men's developing image of an elite AAF. Her position of authority within the air force, especially her close personal working relationship with AAF commanding general Henry Arnold, upset the current military organizational structure and the sexual division of labor with men in top military official positions. Some AAF officials resented Cochran's ability to go directly to Arnold rather than following the chain of command, and perhaps they also questioned her position of authority as a woman. While other military officials were known for their forceful, abrasive personalities, male personnel were averse to these same characteristics in a female leader. These men perceived Cochran as encroaching on their male-dominated space, and they sought to limit the range of her influence.

In addition to facing these perceptions, Cochran tried to change the extent of her powers within the AAF on numerous occasions, an action necessary to redefining women's roles in the military and creating a space for women in aviation. When the WAFS and Women's Flying Training Detachment programs merged to form the WASP, one of her duties was to handle the resignations and transfers of the WASPs. Furthermore, Cochran would also compile statistics on the WASP program, and she wanted to receive immediate notification when a WASP was in an accident of any kind. The Ferrying Division "objected strongly to these proposals" because it was already handling these jobs. General Tunner, the division's head, saw these new roles as an "interference," and he did not want to report to both Cochran and the Air Transport Command. In the fall of 1943, Cochran sent proposed regulations to AAF Headquarters in which she would appoint "administrative officers and field representatives" to each base where the WASPs were assigned. She also wanted to create "ratings," or rankings, for the WASPs, including squadron leader, deputy squadron leader, squadron executive, squadron operations officer, and squadron supply officer. However, Tunner also disapproved of these proposed changes, believing they would disrupt the current chain of command.[132]

AAF officials questioned Cochran's discipline procedure for the WASPs on this basis of her bypassing the chain of command and attempting to expand the boundaries of her position. Cochran's suggested plans for disciplinary action were not approved by the air force. She wanted a disciplinary board specifically for the WASPs that consisted of "three flying officers, the WASP Squadron Leader, and/or the WASP Establishment Officer." Furthermore, while the CO at a base (all of them were men) would be informed of hearings, Cochran wanted to approve his decision before he could take action. These activities would take disciplinary power out of the hands of AAF officials and place Cochran in a position of greater control. General Tunner's response to this plan "was strongly worded," according to the air force historian who wrote the history of the WASP program after it ended. Tunner summarized his opinion by saying that Cochran's changes would be "a direct violation of established military chain of command" and would create an "intolerable" system. Furthermore, he believed women pilots should be under the same authority as male pilots, as they had been for more than a year.[133]

There are instances of WASPs appearing before AAF boards, not Cochran's proposed disciplinary boards, and these illuminate another aspect of the work culture of the program. These WASPs violated rules and regulations—for example, one woman was found drunk in the barracks, and another was dating a commanding officer.[134] In these examples, one of the WASPs resigned, and the other was eliminated from the program.[135] With these actions, the WASPs followed a strict military code of conduct. In her final report on the WASP program, Cochran acknowledged the issue of discipline and argued that, because of women pilots' civilian status, it was easier to maintain "disciplinary control" over them during training, as opposed to after graduation.[136]

In her position of authority as program director, Cochran often attempted to smooth over problems between the WASPs and AAF personnel, but her involvement again led to authority problems with other AAF officials. She made random inspection trips at air force bases to record details about WASP activities, successes, and problems in their roles. Before her arrival, Cochran was supposed to inform the AAF CO when making inspection trips at the base. However, she frequently made spontaneous visits and talked with the WASPs without consulting the CO. Cochran believed these visits were essential to maintaining control over and order among women pilots. Male officers thought she was ignoring their authority and the AAF chain of command. The Ferrying Division made several complaints about this. Its members told AAF Headquarters, "Such practice makes it extremely difficult. . . . to 'keep up' with what is going on in Miss Cochran's mind and it is requested that she be advised to go through channels in the normal manner on all future occasions." In response, Cochran told AAF Headquarters that she only circumvented the chain of command "on occasion" because of her previous experiences on ferrying bases. She claimed that when she tried to talk to the CO at five or so other times, he was "busy," as were the rest of the officers "in order of authority" under him. She said that when she gave advanced notice of her arrival, no one greeted her when she landed on the field.

Regardless of whose story is more accurate, these tensions between Cochran and other AAF officials generated or maintained hostility toward women in the military.[137] Cochran also dealt with other issues, such as AAF officers protesting the incorporation of women pilots on their base. When the US Air Force (USAF) recorded the history of the WASP program in the postwar period, it reached this conclusion about the fighting between Cochran, the Ferrying Division, and AAF Headquarters: "It may be that these unfortunate occurrences will be longer remembered than the contribution to the war effort or the testing of women pilots' abilities."[138] Furthermore, the fighting between these branches of the AAF and Cochran indicates other struggles involving interservice rivalries during World War II.[139] As in the case of the WASPs, some gendered motivations and stereotypes influenced the dynamics at play. Cochran increasingly tried to assert her authority and gain more control in an entirely male realm of AAF officials as she worked to keep the WASPs from being dismissed as mere novelties.

According to AAF bases' histories, some male pilots and AAF officials responded to the WASPs with hostility or skepticism due to their definitions of women's roles or their fears for job security. These reactions were about more than mere job competition, as the WASPs interrupted definitions of heroism. As detailed by the Western Flying Training Command, some men were "professionally jealous or even old-fashioned in their sentiments about the capacities of women." Furthermore, the command's history notes that "prejudices might enter into evaluations made by administrative officers" because of these beliefs, meaning that some of the base histories contain these biases.[140] All Eastern Flying Training Command bases agreed that there was "resentment at their [women pilots'] encroachment into a man's domain."[141] The WASPs remembered male skepticism due to a fear of women taking their roles or jobs and contested notions of heroism. As one WASP explained, "The general feelings of . . . the male pilots was that we were going to nose them out. Which we did not do . . . [but] they were not generally enthusiastic to have us."[142] Overall, the Western Flying Training Command history concludes, there was a "general doubt" among men about the "WASP experiment."[143]

The final, official AAF history of the WASP program, which takes all of the base histories into account, reflects women's successes and the doubts that male pilots had about them. The USAF historian concluded about the program, "It was demonstrated that women are capable of performing a variety of flying and aviation administrative duties. Whether they are equally as capable as male pilots in these respects and other types of piloting and ground activities will perhaps continue to be a point of controversy."[144] In turn, these histories note, the WASPs responded by trying to prove their abilities with "more than average determination." They were "conscientious, and even more significant, they were determined to make good."[145] Women pilots were successful in these endeavors as they proved their abilities, and male pilots found them to be "competent and agreeable coworkers" who were "part of the team working for victory."[146] Interestingly, these AAF reports also note that the WASPs "responded with courage when that was needed."[147] This conclusion acknowledges that women pilots also possessed a characteristic often attributed to male veterans of war.

Filled with gendered language, the AAF histories of the WASP program illuminate the ways that female pilots were constantly considered an experiment, being observed both as women and as pilots. The reports seem to focus on those issues of sexuality, reproduction, and the body that men and the general public found most troubling. Keeping their status experimental kept the WASPs from challenging definitions of what it meant to be a hero. For example, one AAF official stated, "There were naturally evidences of typical female behavior such as tardiness, emotional outbursts, and impatience with military customs and channels of communications, but these were of little overall importance."[148] Although this comment stereotypes certain behaviors as "female," it does not seem to undermine women's work as pilots, since this report labels such behaviors largely unimportant. When making conclusions about WASP performance, the Eastern Flying Training Command reported that the "majority" of its AAF bases noticed the WASPs "compared unfavorably to men in emotional stability under unusual situations and in emergencies."[149] Again, this observation reveals biases that the AAF acknowledged in base histories, and it is one that frequently haunted the WASPs, alongside arguments about their intelligence and physical abilities.

The AAF also continued to track the WASPs' physical capabilities via flight surgeons' medical records on bases where the women served. When compiling medical records from each base, the AAF concluded that the WASPs had excellent "physical stamina." Some even "took their work too seriously and probably in some cases should not have undertaken long flights or extended hours." Furthermore, the WASPs had "very few cases of loss of time on the job due to illness."[150]

In addition to noting the WASPs' physical capabilities, the AAF flight surgeons also recorded instances of pregnancy and abortion among the pilots. As previously mentioned, pregnancy was one of the reasons that WASPs resigned during the war.[151] One base allowed a pilot to continue to fly for an unspecified length of time after she reported her pregnancy, but she eventually had to resign. Although there were questions about WASPs' abilities and the impact of flying on their reproductive organs, at least one flight surgeon allowed a woman to fly even though she was pregnant. However, it is also possible that the pilot did not report the pregnancy until she started to show.[152] There is also one mention of abortion in the AAF base histories. The senior flight surgeon at an airfield in Texas reported that there was "an abortion performed for a legitimate pregnancy," and the WASP could not fly "for several months."[153] This record gives no other details about the abortion or the pilot, but it does illuminate the AAF's desire to record as much as possible about women's bodies in relation to flying.

In addition to closely monitoring women's bodies, the AAF observed dating between pilots, which illuminates other male attitudes about women pilots. The Eastern Flying Training Command said about these interactions, "Almost all WASPs were very popular with flying and administrative officers, spent much time in their company, and considerable numbers of WASPs assigned to this command became engaged to or married officers."[154] Although there were strict rules about WASPs dating AAF men, it seems that trainees were held more closely to them than program graduates were. In a letter home to her parents, WASP Betty Budde talked about dancing at an officers' club with male pilots, remarking, "Everybody's so thrilled about having girls on the base, we could have dates practically whenever we wanted."[155] Although in some cases, male AAF officers criticized or viewed WASPs as less professional for their dating. A major at Foster Army Airfield in Victoria, Texas, thought the best women pilots at the field were those who "did not fool around with any of the officers."[156]

There are also playful stories about the self-assuredness of male pilots. Teresa James related a humorous memory about having to land at a field to go to the bathroom. When she got to the field, the man at the flight desk was busy on the phone, and so he hastily gave her directions to the nearest "ladies' room," or so she thought. James found a stall and a couple of urinals in the bathroom, although this was not new to ferrying pilots. When she finished going to the bathroom in the stall, she noticed a man peeing in a urinal. She said, "Oh my god, I thought this was for ladies." He replied, "So is this, but I wanted to run a little water through it." When recalling this story years after the war, James considered that "a real smartass answer."[157] This event was also so memorable that she was able to recall it decades after it happened.

Since "war and Army flying . . . had been looked upon as a man's game," the WASPs were perceived as disruptive to definitions of heroism and to the developing AAF image that centered around a high level of professional prowess.[158] As they sought to reconcile reversed positions of authority and maintain their desire to be heroes, men expressed surprise, hostility, skepticism, and acceptance concerning the presence of women pilots in the AAF. Alternatively, in instances of sabotage, male pilots took aggressive misogynistic actions toward women. The WASPs asserted their roles as professional pilots in these AAF assignments by excelling in their work and proving their abilities to male pilots. According to several AAF officers, the WASPs focused on demonstrating their skills when confronted with men who were critical of or skeptical about women's roles in the AAF. During their ferrying assignments, the WASPs had the same fatality and accident rates as male pilots. The WASPs' performing at the same level as male pilots also threatened the elite hypermasculine AAF image. When women aviators' work assignments were described as tasks or simply women's work, the danger and the high skill set involved were hidden and minimized. While the WASPs successfully struggled in the contested airspace, they were never granted status as male pilots' equals during the war, and they were continually considered an unusual phenomenon in the AAF. Instead, the media cast women pilots as glamorous girls, not military personnel.

WASP trainees threw coins into the wishing well at Avenger Field in Sweetwater, Texas, as a symbol of good luck before a flight. They would also throw a trainee into the wishing well after she completed her first solo flight. Pictured here are some of the WASPs, their instructors, and director Jacqueline Cochran. Image courtesy of Libby Gardner and WASP Archive, the TWU Libraries' Woman's Collection, Texas Woman's University, Denton, TX.

Graduating class 44-W-4 in their Santiago blue uniforms at Avenger Field in Sweetwater, Texas, on May 23, 1944. This photograph captures the flat, dusty landscape of West Texas that marked the women's training experiences. The graduation ceremony and celebrations reinforced their embrace of a military sisterhood. As they donned their uniforms after graduation, the WASPs constructed an identity that denoted status, citizenship, and the culture of the military. Image courtesy of WASP Archive, the TWU Libraries' Woman's Collection, Texas Woman's University, Denton, TX.

Eight WASPs in Enid, Oklahoma, pose in front of an AT-6, one of the women pilots' favorite planes to fly. Stationed at Enid Army Airfield, the WASPs held assignments including ferrying, testing, and administrative flying. Pictured left to right: Evelyn Stewart Jackson, Meriem Lucille Roby Anderson, Jean Moore Soard, Flora Belle Smith Reece, Lucille Carey Johnson, Juner Bellew, Mary Abbie Quinlan, Sylvia Miller Reich Burrill. Image courtesy of WASP Archive, the TWU Libraries' Woman's Collection, Texas Woman's University, Denton, TX.

Four WASPs examine the "Operations Tow Target" board featuring the daily flight schedule. The columns provide the following information from left to right: identification number of the aircraft, name of the assignment, takeoff time, mission altitude, name of the radio contact on the firing line, radio frequency for the radio contact, and the scheduled concluding time of the mission. Towing targets was a dangerous but important assignment that prepared men for combat. Image courtesy of Laurine Nielsen and WASP Archive, the TWU Libraries' Woman's Collection, Texas Woman's University, Denton, TX.

Dorothea Johnson Moorman, Colonel Paul Tibbets, and Dora Dougherty Strother McKeown stand in front of B-29 Superfortress *Ladybird* with Walt Disney character and WASP mascot Fifinella featured on the side. The WASPs demonstrated the safety of the B-29 to male pilots who initially considered this bomber unsafe because its early iterations developed engine fires. Colonel Tibbets was the check pilot for Moorman and McKeown, and later in the war, he would fly the B-29 *Enola Gay* to drop an atomic bomb on Hiroshima. Image courtesy of Laurine Nielsen and WASP Archive, the TWU Libraries' Woman's Collection, Texas Woman's University, Denton, TX.

HOW TO GET IN THE AAF

This political cartoon, "How to Get in the AAF," was published in *Contact* magazine in June 1944 while the WASP militarization bill was before Congress. The government shut down the Civil Aeronautics Administration–War Training Service (CAA-WTS) program in 1944, leaving male civilian pilots eligible for the draft. *Contact* magazine was a fierce opponent of the WASPs receiving military status and benefits. Featuring a CAA-WTS pilot leaving the store dressed as a woman, this cartoon played on societal fears over gender roles and implied that women were taking jobs from men. Image courtesy of WASP Archive, the TWU Libraries' Woman's Collection, Texas Woman's University, Denton, TX.

Senator Barry Goldwater was an unlikely and fierce champion for the WASPs in the 1970s. Although he was opposed to women's entrance into the service academies and was one of only eight senators who voted against the Equal Rights Amendment, he was a staunch advocate for the WASPs because he had flown alongside them while stationed at New Castle Air Force Base in Delaware during the war. Pictured here with Senator Barry Goldwater (seated) are members of the WASP Militarization Committee (left to right): Lee Wheelwright, Dora Dougherty Strother McKeown, Bee Falk Haydu, Byrd Howell Granger, Margaret Ellis Kerr Boylan, Doris Brinker Tanner, and Colonel Bruce Arnold. Image courtesy of WASP Archive, the TWU Libraries' Woman's Collection, Texas Woman's University, Denton, TX.

During their fight for veteran status, the WASPs organized and executed strategies to prove the military nature of the program. In the process, they illuminated masculine privilege and contested understandings of what it means to be a veteran. Colonel Bruce Arnold, General Henry "Hap" Arnold's son, wanted to continue his father's legacy in helping the WASPs during the 1970s. Pictured here are Margaret Ellis Kerr Boylan, Dora Dougherty Strother McKeown, Bee Falk Haydu, and Colonel Bruce Arnold, with additional WASPs and other supporters in Washington, DC, in 1977. Image courtesy of WASP Archive, the TWU Libraries' Woman's Collection, Texas Woman's University, Denton, TX.

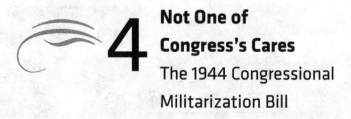

4

Not One of Congress's Cares

The 1944 Congressional Militarization Bill

Oh, we were very sad. Very sad because—well, we were living it and had been all through training, and then our different assignments. It was our—it was all we talked about, thought about. . . . Suddenly, in a few days' time, here you are, completely nothing. . . . It's such a transition that we have to go through afterwards. I mean, to this day all I have to do is hear a plane go overhead and I'm right with that pilot up there.—WASP Lorraine Zillner Rodgers

When Catherine "Cappy" Vail Bridge learned that Congress failed to grant the WASPs military status in 1944, she felt devastated. As she flew her very last assignment as a WASP, ferrying a P-51 to Palm Springs, she overheard a male pilot at the field jokingly remark, "You're never going to catch me flying one of those." After a conversation with him, she learned that he had only been flying training planes and not pursuit aircraft. Regardless, the conversation left her heartbroken, believing it was likely her last chance to fly military aircraft at high altitudes. In an interview decades after the war, Bridge recalled that it was hard to talk about her experiences as a WASP in the postwar period, and that she knew there were other WASPs who also could not talk about their service "for years." She revealed the depth of her disappointment that as a professional, she could not continue in her craft: "I understood how the Vietnam veterans felt, you know, just a complete rejection after doing a good job."[1]

During the 1940s, all branches of the US military were required to obtain authorization from Congress before granting the women in their military unit(s) benefits.[2] The failure of the bill for the WASPs in Congress resulted from numerous factors, including the media's coverage, the end of the War Training Service program, which meant male pilots were eligible to be drafted into the army, and the actions of WASP director Jacqueline

Cochran. Despite women pilots' wartime successes and accomplishments, men in Congress viewed the WASP program as a threat to established gender roles, and they chose to listen to falsified testimony rather than to the accounts of top Army Air Force officials.[3] The AAF disbanded the program on December 20, 1944, and women were excluded from military flying until the early 1970s. This prohibition left high altitudes as spaces literally for men, who dominated jet and space aviation and new challenges in the 1970s.

The defeat of this militarization bill in 1944 led women pilots to rekindle the bonds of their military sisterhood over their lingering discontent and disappointment. Learning of the failure of the bill and the end of the WASP program in 1944, the last WASP class sang, "You fearlessly conquered the realm of the skies, / And sidestepped the check pilot's snares. / Rewards are in order for the trainee who tries, / But you're not one of Congress's cares." The last lyrics of this song reflect their desire and "hope" to stay connected with the other WASPs despite the program's disbandment.[4]

The WASPs were the last group of women in the military to have a militarization bill introduced to Congress. During World War II, women in every other branch of the military, including the army (Women's Army Corps [WAC]), navy (Women Accepted for Voluntary Emergency Service [WAVES]), marines (Women Marines), and coast guard (United States Coast Women's Reserve), as well as women in the Army Nurse Corps and Navy Nurse Corps, received militarization. Although the WASPs were under the army, since the air force was not yet a separate branch of the military, they did not receive militarization with the WAC because the militarization bill did not include the WASPs.

The AAF did discuss placing the WASPs under the WAC to gain militarization. Cochran adamantly opposed being second-in-command under WAC director Colonel Oveta Culp Hobby. She did not think Hobby should make decisions about the WASPs since she did not have any aviation experience.[5] She also did not respect the colonel's leadership decisions. According to Cochran, when she discussed her concerns with General Arnold, she told him, "[The WASP program] will become part of the Women's Army Corps over my dead body. . . . Hobby has bitched up her program and she's not going to bitch up mine."[6] Arnold also disapproved of the proposed plan. He did not want the WASPs under the WAC because the WACs were performing "administrative, clerical and technical duties," whereas the WASPs "were professional personnel with specialized skill in the same sense that female doctors and nurses were commissioned."[7] As such, the

WASPs had a separate militarization bill from the WACs. Some female pilots blamed the WASP program's conclusion on Cochran's desire to maintain leadership. They thought that if Love had not been in a position of authority beneath Cochran, things might have worked out differently.[8]

The 1944 militarization bill would have granted the WASPs military benefits, including access to medical care under the AAF. In the event of a WASP's death, this would include a military funeral, financial compensation for her family, and the option for her family to display a gold star, which is indicative of the death of a family member in military service. The thirty-eight WASPs who died during military service "had no right to military funerals, their survivors received no death benefits, and their families could not even display the Gold Star."[9] Furthermore, the bill would have given WASPs access to the GI Bill of Rights in the postwar period, allowing them to apply for government loans and seek a college education.[10]

During World War II, the two WASP militarization bills presented in the House and Senate would have given the WASPs these benefits. On September 30, 1943, Congressman John Costello introduced House Resolution 3358 for WASP militarization. This measure stated, "[The WASPs] shall be commissioned in the Army of the United States and shall receive the same pay and allowances and be entitled to the same rights, privileges, and benefits as members of the Officers' Reserve Corps of the Army with the same grade and length of service."[11] After this initial introduction, the War Department asked Costello to include a few revisions in the bill. On February 17, 1944, he submitted the longer House Resolution 4219. This updated legislation gave more specifics on rank for women pilots and specified that the WASPs could only command other women. It was sent to the Committee on Military Affairs in March for hearings.[12]

During these hearings, AAF commanding general Henry Arnold was the only witness who testified, and the meeting lasted less than one hour. Arnold expressed support for the militarization of the WASPs. He also discussed the Civil Aeronautics Administration–War Training Service (CAA-WTS) pilots and argued that they were desperately needed in the ground forces overseas, while the WASPs should continue their work on the home front.[13] As a result of Arnold's testimony, the House Committee on Military Affairs recommended House Resolution 4219 for passage. Representatives concluded that the WASP program should be militarized because of wartime shortages overseas and because women pilots were performing work essential to the war effort. The committee suggested a vote before Congress took a summer recess.

Two days after the House Committee on Military Affairs held hearings, Senators Joseph Hill and Harold Burton introduced Senate Bill 1810, equivalent to House Resolution 4219. The bill was sent to the Senate Committee on Military Affairs.[14] With the progress in the House and the support of the War Department, the chances for the passage of the WASP militarization bill seemed promising. However, events occurring simultaneously in the spring and summer of 1944 caused a shift in the legislation's progress.

While the bill was in Congress, the government had decided to shut down the Civilian Pilot Training Program (CPTP). This same program trained most of the women who became the WASPs before the United States declared war. After America entered World War II in December 1941, women no longer received admittance to the CPTP, and the program was renamed the CAA-WTS in 1942. Thus this name change signaled the United States' preparation for battle and the program's focus on training male pilots for combat. As war mobilization increased and the need for pilots overseas was less intense, the AAF decided that the CAA-WTS was "exceedingly burdensome and not cost-effective."[15] From early 1944 through June 30, 1944, the AAF slowly shut down the WTS course across the country.

The male instructors of these WTS programs were civilians who had draft deferment during their service, but they were eligible for the draft once the programs shut down.[16] They could only join the air force as pilots if they passed the flight and physical examinations. The AAF made it clear to the instructors that they were not automatically "guaranteed" a position in the force.[17] Most of those men were unqualified to serve in the same capacities as the WASPs, mainly because they did not meet physical or age qualifications.[18] However, these pilots falsely protested that the WASPs took jobs from men.[19] These men argued that the WASPs held positions that they themselves could fill.

The CAA-WTS pilots successfully lobbied the Committee on the Civil Service, chaired by Representative Robert Ramspeck. Ramspeck investigated the WASP program based on the male aviators' concerns, and he wrote a report based on his findings. Much of his narrative was inaccurate, and it extensively covered the CAA-WTS pilots rather than the WASPs. Ramspeck argued that the AAF was "dismissing, or failing to properly utilize, large numbers of male civilian pilot instructors."[20] He made this comment in direct contradiction to Arnold's testimony. On June 5, 1944, Ramspeck announced his findings. When the Costello bill went to the House floor later that month, it fell nineteen votes short of passage.[21] Thus, instead of arguing that these pilot instructors should uphold their patriotic duty to their country and serve overseas, enough congressmen supported the male civilian pilots for the bill to fail. It is this situation that makes the reasons for the failure of the WASP militarization convoluted and murky.

Despite top military and government officials' support and women pilots' successes, the AAF disbanded the WASP program in December 1944. High-ranking AAF officials, including Commanding General Henry Arnold, Secretary of War Henry Stimson, and Ferrying Division head General Tunner, supported WASP militarization in 1944.[22] Stimson wrote a letter to the Honorable Andrew J. May to let him know that the War Department supported the militarization bill. Stimson clarified what the measure would accomplish if passed: "The integration into the Army of this personnel will not create a new women's organization. It will eliminate an existing civilian organization."[23] Thus, the WASPs would be official military pilots of the AAF rather than retaining their current civilian status. General Arnold called the WASP program a success, partly because female pilots' records matched male pilots', proving that women had equal flying abilities. As he made this point in a speech at the last WASP graduation ceremony: "Frankly, I didn't know in 1941 whether a slip of a young girl could fight the controls of a B-17 in the heavy weather they would naturally encounter in operational flying. . . . Now in 1944, it is on the record that women can fly as well as men."[24] Furthermore, Arnold's testimony to the House Committee on Military Affairs influenced representatives' recommendation of House Resolution 4219 for passage. In addition to gaining this support, the WASPs had also proved their success to the AAF.

For bureaucratic reasons and to keep officials updated, Jacqueline Cochran continuously submitted reports to the air force about WASP performance, which led the AAF and War Department to support militarization. At the conclusion of the program, Cochran published a report on the trainees' achievements. Medical studies conducted on female pilots, including aptitude and psychological tests, showed equivalent endurance and consistent flying for the same number of hours as male pilots. WASPs' test scores and performance and elimination and graduation rates were comparable to those of the male pilots. At times, the WASPs even had lower elimination rates than male aviators.[25] There are a few theories as to why the militarization bill did not pass Congress, despite these successes of the program and the support of AAF officials.

Unlike women in other military units during the war, the WASPs performed completely nontraditional work and faced further resistance with their militarization bill. Most women serving in the army, navy, marines, and coast guard were in fields that seemed natural extensions of women's work, including communications, health care, or secretarial jobs.[26] In the WAC, the majority of women worked in stereotypically female roles, including file clerks, switchboard operators, and executive secretaries. As many as 90 percent of the WACs serving overseas were engaged in office and administrative work. Historian Leisa Meyer argues these assignments were a result of the army's "need to preserve distinctions between male and female soldiers."[27]

WAC director Hobby intentionally emphasized women's role in the army as motivated by self-sacrifice, and not by career advancement. She sought to alleviate congressional fears over wartime-disrupted gender roles, but she also believed that women's wartime service should be temporary, with women assuming duties as wives and mothers after the fighting ended.[28] Women who served as nurses in the US Army and US Navy were considered traditionally feminine and unthreatening to gender roles, even when they performed work that deviated from societal conventions (e.g., as POWs overseas). This was due to the media's image of them as sacrificial, caring, and feminine.[29] Ultimately, the service of these women as nurses and in other predominantly traditional roles was not seen as challenging men's positions in the military.

Other women worked as civilians for the government or military in nontraditional roles, but due to the secrecy of these positions, their work was unknown to the American public and therefore not subject to debate. Women served as code breakers for the army and navy during World War II because of their expertise in math, statistics, and technology. Female civilians were also employed as chemists, operators, administrators, personnel processors, and janitors under the Manhattan Project. Yet thanks to the classified nature of the Manhattan Project and intelligence work, these workers kept their positions secret from even their closest family members.[30]

The work of women serving as WACs in the army was highly visible to the American public, and debates in Congress over militarization centered around fears about military women's sexuality and disrupted gender roles. Because of fears over military authority, southern Democrats edited the WAC bill to ensure that women did not command men.[31] Despite these debated fears, the militarization bill passed, granting the WAC military status. Afterward, a bill for the navy's WAVES faced "little resistance" in getting through Congress.[32] This success for the WAVES did not happen for the WASPs.

Scholars have offered explanations for the defeat of the WASP militarization bill, although they do not answer this complicated question fully. One argument is that gender constructions in the wartime era led to the failure of the 1944 militarization legislation and the subsequent disbandment of the WASP program. Militarization failed because the WASPs went "beyond culturally constructed normative boundaries of how women were expected to behave, and who were serving in what were constructed to be male roles."[33] While this is true, it does not consider that high-ranking male AAF officials supported women pilots.[34] Furthermore, intense media scrutiny of the program resulted in national media falsities, and congressional representatives listened to inaccurate claims about the program rather than to AAF officials. Yet these accounts were *not* the "only press the WASP received" during the war.[35]

Perhaps some of the blame for failed militarization can be placed on Cochran's position of authority. Like WAC director Hobby, Cochran was "one of the few women who held positions of power within the state during World War II."[36] Both leaders had direct communication with the most powerful men in the army and AAF. General George C. Marshall personally recruited Colonel Hobby, while Cochran worked directly with General Henry Arnold. Cochran's driven, ambitious personality was often abrasive to other military officials. She used her political connections and close relationship with Arnold to circumvent the AAF chain of command, in the process alienating several AAF officials during her time as WASP director. Cochran's presence as a woman in a position of authority, particularly regarding high-ranking military officials, was threatening to the male hierarchy of the AAF.

Congressman John Costello, who introduced the WASP bill to the House, believed that Cochran's potential to be promoted to a higher rank played a significant role in the bill's failure. In an interview years after the war, when asked about Congress's "rationale for opposing" the WASP legislation, Costello argued that young AAF officers feared Cochran's potential promotion above them. As he detailed, "[Cochran] had a terrific personality. A very outgoing person, easy to talk to. She made everybody feel that she enjoyed being with them." She was so adept at her job that some worried "the AAF might even make her commander at a higher rank than the others, and that wouldn't sit well anywhere if that happened."[37] Thus, servicemen felt threatened and wanted to force Cochran out. As Congressman Edouard Izac, who represented the strong opposition toward the bill, proclaimed, "It is the most unjustified piece of legislation that could be brought before the House at this late date. I know that any woman would like to have 2,500 girls under her and be a colonel."[38] (He said this in spite of the fact that WAC director Hobby was promoted to the rank of colonel.) He continued, "It is not going to help the course of the war one bit, and I am sorry to see Hap Arnold lose his balance over this proposition."[39] Izac reflected his own gender bias as he insinuated that power or authority was Cochran's motivation for desiring military status.

Further insight into the congressional decision to listen to the CAA-WTS voices rather than the AAF and War Department lies in the history of the CPTP. When the CAA-WTS program shut down in 1944, those in the War Training Service knew that it was due to the air force's "dissatisfaction" with their program.[40] This hostility was coupled with the fact that many in the CAA-WTS felt entitled to become AAF pilots and were offended by the AAF's treatment. Since the AAF shut down the program quickly, there was no plan to integrate the CAA-WTS trainees and instructors into the AAF. These instructors thought that the CAA-WTS was concluded in a "haphazard manner" that left them feeling "badly used" by the AAF.[41] These male pilots then turned to Congress for recognition and claimed positions in the air force they believed were rightfully theirs. This tense situation, joined with Cochran's position of authority that threatened male officials and congressmen and the media's coverage of the WASPs, contributed to the failure of the WASP bill and made the WASPs discarded weapons of war.

Although select AAF and government leaders supported the WASPs, congressmen, negative influences in the media, and civilians silenced them. Those against the militarization of the WASPs clung to established gender assumptions, the false claim that women took jobs from men, and the romanticized image of female aviators presented in the media.

Newspaper and magazine articles referred to the physical characteristics of the WASPs, emphasizing their femininity to reassure the American public about women's new wartime roles. These images created a veiled illusion of female pilots, as they discussed women's hair, eyes, weight, height, and potential jobs as models or pasts as beauty queens.[42] Journalists sent requests to the AAF for "photogenic" women to photograph when visiting various AAF bases.[43] The resulting articles described various female pilots' appearances with phrases such as "pretty and blond," "voted the best-dressed gal on the campus of the University of Nebraska," a former "beauty queen," a "slender, brown-eyed brunette."[44] Numerous articles mentioned women's tanned skin from exposure to the sun while flying. A writer for *Strictly GI*, a newspaper published by the Grand Island

Army Air Base (GIAAB) in Nebraska, interviewed four WASPs stationed at GIAAB. This fellow AAF serviceman mentioned women's appearances numerous times and called them "trim-looking lassies" in the caption for the article's photograph. These gendered descriptions provide a stark contrast to what the serviceman deemed the "masculine job" of AAF flying. National media attention on Jackie Cochran and Nancy Love also focused on their appearances.[45] This emphasis on women's physical traits in media coverage undermined and distracted from their professionalism.

Throughout 1944, while several newspapers endorsed the WASP program and militarization bill that would grant women pilots benefits, publicity against the bill often overpowered those in support of it. *Contact* magazine and journalist Drew Pearson's "Washington Merry-Go-Round" column were two of the most vocal opponents of the WASP program. *Contact*, a monthly magazine, hailed itself as a news source for "business and professional people" in aviation, including "flight instruction and air transportation." The periodical published a series of political cartoons and articles in 1944 arguing against the militarization bill. These publications urged male pilots, especially those previously in the CAA-WTS program, to write their congressmen to protest the measure. *Contact* also attempted to investigate the WASP program and often published falsified information about it. Despite the inaccurate statistics incorporated in its articles, *Contact* attracted widespread attention for its fierce stance against the legislation. Even in late 1944, when the WASP bill had already failed, *Contact* continued in this endeavor by complaining that women pilots still worked while many CAA-WTS instructors did not have AAF positions.[46] For example, the magazine reprinted a series of cartoons rationalizing how its publicized efforts contributed to the bill's demise.

According to the American Legion, some newspapers also printed these cartoons, and one cartoon caught much congressional and public attention. Entitled "How to Get in the AAF," it portrayed a CAA-WTS pilot leaving a store dressed as a woman.[47] This sketch played on fears that women were taking jobs from men, and fears that women's presence in the military disrupted ideas about masculinity and femininity. It implied that women now received preferential roles over men in the US military.[48] A *New York Times* article that opposed the militarization bill also flipped gender roles, arguing, "[CAA-WTS pilots] may soon be cleaning windshields and servicing planes for 'glamorous women fliers.'"[49] This journalist implied that male aviators would have to work for women in subservient positions, a possibility that horrified many in the American public and Congress.

Although many *New York Times* journalists supported the WASP bill, this opposing voice represented concerns of a segment of the American public.

Far from objective, *Contact* obstructed the women pilots' professionalism by printing numerous inaccurate articles or completely falsified information. A letter to the editor in the "Voices from on High" column provides an example of the erroneous material found in the magazine. Mary Elizabeth McConnell, a female pilot whose acceptance to the WASP program was revoked after the failure of the militarization bill, wrote the editor of *Contact* in October 1944. She argued that the magazine failed to uphold its motto of being a "service to aviation" because of its opposition to the WASP program. In essence, she argued that the magazine only supported the interests of male pilots who felt threatened. Furthermore, McConnell contended that the WASPs did not keep jobs from the CAA-WTS male pilots. In response, the editor argued, "Glamour had something to do with the desire of many of them [WASPs] to displace these experienced men pilots." The editor further suggested the WASPs leave the AAF to become nurses overseas, "where [their] feminine touch" could be useful. With these statements, he supported *Contact*'s stance that a woman's place was not in the field of aviation. Furthermore, the editor bought into cultural images of the WASPs as glamour girls, not aviators, that were so prevalent in wartime and prewar media.[50]

Like *Contact*, journalist Drew Pearson's "Washington Merry-Go-Round" column gained widespread national attention during the summer of 1944 for portraying the WASPs as keeping jobs from male pilots.[51] The feature had millions of readers and was published in over 350 papers around the country, and Pearson also made regular broadcasts on an NBC radio show. Scholars have described "Washington Merry-Go-Round" as a "gossip-ridden news" column.[52] Pearson argued, "Arnold's efforts [at WASP militarization] sidetrack the law by continuing to use the WASPS while more than 5,000 trained men pilots, each with an average of 1,250 flying hours, remain idle."[53] The reporter was referencing the recently released CAA-WTS male instructors, and he mocked the AAF for requiring the men to pass examinations before their admittance as AAF pilots. He believed that the male aviators had proved their service to the country and should be automatically incorporated into the air force. To get readers to sympathize with the CAA-WTS instructors, Pearson described them as "thrown out of work, to start their military service all over again."[54] He called the instructors "the unhappiest, most disillusioned men in the country," and he argued that the WASPs made these men's problems "worse."[55]

Pearson further contended that the only reason the WASPs were still flying was that Cochran exploited her political and military connections to get them flying time. The journalist also claimed that only eleven WASPs could fly twin-engine aircraft, and that only three flew four-engine bombers. These distorted statistics failed to support his argument that "hundreds" of male pilots returning from combat were "anxious to stay in the Army as transport ferry pilots."[56] With this last comment, Pearson created an argument that would outrage many Americans—that the WASPs were taking jobs not just from civilian men but from veterans.[57]

Journalists who supported the WASPs revealed their awareness of the role of gendered fears in the militarization bill's failure. One WASP, Barbara Poole Shoemaker, wrote an article published in *Flying Magazine* that claimed the CAA-WTS pilots' demands for WASP jobs were "a little far-fetched." She argued that the situation would not have worked for men in other professions if they tried to avoid the draft.[58] Shoemaker also combated many inaccurate statistics about the WASP program by acknowledging that its graduates flew heavy aircraft and had a comparable fatality rate to male pilots. She contended that the failure of the militarization bill resulted from a "battle of the sexes."[59]

Texas's *Fort Worth Star-Telegram* argued that it was "strange" Congress did not grant militarization to the WASPs, stating, "Predominantly male Congress could not bear to see women working when there were men wanting their jobs, and therefore denied them the status." *Liberty* magazine arrived at a similar conclusion, claiming that while Congress should be respected, every so often "a measure comes up for consideration which stands or falls not on its merits but upon whatever emotional mood happens to grip Congress at the time."[60] With this insightful description, the magazine also saw past the inaccurate claims that women were taking jobs from male pilots. Arguing that the WASPs "performed valiantly in many types of war service," a *New York Times* article declared, "Thus far these able and patriotic women have not received the award they desire and deserve—namely, military status."[61] These supportive articles disrupted the distorted media coverage of *Contact* and Drew Pearson while also contending that the WASPs deserved military status.

Media sources continued to support the WASPs even in the final days of the program in December 1944. Several radio shows issued tributes to the WASPs when the program disbanded. In *Your Radio Hostess*, the presenter interviewed four WASPs and played a "musical salute" to them afterward. Another broadcast, *America on the Air*, discussed the success of the WASP program and asked Americans to "pay honor . . . to the gal-lant women who have served so well." Robert St. John, an NBC journalist, called the WASPs "vitally important" and supported this assertion with statistics about women pilots. He argued the WASPs had "one-seventh of the MASCULINE record of errors." About the conclusion of their program, he appallingly noted, "I was told there isn't going to be any CEREMONY! Just some tearful farewells . . . and . . . one thousand WASPS go back . . . into civilian clothes, because Congress doesn't think they're any longer needed!"[62] This emotional plea illuminates the journalist's perspective of the injustice of WASP disbandment.

In addition to job competition, congressmen mentioned the media's glamorized portrayal of the WASPs as a reason not to militarize the pro-gram. One representative pointed out that this image derived from maga-zines and a movie, presumably *Ladies Courageous*. This 1944 film produced by Universal Pictures intended to provide a story of the Women's Auxiliary Ferrying Squadron (WAFS), and it was even "sanctioned by the United States Army Air Force" in its early stages. However, it offers a drastically inaccurate representation of the women's pilot program, making aviators look petty, selfish, and inconsequential. Several of the WASPs who watched this movie in the theaters were horrified by its portrayal of their work.

In the film, the supposed WAFS pilots chase and date military men, implying that women only joined the armed forces so that they could get a man. These fictional pilots also have irresponsible accidents, including stealing an airplane (which the actual women pilots respected as govern-ment property) and crashing it. Far from portraying the WASPs as military pilots, the characters in the film do not take their work seriously, and they do not accomplish any serious assignments for the AAF. A March 1944 review in the *New York Times* also expressed disgust at the dramatic inac-curacies, arguing, "[*Ladies Courageous*] will give many moviegoers a very bad impression of our women pilots" as "a bunch of irresponsible nitwits." Since the film's producer, Walter Wanger, was a World War I air veteran, the American public likely assumed his depictions were accurate based on his background. The *New York Times* reviewer concluded, "[Women pilots] have pitched in and done their country a very valuable service delivering planes . . . and not without considerable personal risk and sacrifice of customary comforts."[63] Cochran tried unsuccessfully to delay the release of *Ladies Courageous* until Congress voted on the militarization bill.[64]

Many of the WASPs followed the progress of the militarization bill in Congress, although they could not participate in the debates per Cochran's orders. In the summer of 1944, months before the legislation's failure, the trainees began including national newspaper articles about the congressional debates in their newsletters. The articles depicted the WASPs far more accurately, as the newsletter excluded pieces by the famous "Washington Merry-Go-Round" columnist Drew Pearson. Although it is not clear how the WASPs obtained the national newspaper coverage or received permission to reprint it, the fact that they did so is evidence of their concern over and interest in the congressional debates. Perhaps the reprinted material also served as a form of encouragement for women pilots, as General Arnold and Secretary of War Henry Stimson both supported the militarization of the WASPs.[65]

Without militarization, the WASP experience ended up being temporary, as in the experience of other women wartime workers. In the *Army-Navy Screen Magazine* film recorded in Sweetwater during WASP training and later shown in movie theaters, the narrator hints at the public's belief that women's wartime roles were temporary. He tells women pilots, "Someday you'll sit in the evening with your husband and remind him that you did your part during the war."[66] This response reflects the larger American public's perspective that all women's wartime service should be temporary to allow men more jobs after the war. It also undermines the accomplishments of women in aviation.

The last class of WASPs who graduated just before the program's disbandment did not receive assignments at the AAF bases. These pilots expressed their disappointment and heartache through their class songs. Unlike the other military songs, which offered encouragement or advice to the following classes, these are full of bitterness. In one song the WASPs proclaimed, "We earned our wings now they'll clip the goldarned things, / How will they ever win this war?"[67] These lyrics reflect resentment about being cut off from the war effort since serving their country was a motivation for many women's service, and one that many trainees viewed as invaluable. Other songs reflected women's uncertainty about their future role in the military and their anger about returning home with no prospective aviation jobs.[68]

The disbandment of the WASP program generated tremendous disappointment among many of its members. In a postwar newsletter, one WASP wrote about the difficulties of readjusting to life after her service and missing "flying those beautiful airplanes." She received the following advice from a fellow WASP that helped her keep the situation in perspective. This comrade told her that she should "keep flying," even if she had "to pawn the family jewels" to pay for it. In addition, she should keep reminding herself that she was lucky she had received the "wonderful training and experiences" during the war.[69]

There are numerous stories about female pilots' disappointment over the conclusion of the WASP program, particularly concerning the difference in civilian flying as compared with military flying. Women who worked in factories also encountered setbacks at the end of World War II, as they were forced out to allow returning male veterans to have their jobs.[70] For many WASPs, the program's dissolution felt like an abrupt end to their short military service and aviation careers. They worried about finding jobs in the postwar period and frequently complained about not finding advanced aircraft to fly in "civilian life."[71] The WASPs knew that the only planes they could fly after the war would likely be low-altitude single-engine aircraft. Of her life before World War II, one WASP remarked, "My whole salary used to go for flying, and I never flew anything as big as this [a military plane]."[72] Postwar flying felt "tame" in comparison, and these aviators thought their years in the AAF "spoiled" them.[73] A few of the women pilots felt less grief over the end of the program because they were hired as civilians to stay on the same base as their WASP assignment, although in nonflying capacities such as a Link Trainer instructor for male pilots. However, for most, it felt "traumatic . . . to have to return home," and they felt "devastated" adjusting to life after deactivation.[74] They missed the space of the sky.[75] Some WASPs coped with this desolation by not speaking about their wartime service.[76] They were disappointed that their professional careers were cut short, and postwar opportunities were severely limited.

When the WASP program disbanded, most of its members desperately wanted to remain pilots after the war. One journalist interviewed WASPs at Sweetwater and asked them what they wanted to do after the war, to which they "responded in chorus, 'Fly!'"[77] For many, their opportunities in the military in World War II offered them the hope of career advancement, despite exclusion from military and many civilian flying opportunities. Women could no longer fly military aircraft for the next three decades. Shortly after World War II, the air force began including jet experience in its training. With few exceptions, women were excluded from progressing to the next stage of aviation—jet flight. As a result, when NASA announced the opportunity to fly in space, women were unqualified because they did not have jet experience.[78]

Several of the WASPs wanted to continue flying during the war, whether with the AAF or with an Allied country's air force. They asked the AAF whether they could fly at a salary of just one dollar a year, yet the AAF declined their offer.[79] Others tried to fly for the Chinese air force at the end of the war. Hazel Ying Lee and some of her fellow WASPs decided that since the WASP program was ending, they wanted to serve as pilots for another of the Allies. Lee suggested China since her parents were natives of the country, and she had previously tried to fly for the Chinese air force, although it were not accepting women pilots at that time. In a letter to a fellow WASP, Lee outlined her actions and proposed a plan of action. She wrote, "Now that we're to be inactivated by Dec. 20th, all of us are deciding what to do in the future. Most everybody wants to go to China."[80]

The other WASPs agreed that this was a good option, so Lee wrote Madame Chiang Kai-Shek, wife of the Supreme Commander of Allied forces in the China war zone. Chiang's secretary sent her letter to General Pang-Tsu Mow of the Chinese air force in Washington, DC. General Mow told Lee that she could work for the Commission on Aeronautic Affairs in China, and they planned to meet after the WASPs disbanded to discuss the ex-WASPs flying with him.[81] However, on November 25, less than a month after sending her letter, Lee was killed in an airplane accident.[82] There is no evidence that any of the other WASPs contacted the Chinese air force separately. After their options for flying fizzled out and the war ended in August 1945, the women pilots were left to find jobs in the civilian sector.

The former WASPs aggressively pursued aviation jobs, but few were successful, because of the discriminatory hiring practices of commercial airlines.[83] Like male veterans after the war, many women felt determined to find work as pilots, as they could not imagine leaving aviation or working a desk job. As one female pilot poignantly stated, "If they disband us . . . I want to go to South America. I think I'd die if I had to work in an office or something. We all look at each other blankly when we think of an office job."[84] Some WASPs wrote letters to airlines asking about employment as pilots, but they were turned down or encouraged to apply as flight attendants.[85] Others volunteered for the Civil Air Patrol as a chance to remain in aviation, even though they were not paid.[86] In the 1960s, when the National Aeronautics and Space Administration (NASA) announced an experiment for women's astronaut training, WASP Elaine Jones wrote and asked for the opportunity to participate. When told that she was too old to complete the training, she wrote a letter back stating, "When the youngsters poop out, I'll still be waiting."[87] Jones's response is evidence of her frustration at the lack of opportunities and persistence at wanting a career in aviation even decades after World War II.

Several of the WASPs found careers in aviation or aviation-related fields as flight instructors, ferry pilots, or writers for aviation media sources decades after their military service. One started a television show for Columbia Broadcasting System to help "dispel [a] fear of flying through knowledge" about aviation.[88] Another former WASP held the creative position of professional skywriter.[89] Still other WASPs set flight and aviation records or flew in air races.[90] Some inspected airplanes for major concerns like the Douglas Aircraft Company.[91] In the immediate postwar period, a few female pilots sought to improve the future for younger generations by teaching Girl Scouts about flight. They hoped "it [would] mean more women fliers in the future" if they encouraged girls' interest in aviation.[92] At least two WASPs made careers as helicopter pilots. Dottie Young became the world's first helicopter transport pilot.[93] Dr. Dora Dougherty Strother McKeown flew for Bell Helicopters for twenty-four years, during which time she broke several helicopter records.[94] Despite these examples, the majority of the WASPs turned to careers outside of aviation.[95] Some were motivated to return home and have families in the postwar period, and some women industrial workers did the same.[96]

There were two notable exceptions to women's participation in the jet age.[97] WASP Ann B. Carl was the first woman to fly a jet, although she flew these experimental aircraft before the disbandment of the WASP program. Her WASP assignment was at the Wright-Patterson Air Force Base, where she flew jet fighters. However, she did not have a career in aviation after the war.[98] After disbandment, Jacqueline Cochran turned to other aviation pursuits and became the only woman to fly jet aircraft until the 1970s. Using her political connections, billionaire husband's financial support, and the profits from her own makeup company, she pursued a successful aviation career for the rest of her life. Cochran won national and international awards, set flight records, and even tried to participate in NASA's women in space flight training program, although she did not meet the qualifications for medical reasons. She set several specific jet-aircraft records in her lifetime, and she was the first woman to break the sound barrier, land a jet on an aircraft carrier, and pilot a jet across the Atlantic. She was also a test pilot for the air force when she flew the F-104 Starfighter.[99] In addition to these accomplishments, Cochran negotiated an opportunity for the WASPs in the US Air Force Reserves (USAFR) after the war.

In the summer of 1948, Cochran inquired about the possibility of the WASPs entering the USAFR.[100] In early 1949, the US Air Force was accepting applications from the former WASPs, offering positions to "all Ex-WASP who meet the standards and qualifications a commission of 2nd Lieutenant in the United States Air Force on a *non-flying* status or in the USAFR on a *non-flying* status."[101] Cochran encouraged the WASPs to take advantage of this "privilege" and "important" opportunity since women might be placed on flying status in the future.[102] Despite the emphasis on "non-flying" in her letter, this prospect left the WASPs with a hope for future military aviation careers. As of the fall of 1949, almost 200 WASPs had applied for the USAFR. Depending on their number of flying hours, the WASPs received varying ranks within the air force. Barbara London and Betty Gillies of the WAFS had the highest level of experience and were commissioned as majors. A few other women pilots started as captains, while the rest were commissioned as second lieutenants.[103] There were 156 WASPs commissioned as officers in the USAFR, but only 112 served because the air force discharged those who had young children.[104]

During their time in the USAFR, the WASPs served both within the United States and overseas. Most of them worked in traditional women's jobs—for example, as administrative assistants. Some of the WASPs were dissatisfied with their service. WASP Elaine Harmon never received any assignments, and she was disappointed in the lack of opportunities.[105] WASP Mary Carolyn Clayton applied for commission in the air force because she hoped that "flying or . . . military service would always be a part of [her] life." Unfortunately, she never had the opportunity to fly during her service at Langley Air Force Base in Virginia, in Wiesbaden, Germany, or at Hamilton Air Force Base in California. Disappointed, Clayton told a journalist, "I wanted to fly as a career. . . . I guess you can't have everything."[106] The WASPs were also restricted in their USAFR positions since they had to resign when they had a child under eighteen years of age.[107] Thus, while some experienced travel to different countries, they never could create a military aviation career.

During the debate over the 1944 militarization bill, WASPs' roles as military servicewomen were contested. Congress supported the voices of male CAA-WTS instructors. Instead of focusing on the fact that these men avoided the draft, representatives concentrated on implications that women were holding jobs claimed by men and that the WASPs were more qualified than the CAA-WTS pilots, according to AAF regulations. The militarization bill also failed because of Cochran's actions transcending roles of authority, the hostility between the AAF and CAA-WTS, and the glamorized image of the WASPs in the media. As discarded weapons in the postwar period, women had no access to high altitudinal spaces, including jet aviation and space flight, and they had no success with their aviation goals through their USAFR service. Through their continued camaraderie and efforts to network, the WASPs organized and fought for status as veterans in the 1970s, during the women's liberation movement when other women made similar demands.

5 I Never Flew an Airplane That Asked If I Were a Mr. or a Mrs. or a Ms.

Contesting Definitions of a Veteran and Receiving Veteran Status

> The point was that the government owed us. They did! We worked for the government. We flew for the government. We died for the government. The same as men. We, many of our people got killed. So it's no different when it's a WASP getting killed than when it's a man getting killed. They're just as dead. Their families are just as bereaved.
> —WASP Lillian Roberts-Risdon

At a WASP reunion business meeting in 1975, Bruce Arnold, son of World War II general Henry "Hap" Arnold, stood up and said that he knew his father wanted the WASPs to receive military status during the war. To finish his father's legacy, Arnold promised to do everything in his power to help these pilots finally become veterans. While the WASPs had already worked toward getting a militarization bill before Congress, this was when their organization gained momentum. As president of the WASP organization, the Order of Fifinella, from 1975 to 1978, Bee Falk Haydu was at the forefront of these efforts. She and other WASPs appeared on national television outlets like *Good Morning America* and gave or wrote radio, magazine, and newspaper interviews. In explaining the extent of this massive undertaking, she said they burned "a lot of midnight oil." In an era without email or cell phones, Haydu argued that one of the "biggest problems" organizationally was informing fellow WASPs of what actions to take next in the fight.[1]

In the 1970s, amid the women's liberation movement and a country reeling from Vietnam, the WASPs organized and presented another militarization bill before Congress. As they put together evidence of the military nature of the WASP program, the women answered questionnaires about their wartime service and how they viewed militarization. In her answer to the militarization question, WASP Gini Alleman Disney stated, "I most certainly did expect to be militarized and was most disappointed when we were disbanded. I did not join, train, and serve to become [anything] other than a pilot and I wanted the opportunity to continue to serve in an airborne capacity. . . . I never flew an airplane that asked if I were Mr. or a Mrs. or a Ms."[2] Disney's expectation of militarization and her perspective that an airplane never needed to know her sex or marital status illustrates many women pilots' frustration over a lack of veteran status and what they considered to be full citizenship. Veterans organizations fought against the WASPs to protect their own narrow definitions of heroic military service and positioned themselves as stakeholders of the title "veteran." In this fight for militarization, the WASPs organized and executed strategies to prove the military character of the program. In the process, they illuminated masculine privilege and contested understandings of what it means to be a veteran.

The WASPs maintained their identity as military pilots in the postwar period. They possessed pride in their wartime service, as they kept their uniforms, attended reunions, and maintained long-distance friendships to reassert their sense of military sisterhood. Increasing numbers of WASPs became passionate about trying to fight for militarization in the decades after the war. When Marty Wyall discussed her service as a WASP, she proudly took her uniform out of the closet and tried it on for an interviewer while posing for pictures.[3] Another female pilot framed a piece of the fabric from the government-issue coveralls that she wore during training.[4] One bought a license plate for her car, 43WASP6, which incorporated her veteran identity via her training class, 43-W-6.[5] Thus the WASPs kept reminders of their identity as pilots. It was this pride in their wartime service that would motivate them to fight for militarization.

A year after the conclusion of the WASP program, its members began discussing militarization as they developed networks of communication among their former classmates. Before disbandment, the WASPs created an organization called the Order of Fifinella, named after the Walt Disney character that was their mascot and on their AAF patches, and they met for reunions.[6] The Order of Fifinella also published a newsletter that printed information on aviation jobs or "other pertinent information relative to women in aviation."[7] As early as 1946, the WASPs began gathering annually.

WASPs' creation of newsletters and participation in annual reunions highlight their identity as veterans, just as other veterans of war have formed their own organizations. Sociologists argue that former members of the armed forces create organizations because military service "lends itself to group formation." Veterans "collectively attach social and political significance" to their experiences.[8] With the Order of Fifinella, the WASPs continued the camaraderie they had built during the war, and they helped one another further their aviation careers. While attending reunions, WASP Elaine Danforth Harmon got reacquainted with old friends from her WASP training class, many of whom she kept in close contact with, and she also met women from other classes. Of the fellowship among these pilots, she passionately remarked, "Even if I don't know a WASP, I feel like she's a good friend."[9] With this description, Harmon illuminated the ways the WASPs were a military sisterhood. Speaking of her attendance at reunions with classmates, one WASP noted that "it was just as if that twenty years [since their service] had not passed."[10] Another remarked that when people attend WASP reunions, they can tell that flying during the war was the "highlight" of the pilots' lives.[11] Harnessing these friendships, the WASPs not only reminisced about their wartime experiences, but they also began making plans for militarization.

Less than a year before the first national reunion, the WASPs started discussions of military status, but fears of losing any current aviation jobs they held kept them from moving forward. Their December 1945 newsletter outlined arguments for and against legislation that would grant the WASPs veterans benefits. The measure would grant the thirty-eight families of deceased pilots compensation and provide the WASPs with medical and educational benefits. Furthermore, if placed on reserve status with the air force, the WASPs could be engaged as military pilots in the next war. Those opposed to the legislation emphasized that it would be "almost impossible to pass." Moreover, they remarked that GI loans were often just as challenging to obtain as civilian ones, and that education was "more acute for veterans whose training was for combat" but had no "peacetime skill." In addition, some of the WASPs were currently unavailable for reserve status because they had children under the age of eighteen. Finally, the executive board of the Order of Fifinella noted that the legislation's timing might not be ideal: "There is a strong possibility of harm being done to WASP now engaged in competitive commercial flying, by renewal of the old feud, prejudice and criticism, directed at [the] WASP as a group." This "old feud" references the struggle between the male Civil Aeronautics

Administration–War Training Service pilots and the WASPs over rights to AAF jobs.

Furthermore, the WASPs currently working in commercial flying or attempting to enter the field competed against the over 190,000 male pilots discharged from the AAF at the end of the World War II. As of 1950, there were only around 37,000 total jobs for pilots—men and women—in civilian aviation. Some of the former WASPs held jobs as flight instructors, ferry pilots, or helicopter pilots. They feared losing their commercial employment if they pushed for a legislation bill.[12]

After detailing the two sides of the militarization argument, the Order of Fifinella also sent out a questionnaire asking WASPs about their education (whether they were currently attending college, or whether WASP service disrupted it), any disabilities they acquired while in the WASP program, their medical care, and their interest in government loans. The GI Bill covered these services for other veterans. The last questions asked about WASP interest in a "campaign . . . for legislation" so that the pilots could have access to the GI Bill or admittance to the US Air Force Reserves.[13] This questionnaire is the first recorded mention of women's organization and planning for militarization. In February 1946, former WASPs met with other women's aviation organizations, including the Ninety-Nines and Texas Wing of Women Fliers, to discuss the possibility of veterans benefits for the WASPs.[14] When the Order of Fifinella organized the first WASP reunion in August 1946, part of the agenda discussed the possibility of militarization.[15] This latter discussion meant that the Order of Fifinella's questionnaire yielded enough positive opinions that the organization's members considered legislation worth pursuing, although there were a few voices of dissension. Some did not want a militarization bill and thought that pursuing additional benefits would be "selfish."[16] Perhaps their perspectives reference societal opinions about women's self-sacrifice in times of war, or perhaps these WASPs did not need the additional benefits offered to male veterans.[17] These concerns would be addressed by the Order of Fifinella later, in the 1970s.

Despite the data collected via questionnaires and despite the amount of interest in militarization, the WASPs did not launch a campaign to pursue veteran status until the 1970s. In the decades from 1945 to the early 1970s, the WASPs continued to produce newsletters with detailed information about aviation jobs and updates on their personal lives. The newsletters facilitated a continued camaraderie between the women while also making them aware of opportunities in aviation. These publications and the annual reunions became a political space for the pursuit of militarization in the 1970s.

The WASPs maintained the close friendships formed during the war as they met for reunions and continued their newsletter tradition from 1944, the year the program disbanded, until 2011. Their maintenance of these networks and friendships led to discussions of another militarization bill and WASPs' foray into politics. During the 1970s, the WASPs increased these discussions and urged one another to network with representatives and senators. Eventually, they began lobbying Congress, speaking with media outlets about the bill, and collecting documentation to provide evidence to congressional representatives. Colonel Bruce Arnold helped the WASPs navigate this political landscape. Thus, through their political connections, consistent networking, and drive to receive veteran status, militarization became a reality for women aviators in the 1970s.

Women pilots began writing letters to representatives in the late 1960s, amid a growing women's movement pushing for equal rights for the sexes. Many of the WASPs dissociated themselves from the political agenda of the feminist movement, much as female military leaders did in the 1970s. Both the female veterans and current service members were concerned over politicization. Current servicewomen worried that politicization would invoke "knee-jerk changes" that would create an obstacle to "real, lasting progress toward women's equality."[18] The WASPs were concerned politicization would alienate supporters of the bills that would granted them veteran status. Despite this distancing, women's liberation must have fostered a sense of consciousness among the WASPs and a desire to fight for their rights as citizens. For example, WASP Gini Alleman Disney's response about planes not asking about her marital or sex status, including her use of the title "Ms.," fits the subtext of second-wave feminism.

Several of the WASPs specifically mentioned that they did not consider themselves feminists or a part of the women's liberation movement. One remarked that her service in the WASP "was not a feminist movement or a Women's Liberation project, in any kind of way."[19] Another WASP reflected that her wartime flying was "an opportunity to do something that was once-in-a-lifetime." She continued, "Of course, you didn't even know it at the time. And it has nothing to do with being a feminist. . . . I never thought of it that way." This description of "opportunity" reflects that flying was a nontraditional career option during a time when few such choices were available to women. In interviews decades after the war, journalists and other interviewers often told this WASP, "You were ahead of your time."[20] She disagreed with this statement and did not think it had any bearing on her decision to join the program. In a media interview in the mid-1990s, one WASP told a journalist, "I'm definitely not a women's libber!" Explaining her belief that being a wife and mother is a meaningful "career," she also advocated women's military career advancement.[21] With their statements, these women articulated their conceptions of equality of the sexes while rejecting the politicization of the term "feminist." during women's liberation.

Despite their dissociation from the feminist movement's political agenda, the WASPs gained a sense of consciousness from women's liberation, along with a desire to fight for their rights as citizens.[22] Cynthia Enloe argues that "women can draw on their own experiences with the military to expose the military for the contradictory and vulnerable patriarchal institution it is and always has been," just as the WASP did in their quest for veteran status.[23] In the 1970s media coverage of the congressional debate over militarization, journalists referenced the impact of the women's liberation movement. One commented, "Finally, in this era of rising concern for women's rights, WASPs are realizing that they were stung."[24] During an interview, a WASP told a journalist, "[My fellow pilots and I] have just started really gearing up and roaring. . . . We have gained momentum since the women's movement."[25] For some WASPs, life experiences and the benefit of hindsight made them realize they should fight for their rights as citizens. As one WASP commented, "What did I know then—I was only 21."[26] Although disdainful of the term "feminism," the WASPs readily employed the language of women's libbers, calling certain World War II–era pilots "chauvinists." Another WASP called a male pilot she served with during the war "one of the male chauvinists. He thought all women were made for him and the kitchen."[27] Some called the wartime years "openly chauvinist days."[28] As other women acquired rights through women's liberation, the WASPs also wanted to seize the opportunity to earn their veteran status.

The language of the congressional debate itself directly reflected the women's liberation movement, as supporters of the bill cited "sex discrimination" as the reason for failed militarization in 1944. Senator Barry Goldwater was an unlikely and fierce advocate for the WASPs in 1977. No feminist, the former presidential candidate was renowned for his conservative politics. He was one of only eight senators who voted against the Equal Rights Amendment.[29] Goldwater opposed women's service in combat roles and their entrance into the service academies. After he flew in formation with the first ten female pilots to graduate from the Air Force

Undergraduate Pilot Training program in 1977, he explained that while women flew as well as male pilots, just as the WASPs had decades earlier, he still did not support their incorporation into combat operations or their entrance into the service academies.[30]

Nevertheless, Goldwater was a staunch advocate for the WASPs because he had flown alongside the female pilots stationed at New Castle Air Force Base in Delaware during the war. Author of Public Law 95-202, Goldwater intended for the WASPs to be "considered active duty for the purposes of all laws administered by the Veterans' Administration." To him, it was clear that the WASPs qualified as veterans under Title 5 of the United States Code, Section 2108(1), which defines a "veteran" as "an individual who . . . served on active duty in the Armed Forces during a war."[31] Goldwater cited several examples of sex discrimination against the WASPs during World War II while concluding, "[These instances occurred] long before the days of women's lib, but every man who wore wings and flew for the Army had and still has an admiration [for the WASPs]."[32] Another senator noted that he witnessed "many blatant cases of sex discrimination which required remedial congressional action," including discrimination against the WASPs.[33] Thus, the rhetoric of second-wave feminism permeated this battle for veteran status, regardless of the female pilots' identification with the politics of the movement.

The new political connotations associated with the term "feminism" and the backlash to the 1970s movement, coupled with the need to appeal to a wide range of political backgrounds in Congress, presumably explains the WASPs' stance. WASPs' attitudes toward feminism and women's liberation might have been due to their political affiliations or their fears of alienating congressional support, including that of Senator Barry Goldwater. With the rise of Phyllis Schlafly's STOP ERA movement, alignment with women's liberation could alienate a segment of the American public and congressional representatives just as the WASPs were garnering signatures on petitions. For the WASPs, their desire for veterans benefits likely outweighed their political interests or desire to gain equality for other women.

WASPs' reactions to feminism and women's liberation are similar to those of army wives in this same era. A "grassroots movement of army spouses" was "fueled" by second-wave feminism, although feminism was not popular among most army wives. These women feared the repercussions of disrupting the military culture that emphasized their supportive roles as essential to the success of their husbands' careers. Other wives had limited understandings of feminism or found the movement offensive due to the National Organization for Women's argument that "traditional service-oriented volunteerism" is an "exploitation of women's labors." Those who were more likely to embrace second-wave feminism were more educated, younger, middle-class wives.[34]

What is striking about the WASPs' and army wives' engagement with or aversion to the label of "feminism" is the fact that female veterans of a previous generation harnessed second-wave feminism. Women who served in the US Army Signal Corps during World War I wanted recognition as soldiers, and in the 1970s they pursued and received veteran status on the same bill as the WASPs. When speaking with congressional representatives, these servicewomen argued that they were "victims of 'male chauvinism' during the war." They sought help from the National Organization for Women at the height of women's liberation, and some even openly embraced the title of "feminist."[35]

Even after the WASPs received militarization, they maintained that they were just women pursuing their interests, isolated from pursuits of equality or women's rights. In the immediate aftermath of the 1977 congressional victory, a journalist interviewed several WASPs in a Washington, DC, restaurant as they celebrated. They "laughed" at his insinuation that they were "early feminists" for entering a male-dominated field. Shocked, the reporter explained that these women had "literally flown in the face of traditional male-female roles all their lives," as many cultivated postwar careers in fields with few women. While some of the WASPs interviewed were willing to admit that they "broke down [a] stronghold" and proved women's abilities, they emphasized that it was not their intention.[36] The WASPs ironically pursued nontraditional careers and veterans benefits, which feminists throughout the twentieth century would have championed and which early female aviators would have considered a missed opportunity for equality.

The campaign for the WASP militarization bill picked up momentum when Women's Auxiliary Ferrying Squadron member Teresa James was able to garner the support of Representative Patsy Mink, who agreed to sponsor the measure in the House.[37] A Japanese American from Hawaii, Mink was the first woman of color and first Asian American woman elected to Congress in 1964. An advocate for women's rights and eradicating gender discrimination in the United States, she coauthored and sponsored Title IX of the Education Amendments of 1972 and cosponsored the Equal Rights Amendment.[38] In May 1972, Mink introduced House Resolution 15035, but it did not reach the floor for debate. If it had, the bill would only have benefited women who served in the US Air Force Reserves (USAFR).[39] The WASPs blamed the bill's failure on the "hostility" of the Veterans Administration (VA).[40] Perhaps this reaction harkened back to the war, when the WASPs caused contested notions of what it meant to be a hero.

After this failure, Colonel Bruce Arnold, General Henry "Hap" Arnold's son, increased his involvement in helping the WASPs, and he worked to prepare a militarization bill for all of the WASPs, not just those in the USAFR.[41] The colonel was instrumental in the passage of the WASP militarization bill in 1977. General Henry Arnold passed away in 1950, and his son wanted to help the WASPs since he knew his father strongly supported them during the war. Arnold acquired an office at the Army-Navy Club in Washington, DC, so that the WASPs could use it as a headquarters for their campaign.[42] When the first women entered the Naval Academy to be pilots in 1973, some media sources proclaimed that these were the first American women to fly military aircraft.[43] These claims motivated the WASPs to fight for not only militarization but recognition of their wartime service.[44]

Problems arose in the 1970s in the political atmosphere of the energy crisis, economic inflation, and the Watergate trials. Because of these issues facing Congress, Colonel Arnold decided it would be best to wait to find more people willing to sponsor the bill.[45] In 1975, he spoke at the annual WASP reunion and asked attendees to wait to contact the media or their representatives or senators until he thought the "time [was] right."[46] That same year, Arnold gained the support of Senator Barry Goldwater, who introduced Senate Bill 1345 in March. In May 1975, Representative Patsy Mink, still interested in helping the WASPs, introduced House Resolution 6595.[47] Unfortunately, Senate Bill 1345 and House Resolution 6595 both remained in the Veterans' Affairs Committees at the end of the ninety-fourth session of Congress.[48]

Despite this failure, Arnold and the WASPs reorganized themselves and prepared for a large-scale effort to lobby Congress in 1976. This organization was time consuming and cumbersome. It took the women pilots about a year to gather contact information for the WASPs currently living, and many of them typed letters on typewriters during this decade.[49] Arnold petitioned the WASPs to write the members of these Veterans' Affairs Committees to emphasize that most of them were "working class" women "who gave up good paying jobs to enter WASP training," that there were plans for the militarization of the program, and that the WASPs now wanted "public recognition" for their wartime service.[50] To update one another on the bill's progress, the WASPs designated women living in some regions of the country to send out "red alerts" via mail to other WASPs in their region whenever essential news about these bills progressed. They hoped that this practice would spread news quickly about the bill. Furthermore, the Order of Fifinella urged the WASPs who had not initially supported the legislation, or who thought that fighting for militarization was a waste of time after "so many years," to at least think about the WASPs who could financially benefit from medical care offered by the VA. As an article in a program newsletter stated, "[Many] are not as fortunate financially." By persuading as many women as possible, the Order of Fifinella wanted to present a solid and unified front for what they hoped would be the final struggle in 1977.[51]

Through this reorganization and increased letter writing to Congress, the WASPs gained additional supporters for the bills introduced in early 1977. In January 1977, Senators Barry Goldwater and Clifford Hansen and Representative Linda Boggs introduced the legislation to their respective Veterans' Affairs Committees. The committees planned to meet on May 25, 1977, to discuss the bills.[52] Colonel Arnold gave the WASPs strategies for navigating Congress, and he used his political connections to support them. In January and February 1977, after the introduction of the measures to the Senate Veterans' Affairs Committee and the House Veterans' Affairs Committee, Arnold strategized with the WASPs and told them to write members of these committees in preparation for their May discussions of the bills.[53] At that time, two members of the Senate committee supported militarization, while five were undecided. In the House committee, thirteen representatives supported it, five opposed it, including Chair Ray Roberts, and ten were undecided. In the final months before the vote, the WASPs hoped to persuade the undecided members.

The WASPs faced resistance from congressional representatives and senators who believed passing a militarization bill for the female pilots would lead to other civilians requesting and earning veterans benefits. Representative Olin Teague, a House Veterans' Affairs Committee member, led the opposition to the bill.[54] Known for his tenacity in Congress, his old college football nickname, "Tiger," followed him.[55] Teague argued that the WASPs should not receive militarization since they "were not subject to any form of military discipline," and "they were not subject to normal military command." These statements are not reflective of the actual WASP experience, as the pilots followed military rules and regulations and were subject to military discipline. Furthermore, Teague viewed the WASPs as being on equivalent civilian status with Red Cross workers and United

Service Organization (USO) entertainers, in that they "received far more rights, rewards, salary and other benefits than individuals who were serving in the army or navy in the enlisted status or on the officers level."[56] However, the WASPs received similar privileges as AAF officers—for example, access to officers' clubs—although they were paid less and did not have any active-duty benefits.

Teague and some veterans organizations feared that if the WASPs received military status, then the same would have to be done for other civilian groups, such as the USO and Red Cross workers, "who served on a similar basis."[57] Unlike most other civilian organizations, the WASP program was unique in that the AAF initially organized it with the assumption of wartime militarization. Representatives Ray Roberts and John P. Hammerschmidt voiced similar concerns while emphasizing combat and overseas service linked to veteran status. These congressmen supported a bill that granted Czech and Polish veterans medical benefits from the VA, provided they had been citizens of the United States for ten years. Their reasoning for extending benefits was that "these persons [had] engaged in armed conflict against enemies of the United States."[58]

Led by WASP Byrd Howell Granger, the WASPs gathered information and documents to prove the military nature of the program to Congress. They sent Granger their wartime documents and materials. The servicewomen collected the following information in support of militarization: The WASPs took an "oath of office" when they arrived in Texas for training.[59] In addition, they were issued dog tags, and they wore their uniforms according to AAF Regulation 40-9.[60] The WASPs also had membership cards for officers' clubs, unlike other civilians in the AAF, who were not allowed access to these establishments.[61] Access to the officers' club was granted to pilots with a rank of second lieutenant, which the WASPs would have received if the 1944 militarization bill had passed.[62] Furthermore, WASPs learned the Articles of War, a code of conduct for the US military. Some women were even issued firearms during the war when they ferried top-secret equipment.[63] These brief examples provided evidence to Congress that the WASPs followed most aspects of military protocol and functioned as AAF officers.

One of the most critical documents collected was the honorable discharge certificate that some WASPs received when the program disbanded.[64] This document persuaded Representative Olin Teague to change his opinion about the bill. As a World War II veteran, he had received an honorable discharge certificate, and he acknowledged that the WASPs were organized as military when he saw the same certificate in the women's possession. His opinion reversal is attributed to the success of the House Veterans' Affairs Committee's support of the militarization legislation.[65] Teague's revelation was made possible through women pilots' organizational efforts.

Amid the backdrop of the women's liberation movement, it is no surprise that the WASPs viewed themselves as veterans and wanted militarization. Byrd Howell Granger sent out questionnaires to women pilots asking for details about their military service. One of the questions she asked involved WASP perceptions of themselves as members of the armed forces: "During your service as a WASP, did you think of yourself as a civilian or as part of the military? Did you expect to be militarized?"[66] Most of the WASPs answered that they "thought of [themselves] as part of the military."[67] Some women believed they were military since they called others in American society "civilians." The WASPs also frequently mentioned the differences between their lives as WASPs and their civilian lives. One even declared that WASP disbandment without militarization would have been equivalent to the US military "kick[ing] out soldiers in the middle of war."[68] Although one WASP did not think of herself as military since the program did not officially receive militarization in 1944, she had hoped it would happen during the war.[69]

In the 1970s congressional debates, representatives and senators literally put a "price on patriotism."[70] Supporters of the bills to grant the WASP veteran status leveraged estimated costs of veterans benefits as an argument in favor of passing the legislation. They estimated that the price of providing benefits for the approximately 850 WASPs still living would be around $80,000 to $120,000 a year.[71] These statistics show the legacy of the cost of American wars, but they also provide a literal financial amount that Congress believed was reasonable to pay for the women's military service three decades earlier.[72]

Many of the WASPs hoped the militarization bill would pass not only because of the medical and funeral benefits but also because they could be called veterans.[73] WASP Dottie Davis created a handout for the public entitled "Who Were the WASPs?" Davis stated therein, "Although some of them desperately need the benefits which currently proposed legislation would provide, the Majority are mainly interested in belated recognition and the right to say, with pride, 'We are veterans!'"[74] Similarly, in a newspaper article, a WASP told a journalist that she felt she and her fellow pilots were "entitled to the title 'veteran.'"[75]

In addition to gathering evidence, the WASPs wrote petitions supporting Senate Bill 247 and House Resolution 3321 and garnered signatures to present to Congress. These petitions stated that the over 850 WASPs were still "in need of veterans' benefits." The documents illustrated the military nature of the program and the fact that the thirty-eight WASP fatalities could not have military funerals, insurance, or benefits that male military pilots received during the war.[76] Some of the WASPs employed creative tactics to get Americans to sign. One attended a *Star Wars* premiere on May 25, 1977, and gathered hundreds of signatures.[77] Another took the petitions to local airports and remarked, "Male pilots were signing our petitions like mad."[78] The fact that the WASPs acquired these signatures illuminates the enthusiasm of people to support World War II participants, perhaps as a part of the "Greatest Generation" myth embraced by the American public, and to help women achieve their goals during women's liberation. WASPs' petition efforts were all a part of their struggle to have access to veteran status.

Several veterans groups fought to protect definitions of the term "veteran" during the congressional debates surrounding the WASP militarization bill, and their concerns were tied to ideas about the family and traditional roles for women. The VA, American Legion, Veterans of Foreign Wars (VFW), and Disabled American Veterans (DAV) were against the WASP militarization bill.[79] Since veterans are not a "monolithic power bloc," in these discussions, veterans within the organizations at national and local levels disagreed on their stance about militarization, with many local chapters supporting the WASPs.[80] Some World War II veterans in these groups held on to generational ideas about women in the military. Others likely had conflicted ideas about veterans and gendered roles due to controversial debates surrounding the Vietnam War and women's liberation. American anxieties over the defeat in Vietnam and the rise of second-wave feminism generated fears of national decline and a "crisis of male authority" within traditional families.[81]

As Representative Teague feared that other civilian groups would also receive militarization, so did the VA, VFW, and national DAV organization. The DAV argued that the WASPs were not "active military." Therefore, granting them veteran status would "violate this nation's historic principle of restricting VA benefits to veterans and their dependents" and potentially lead the way for other civilian groups to get the same undeserved benefits.[82] Another argument against WASP militarization was that men who "chose alternative service" during the Vietnam War would also apply for a similar veteran status.[83] These veterans wanted to protect their status from those in other organizations who they thought had worked in inferior forms of service. Even during World War II, the WASPs faced similar views from male pilots who perceived combat as the ideal heroic military service.

The VA also contended, "If the purpose of benefits administered by the Veterans Administration is one of recognizing and compensating for the unique demands of a military commitment, then surely extending these benefits to those with only civilian service represents something of a departure. It may be said that, in a significant way, the 'Veterans' Administration then becomes something different."[84] The first female chief benefits director of the VA, Dorothy Starbuck, made this statement before the Senate Committee on Veterans' Affairs in 1977. Captain Starbuck was not only the first female benefits director, but she also served in the US Army during World War II as a Women's Army Corps member in England. Instead of seeing the WASPs as sister veterans, she positioned current veterans as separate and indicated that incorporating the female pilots would alter definitions of "veteran."

The WASPs adapted to this situation and set themselves apart from other groups who might want militarization. They made arguments about the AAF organizing their program with the intention of militarization, about the WASPs taking the same oaths of office as male AAF officers, and about the AAF issuing military orders and participating in military ceremonies. However, members of the VA, VFW, and American Legion continued to battle against the WASP fight for militarization as they sought to protect their own veteran status.

Robert Lyngh, the National Headquarters American Legion deputy director, and John Sommer Jr., the American Legion chief of claims, provided testimony in Congress in which they literally offered a definition of the term "veteran." Lyngh and Sommer read from the United States Code, Section 101 of Title 38: "The term 'veteran' means a person who served in the active military, naval, or air service, and who was discharged or released under conditions other than dishonorable." They contended that granting veteran status to the WASPs would "denigrate" the value of the term: "[The word] will never again have the value that presently attaches to it." This American Legion statement also called into question issues of citizenship, directly relating them to a soldier's service during war: "In the history of our Nation, the veteran has, from the time of the Revolution, occupied a special place in relationship to the American people. In the main, our wars have been fought and won by the citizen-soldier, who, in responding to the nation's call, is fulfilling a basic obligation of citizenship. ... He is required to bear arms and engage in combat according to the orders of the officers appointed over him."[85]

With this description, the American Legion directly referenced women's lack of full citizenship due to their exclusion from selective service and combat.[86] Lyngh and Sommer described the process of becoming a veteran, which involved taking an oath, enrolling in the military during a time of war, being subject to military discipline, bearing arms, engaging in combat, and receiving an honorable discharge.[87] According to this definition, the WASPs fit all the criteria except for combat. When women in the other branches of the military during World War II received military status, they also did not meet this condition of combat. Throughout its description, the American Legion referred to this "citizen-soldier" as a "he." Thus, the organization implied that true veterans were male, and it also participated in the memory of war that has often been gendered male.[88] The American Legion's statement could have been a response to the recent women's liberation movement, the fear of gender role reversals, and the disruption of the white middle-class family.

The VFW issued a similar statement outlining how granting veteran status to the WASPs "would destroy the special status of veterans who have made a sacrifice above and beyond that of all other citizens and would eradicate all veterans benefits as known to us today."[89] These claims also connect the term "veteran" to male military service in combat. In the organization's history, only men who served overseas could join the VFW until the 1980s; women were eventually accepted as members in 1981. Although the American Legion allowed women to join as early as World War II, and it incorporated military men and women on active duty anywhere, not just overseas, the organization still did not support WASP militarization.[90] Despite the organizations' lack of support for the bill on a national level, some local chapters of the American Legion and VFW did champion it.[91] The national organizations sought to keep veteran status away from the WASPs or other civilian groups who might also apply for it.

After the American Legion's and VFW's testimony in 1977, the WASPs continued developing strategies for garnering the support of other veterans. Rather than disrupting definitions of veterans outlined by the American Legion, the servicewomen focused on responding to incorrect summaries of the WASP program as they spoke at veterans group meetings and wrote handouts. Although the National Headquarters American Legion never supported the WASP bill, local chapters of the American Legion did.[92] In August 1977, Colonel Bruce Arnold and four WASPs prepared to meet with the American Legion National Veterans Affairs and Rehabilitation Commission. Arnold met with the former national commander of the Legion, General Bob Eaton, to discuss operational procedures. Eaton offered advice since he "remember[ed] the WASP kindly and enthusiastically from his Air Force days," and he told Arnold that the WASPs should lobby as many American Legion members as possible before the meeting with the commission in August.[93]

The WASPs spoke with their local chapters and set up a display at the national convention ahead of the meeting. They wore their military uniforms, displayed *Stars and Stripes* articles that supported the bill, and passed out pamphlets with facts about the WASP program. Since the *Stars and Stripes*, a media source that hails itself as "the only National Veterans' Newspaper," sided with the WASPs, it gave WASP Patricia Collins Hughes a regular column to print information about the legislation's progress.[94]

Two other military and veteran associations supported the WASP militarization bill—the Combat Pilots Association and the Air Force Association.[95] The Department of Defense also acknowledged that the WASPs deserved veteran status and "should be treated as active duty in the Armed Forces of the United States for the purposes of laws administered by the Veterans Administration."[96] By using copies of the *Stars and Stripes* newspaper in their display and wearing their uniforms, the WASPs politically situated themselves alongside other veterans.

At the same time, other congressional support for the WASP bills incorporated a discussion of the first women who had entered service academies the previous year. Representative Margaret Heckler was "disappointed" in the VFW, American Legion, and DAV for their stance against the WASPs. She argued that if these organizations had "any future," they must "incorporate the needs of women" since the all-volunteer force relied on women's service.[97] She also contended that female graduates from the Air Force Academy would "identify" with the results of the 1977 debates about the WASPs.[98]

One senator directly aligned his appointment of a woman to a service academy with granting recognition and veteran status for the WASPs. He argued that both actions were efforts to eradicate past and prevent future "injustices."[99] In a separate discussion on the possibility of women in combat, another senator referenced women in the military during World War II, including army nurses, the Women's Army Corps, and the WASPs. He argued his support for the bill, stating that women had attained success in military roles in the past and that they had sacrificed their lives for the nation.[100] Yet another senator referenced the previous incorporation of women into the military in his rebuttal of two primary arguments against admitting women into the service academies. He first disrupted the argument about combat training, noting that the majority of training is not combat related. Then he explained that while opponents had complained about the remodeling of facilities, women had already been "accommodated in the regular army without a particularly burdensome expense." In conclusion, he stated that Congress needed to "remove" this instance of discrimination against women.[101]

When speaking at the American Legion's national convention, Arnold coached the WASPs on using their language to help them make the most compelling arguments. Most likely in response to Lyngh's testimony, Arnold explained that it was important not "to ask the Veterans' Committees to change their definition of a veteran." Furthermore, Arnold wanted the WASPs to hint at the discrimination against them in the previous 1944 congressional debates by using "subtle" language. These actions were presumably to keep the male veterans from feeling defensive or threatened by gendered arguments. Instead, the strategy the WASPs employed to discuss the 1944 decision was saying that Congress should "right the wrong" that they had endured.

The WASPs emphasized to American Legion members that Congress supported the Civil Aeronautics Administration–War Training Service (CAA-WTS) male civilian pilots instead of encouraging those men to serve in the army ground forces, where the Allies needed them. Again, those men were eligible for the draft, so they tried for draft deferment again by claiming WASP jobs. Colonel Bruce Arnold told the WASPs that they could use him as a personal example. Arnold served in the ground forces during World War II since his poor eyesight prevented him from serving in the AAF as a pilot.[102] In this sense, he viewed himself as being patriotic and serving where he was needed, something that he criticized the CAA-WTS pilots for not doing. So, in these arguments, the WASPs could be patriotic but still appear undisruptive to the American Legion's definitions of "veteran." Although the national American Legion did not end up supporting the WASPs, women pilots continued developing and employing their strategies for proving their military position and rights to the title of "veteran," even when they had to do that in a "subtle way."

After over three decades of hoping and planning for militarization, the women pilots' organization, strategies, and commitment proved successful. In the fall of 1977, the Veterans' Affairs Committees approved the WASP bills. On November 3 and 4, the House and Senate passed the bills (Public Law 95-202) for the women's veteran status. President Jimmy Carter signed the legislation into law on November 23, 1977. Once they received militarization, the WASPs were entitled to benefits and support, including medical services, job training, and educational opportunities from the VA.[103]

Celebratory, the WASPs acknowledged the connection of veteran status to their rights as citizens. In a special "We Salute You, America!" edition of the *WASP Newsletter* in December 1977, the editor announced, "[November 23 is] a day all America will remember as [the one] the WASP came out of the shadows and were finally noted as serving their country when needed." She thanked the WASPs and all who helped them achieve "the ultimate outcome of Victory."[104] These enthusiastic responses, particularly about saluting America, indicate the servicewomen's excitement about receiving veteran status. One WASP explained the significance of the moment by saying, "[It] meant we were shoulder to shoulder with other World War II veterans."[105] In her *Stars and Stripes* column, WASP Patricia Collins Hughes proclaimed, "Our constitutional right to be recognized for military achievement in a time of war has been acknowledged."[106] Hughes tied the passage of the bill directly to women's citizenship. For others, veteran status also meant the recognition of their deceased pilot sisters. They hoped that it would have given the parents of the thirty-eight WASPs who died during the war "satisfaction that their daughters were veterans, that their daughter had served their country; their daughter was part of the military and got killed in the line of duty."[107] All in all, most of the WASPs felt the bill was "long overdue," and most of them desired the medical benefits and ability to be buried with military honors that came with veteran status.[108]

During the debate over the WASP militarization bills of the 1970s, women's roles as veterans were contested. Through their continued postwar camaraderie and networking, the WASPs organized and fought for status as veterans in the 1970s, when other women made similar demands during the women's liberation movement. WASPs' military sisterhood was apparent as they worked toward a common goal and used creative methods to ensure a victory. In the context of the Vietnam War, as AAF men and male veterans tried to protect definitions of "heroic military service" and status as "veterans," the WASPs proved the military nature of their program. For these women pilots, the fight was about military benefits and their access to recognition as veterans, bringing them closer to full citizenship and challenging the military's identity as a hypermasculine space.

When the WASPs received veteran status with Public Law 95-202, others did as well. Among those included were the World War I female US Army Signal Corps operators who served with the American Expeditionary Forces in France; the Women's Army Auxiliary Corps;[109] and World War I occupational therapists, physical therapists, and dieticians.[110] Public Law 95-202 had meaningful implications for other groups labeled civilian and performing work for the US military. The language of the bill explains that civilian individuals who "rendered service to the Armed Forces of the United States" will be "considered active duty for the purposes of all laws administered by the Veterans' Administration," provided the civilians meet a list of qualifications including military training and being "subject to military justice."[111] Historian Jessica Adler calls the bill a "major public victory" because "the nature of an individual's service would—at least officially—trump gender as a means of defining access to military status and veterans' benefits."[112]

Despite this momentous victory, after receiving veteran status in 1977, the WASPs endured continued battles for their rights to military benefits and the title "veteran" in the 1980s. Their next step was to request their DD-214, or proof of military service form, so that they could apply for benefits, employment, retirement, or membership in veterans organizations. In 1979, the Department of Defense approved the WASP legislation, Public Law 95-202, as meeting the requirements and issued the WASPs their DD-214 forms.[113] There were then questions about the interpretation of legislation passed in 1977, which said, "[The WASPs] shall be considered active duty for the purposes of all laws administered by the Veterans' Administration."[114]

When the WASPs applied for military benefits, including applications to civil service jobs and the processing of retirements, some government departments, including the Office of Personnel Management, rejected their claims, citing the fact that the WASPs were "not considered active duty in the Armed Forces of the United States under the veteran preference laws." These departments thereby disregarded the wording of the original legislation.[115] The US Air Force Air Reserve Personnel Center told the WASPs that they were not eligible for retired pay or retirement insurance benefits because they were "only to be considered active service for the purpose of Veterans Administration benefits and . . . not . . . for any other purpose."[116]

In 1981, WASP Elaine Harmon testified before a House subcommittee about these rejections and issues of interpretation. Despite her testimony and evidence in materials submitted for the record, including a letter from the author of the 1977 law, Senator Barry Goldwater, Congress did not pass additional legislation to grant the WASPs equivalent status to male veterans regarding civil service jobs or retirements.[117]

Epilogue

"Flying is the greatest equalizer. The jet really doesn't know if a pilot is male or female—it doesn't. It just expects you to perform the way you need to. Many people don't realize that females are doing this in the industry—we're doing it out in the operational world of the fighter communities." With this statement, former US Air Force (USAF) F-16 Fighting Falcon pilot Monessa "Siren" Balzhiser echoes the sentiment of WASP Gini Alleman Disney on her wartime expectation of veteran status. Balzhiser became the first female F-35 production and training pilot for Lockheed Martin in 2021. In her comments from a media interview, she quoted retired USAF fighter pilot Christine Mau, who became the first woman to fly the F-35 in 2015.[1]

Balzhiser and Mau mirror the sentiments of early female aviators who saw altitude and flight as an "equalizer." Aviation is still a field that female pilots find liberating and exhilarating. Balzhiser relays the experience of jet flight as one of emotional transition from "nervousness when stepping out to the jet, to the pure excitement of being strapped into one of the most powerful fighter jets in the world, to [being] scared of messing up, to [having] a huge adrenaline rush."[2] Nevertheless, the current low numbers of female civilian and military pilots, and the fact that women are still making headlines for flight achievements, indicate that female pilots are still primarily seen as a "novelty." These and other factors reveal the long-term impact of women's exclusion from high altitudinal spaces for almost three decades, as well as the continuing struggle of military culture to equally and fully embrace all its service members.

As of 2016, the WASPs again found themselves defending their rights as veterans by fighting for inurnment at Arlington National Cemetery (ANC). While Public Law 95-202 in 1977 granted the WASPs veterans benefits, it was not until 2002 that the family of a WASP (Irene Englund) requested inurnment at ANC. Englund was initially denied this honor, but after protests from the WASPs and her family, the army approved military funeral honors for the WASPs and other active-duty designees.[3] However, in 2014, when the family of WASP Ruth Glaser Wright Guhsé applied for her inurnment at ANC, they were denied twice.[4] In March 2015, the 2002 policy again changed, and Secretary of the Army John Hugh issued a memo denying the WASPs the right for inurnment at the cemetery.[5] In September, the army rejected WASP Elaine Harmon's family's request for inurnment. Her family, including her daughter Terri Harmon and granddaughters Erin, Tiffany, and Whitney Miller, organized and fought this latest ruling.[6] Former USAF fighter pilot and US representative Martha McSally joined the fight and introduced legislation to the House.[7] Through their efforts, by March 2016, the House and Senate had unanimously passed a bill allowing the WASPs the opportunity for inurnment at ANC. On September 7, 2016, Elaine Harmon finally received a military funeral and inurnment her family requested. Without political resistance from her relatives and fellow WASP veterans, this would not have been possible.

While the WASPs identified as veterans and fought for recognition of their wartime service, today's servicewomen are statistically less likely to claim veteran status or veterans benefits. According to the Department of Veterans Affairs, less than 30 percent of female veterans "self-identify as veterans in their community and they are often unaware of the benefits and services that are available to them."[8] Self-identifying is defined as claiming veteran status on employment forms, using veterans benefits, and participating in military or veterans organizations.[9] Veteran and policy advisor Andrea Goldstein argues that many women choose not to self-identify due to the devaluation of their service in the American public. Female veterans feel exhausted from the civil-military divide and confronting public perceptions of a veteran as a man with combat experience, or from trying to fit into male-dominated veterans organizations.[10] The women who served in the WASP program created their own veterans organizations and reunions.

The camaraderie between the WASPs continued through the postwar period in the form of yearly reunions that are still held today. In interviews decades after their training, the WASPs still remembered the "wind and sand" of Sweetwater, Texas. When they gather at yearly reunions or air shows, they reminisce about learning how to fly "the army way," recalling their daily struggles and the lessons they learned in the process.[11] They also sing their class songs and the current official air force song, written during World War II.[12] WASP director Jacqueline Cochran even had the air force song as the benediction at her funeral.[13] The guest speakers at these reunions are often the WASPs' successors—USAF female pilots, including Christine Mau and former USAF Thunderbirds pilot Caroline Jensen.

Decades after the war, the next generations of women aviators turned to the WASPs for inspiration. Some current USAF pilots wear a Fifinella patch on their uniforms. On her way to the Air Force Academy for pilot training, Caroline Jensen dropped a coin in the wishing well at Sweetwater to symbolize the WASP tradition of dunking trainees who completed their first solo flight.[14] Several female air force pilots and cadets recently served as escorts at WASP reunions and the WASP Congressional Gold Medal ceremony. These women view the WASPs as paving the way for them and making it possible to hold aviation and military positions.

After the 1977 passage of the congressional militarization bill, the WASPs received additional recognition that granted them veteran status. On March 10, 2010, the WASPs received the Congressional Gold Medal, the highest honor awarded to American citizens. President Barack Obama signed Senate Bill 914 into law on July 1, 2009. WASP Elaine Harmon was one of the three WASPs present at this signing, and she said she felt "extremely honored" to receive the award.[15] On January 1, 2014, mainly thanks to the organization of Albert "Chig" Lewis, WASP Dorothy "Dot" Swain Lewis's son, the WASPs had a float in the 2014 Tournament of Roses Parade in Pasadena, California. The float featured an image of the Congressional Gold Medal that the WASPs received.

The design of the Congressional Gold Medal represents several aspects of the WASP program. The front of the medal features a portrait of a nondescript woman pilot's face. Wearing goggles and a flying cap, she is staring into the distance as though imagining her next flight. This image represents women pilots as a unified group, since it is not modeled after a specific woman's face, and it also represents the WASPs' love of flying. The front of the medal also contains an image of three women pilots walking with their flight gear on while an AT-6 flies overhead. These women's attire affirms their professionalism. Furthermore, the image of the AT-6 crosses the border of the circle around the medal, representing women pilots' work crossing accepted boundaries and flying in high altitudinal spaces. Finally, the AT-6 was one of the WASPs' favorite planes to fly.[16] They flew this aircraft during the advanced stage of training, just before graduation.

The back of the WASP Congressional Gold Medal reads, "The first women in history to fly American military aircraft." This medallion therefore provides the recognition these servicewomen sought in the 1970s, when the media inaccurately described contemporary women as the first female military pilots in America. The back of the medal also features a picture of the silver wings the WASPs received during a graduation ceremony; Cochran or an Army Air Force official pinned them on the women's military uniforms. The WASPs wore their wings proudly and viewed them as a symbol of success and accomplishment. In addition, the medal's back displays three different types of aircraft that the WASPs flew, all of them midflight—a pursuit (P-51), a bomber (B-26), and an advanced trainer (AT-6). The WASPs flew demonstrations of the B-26 to men who called it a "flying coffin," and they successfully convinced male pilots that the plane was safe to fly.[17] Thus this medal encapsulates several critical aspects of the WASP program—the women's love of flight, the ways they entered previously uncharted boundaries for women, the military aspects of their program, and their professionalism in the field of aviation.

The history of female airline pilots is reminiscent of the WASP story, as women are in the minority in this field, and they still experience sabotage and male hostility. Just as women were not readmitted as military pilots until the early 1970s, the same was true of commercial aviation. In 1934, Helen Richey became the first female airline pilot, and women were not employed in this capacity again until 1973, when US airlines hired two women.[18] As of 2020, women accounted for a mere 5.7 percent of all pilots.[19]

Current percentages of women pilots in the military are not far removed from those in the civilian sector, as approximately 6.5 percent of all USAF pilots are women, for example.[20] For perspective, in 2020, women made up 16 percent of enlisted forces and 19 percent of the military's officer corps.[21] In commercial airlines, female pilots are still the minority. According to the Federal Aviation Administration's data from 2020, of the over 170,000 certified airline pilots in the United States, only 4.6 percent are female.[22]

Female airline pilots still experience vandalism of their planes and encounter men who refuse to fly with them, just as the WASPs did over seventy years ago. Retired pilot Kathy McCullough flew for Northwest Airlines in the 1980s and 1990s. During this time, she caught a male pilot attempting to adjust a panel on the plane "just to see if she would catch it during the pre-flight check."[23] In the late 1990s, American Airlines pilot Susan Warren had male passengers who refused to fly with her.[24]

Similarly, when the first female astronaut went to space, she was barraged with questions voicing stereotypical concerns about women pilots that the American public refuses to accept, despite women's century-long accomplishments in aviation. In 1962, NASA sent the first astronauts into space, but it did not send the first American female astronaut, Sally Ride, until two decades later, in 1983.[25] When Ride went into space, the American public once again questioned women. Ride was not even the pilot of the mission, although she had a pilot's license. During a press conference, journalists asked her, "Will the flight affect your reproductive organs?" She replied, "There's no evidence of that." Another questioned her emotional strength: "Do you weep when things go wrong on the job?" She quipped in response, "How come nobody ever asks Rick [Hauck, the pilot] those questions?" A reporter even wanted to know about Ride's plans to become a mother, implying they were relevant to her mission or job. Ride refused to respond to the question and replied, "You notice I'm not answering." Of the experience with the media, Ride lamented, "It may be too bad that our society isn't further along and that this is such a big deal."[26] These 1983 inquiries ignored the history of women in aviation. The WASPs and later women astronaut trainees in the 1960s had undergone medical and psychological testing. Furthermore, women were again serving in the military as pilots.[27]

The history of the WASPs has ramifications for understanding today's issues of women's equality and citizenship in aviation and US military culture.[28] The US military has often been at the vanguard of civil rights, influencing public debate on "affirmative action, integration, marriage, reproductive rights, and sexual harassment."[29] At the same time, military culture still favors white heterosexual male service members, as in the example of the language of military cadences.[30] As women navigate this culture, they often choose between minimizing or emphasizing their femininity.[31] The military has highlighted gender difference in its recruitment and training of women in the era of the all-volunteer force.[32] Service members are still not adequately protected from sexual assault.[33]

Recently, historians and female veterans have argued their concerns about 2021 plans to disband the Defense Advisory Committee on Women in the Services (DACOWITS) and merge it with the new Defense Advisory Committee on Diversity and Inclusion. The army eventually reinstated the committee after female veterans in Congress advocated for its restoration.[34] Since the DACOWITS was created in 1951 to ease the transition of women into the military after the 1948 Women's Armed Services Integration Act, it has effectively brought about change for servicewomen in areas including educational opportunities, promotion, and job assignments. As is the trend in American society, women of color are particularly behind in these and other areas. Of late, the DACOWITS has investigated the impact of motherhood and pregnancy on women's careers.[35]

Some recent changes to military culture that are more inclusive for women are new grooming options, the removal of combat exclusion, and the incorporation of women into new military roles. In 2021, the army announced changes to regulations on hair length and hairstyles, and it provided the option to wear certain types of earrings and additional colors of nail polish and lipstick, something the DACOWITS recommended in its annual reports.[36] In addition to being "more practical" for female service-women, the "healthier hairstyle options . . . are more inclusive of various natural styles in an effort to stop hair damage and loss stemming from styles like the bun."[37] Another form of inclusivity is the navy's construction of more "gender neutral" submarines as a part of a continued decade-long effort to integrate women into the submarine force.[38]

While the 2015 end of combat exclusions removes another obstacle to women's full equality in the military, today's military women still face the same stereotypical concerns over issues of protection, sexuality, and their ability to meet specific standards.[39] Evidenced most recently with the first female graduates from US Army Special Forces training as a Green Beret in 2020 and from the US Army Ranger School in 2015, as well as the first woman accepted into the army's Seventy-Fifth Ranger Regiment in 2017, figures in the American media and public questioned the women's capabilities.[40] As weapons of war, women are still battling against gendered assumptions and sexual harassment, while their rights to military spaces, including combat and elite combat forces, are in a constant state of experimentation and negotiation.

Acknowledgments

Thank you to all of the WASP and their family members who welcomed me into their homes and lives (or greeted me at homecomings and air shows) and patiently answered all of my questions. Special thanks to Mary Anna "Marty" Martin Wyall and her grandson Jonny Wyall (who, as fate would have it, I met on a plane!); Vi Cowden and Mary Helen Foster; Elaine Danforth Harmon, her daughter Terri Harmon, and her granddaughter Erin Miller; Bernice "Bee" Falk Haydu; Dorothy "Dot" Swain Lewis and her son Albert "Chig" Lewis; Jean Terrell McCreery; Flora Belle Smith Reece and Florence "Shutsy" Reynolds; Elizabeth "Liz" Wall Stohfus; Mary Alice Putnam Vandventer; Lucile Doll Wise; Lillian Lorraine Yonally; and *Gilmore Girls* extra Eleanor "Gundy" Gunderson. Thanks also to Meriem Lucille Roby Anderson, Nell "Mickey" Stevenson Bright, Edna Davis, Mildred "Jane" Doyle, Ann (and Harry) Hazzard, Betty Jo Streff Reed, Alyce Stevens Rohrer, Dawn Seymour, and Millicent "Millie" Young. Thank you to West Texas flight instructors Tom Moore and Weldon George for our conversations on your experiences training the WASP at Avenger Field, and to John McCullough for putting us in contact. I would also like to thank Senator Kay Bailey Hutchison and her staff for extending an invitation to attend the 2010 Congressional Gold Medal Ceremony for the WASP. It is an experience I will never forget.

Several academic opportunities fostered new ways of thinking about this project. A 2016 National Endowment of the Humanities Summer Institute, "Veterans in Society: Ambiguities & Representations," generated ideas about the formation of veterans studies as an academic field and provided much of the framework for the discussion of the WASP as veterans. A special thank you goes to Jim Dubinsky, Bruce Pencek, Eric Hodges, and Heidi Nobles for their organization and operation of that institute, as well as the community they created among the attendees. I am also appreciative of Corinna Peniston-Bird and Emma Vickers for their encouragement toward historians of gender and war. A 2020–22 National Endowment of the Humanities Dialogues on the Experience of War grant allowed me to collaborate with scholars, veterans, and mental health professionals on the experiences of female veterans. My gratitude toward colleagues who engaged in deep conversation with this grant include Jessica Adler, Greg Daddis, Susan Eastman, Judy Giesberg, Alexis Hart, Leisa Meyer, BaDonna Mitchell, G. Kurt Piehler, and Kara Dixon Vuic. Kara and Greg, I really enjoyed collaborating with you on this endeavor! Kurt, thank you for the initial conversations and for always encouraging me to pursue professional development.

Discussions with colleagues from the Society for Military History, the West Point Summer Seminar in Military History, and the University of California, Berkeley's Advanced Oral History Summer Institute facilitated and sustained the momentum for this project. Kara Dixon Vuic, thank you for all the opportunities, letters, and consistent encouragement over the years. Heather Stur, thank you for your investment in getting this manuscript to publication. Ron Milam, it is an honor to know you and to have worked with you. I also appreciate those of you who carved out time for conversations on gender and war, writing, and veterans: Jonathan Abel, Jessica Adler, Beth Bailey, Bruce Cohen, Colin Colbourn, Susan Grayzel, Mike Hankins, Jason Herbert, Jason Higgins, Chris Juergens, Kate Lemay, Austin McCoy, Chris Menking, John Mortimer, Michael Neiberg, Stephen Ortiz, Jorden Pitt, Ryan Reynolds, Amy J. Rutenberg, Tanya Roth, Allyson Stanton, Luke Truxal, Jason Vuic, Ryan Wadle, Jackie Whitt, and Corbin Williamson. At Texas Tech University, Ron Milam, Amber Batura, James Sandy, Jacynda Ammons, Ming-Syuan Jhong, Uyên Carie Nguyên, Justin Hart, Julie Willett, Randy McBee, Gretchen Adams, Lynne Fallwell, Annalysa Owen, Barton Myers, Emily Skidmore, Tiffany González, Krystal Humphreys, Erin-Marie Legacey, Robert Weaver, Matt Kocsan, Autumn Costa Lass, and Cody Lass were influential in my development as a historian. A special thanks to Annie Williams, Holly Baggett, Bill Piston, Steve McIntyre, and Sam Rohaus for discussions at Missouri State University. Thank you to my copyeditor, Elizabeth Crowder, and everyone at UNC Press, including Erin Granville, JessieAnne D'Amico, and especially Debbie Gershenowitz, whose enthusiasm for the project encouraged me, and to the anonymous reviewers whose comments made this work stronger.

Colleagues and friends at Messiah University and in central Pennsylvania whose encouragement propelled me forward include Jason and Grace Renn, John Fea, Joseph Huffman, Bernardo Michael, David Pettegrew, alum Ken Stern, Allyson Patton, Robin Lauermann, Paul Rego, Chloe Dickson, Mary Culler, Sydney White, Jenell Paris, Brent Good, Rebecca and

JR Harris, Cindy Devine, Jeremy Hileman, and Eric Brunner. At Saint Francis University, thank you to Denise Damico, Art Remillard, and Ani Bose for your encouragement and mentoring. Denise, thank you for believing in me, always cheering me on, and making me laugh! I am grateful for our friendship. I also appreciated the kindness and support of Joe Melusky, Mark Gentry, Roxana Cazan, and Ed Mihelcic. As a former director and curator of the Keirn Family World War II Museum at SFU, thank you to the individuals who made that work possible and offered engaging conversations on public history and war. Cody Turnbaugh, I truly could not have done it without you, especially in those early days! To Cody, Cory Kumpf, Jesse Turnbaugh, Eli Norman, and Jalen Wells: may we always remember tanks and that leg! Lucy Rojas, you are the most hardworking person I know, and I am grateful to call you a friend. M. Alison Reilly, you have an exceptional eye for design, and your vision for the museum reflected that. Harry Olafsen, you were there right from the beginning, and I appreciate your consistent cheerleading! Bailey Edwards, you were a joy to work with. US Army Rangers Vince Hagg and Sheldon Bare, and Altoona US Army Reserve veteran Travis B. Young, I am honored that you shared your stories and lives with me.

This manuscript would also not have been possible were it not for the tremendous help and support from archivists and staff at the WASP Archive at Texas Woman's University, the National Archives in College Park, Maryland, and Washington, DC, and the Eisenhower Presidential Library. I also received tremendous help and support from Tammy T. Horton and Sylvester Jackson Jr. at the Air Force Historical Research Agency at Maxwell Air Force Base, from archivists and staff at the Smithsonian Air and Space Museum Archives in the Stephen F. Udvar-Hazy Center and the Betty H. Carter Women Veterans Historical Project, and from Anne Marsh at the Institute on World War II and the Human Experience at Florida State University.

Thank you to my family and friends, without whose support none of this would have been possible, including my parents Wayne and Jo Lynn Parry; brother and sister-in-law Caleb and Brittany Cox Parry; my gram Jean Shelton Atkinson; and my lifelong cheerleaders Aunt Jan, Uncle Kenny, Erik, and Kayla Liebel; as well as my nephews Hatcher, Bridger, Ephraim, and Isaiah. I am especially grateful to my dear friends and cultivated family. Amber Batura and James Sandy: y'all will always be my ride or dies. Thank you for your unconditional love and support. Kara Dixon and Jason Vuic (and Imogene and Asher): life with you is just more fun! Our Thanksgiving tradition is my favorite. Rachel Alden, thank you for being there for me through all the hard things. Annie Williams, you are the absolute kindest, and I always look forward to our conversations. Colin and Rachel Colbourn, I am so grateful for our friendship. Lewis Hamilton fans for life. Still We Rise!

Notes

Abbreviations

AFHRA

Air Force Historical Research Agency, Maxwell Air Force Base, Montgomery, AL

EPL

Eisenhower Presidential Library, Abilene, KS

NARA

National Archives and Records Administration, College Park, MD

NARA-DC

National Archives and Records Administration, Washington, DC

NASM

Smithsonian National Air and Space Museum Archives, Stephen F. Udvar-Hazy Center, Chantilly, VA

TWU

Texas Woman's University, Denton

TWU MSS 300

MSS 300: Oral Histories and Letters at Texas Women's University, Denton

TWU WASP Collection

MSS 250: Women Airforce Service Pilots of World War II Collection at Women's University, Denton

Introduction

1. Florence Shutsy Reynolds, interview by the author, August 27, 2017, digital recording, Keirn Family World War II Museum at Saint Francis University, Loretto, PA.

2. Reynolds, interview.

3. In June 1941, the Army Air Force replaced the Army Air Corps.

4. Eleanor Roosevelt worked as an advocate for female aviators in the Civilian Pilot Training Program during World War II. She questioned the exclusion of women from the CPTP after the program began requiring students to enlist in the military. Weitekamp, *Right Stuff, Wrong Sex*, 22–23; Pisano, *To Fill the Skies with Pilots*, 76.

5. Kinder, "Embodiment of War," 225.

6. Focşa, "The White Squadron."

7. Zegenhagen, "German Women Pilots at War"; Zegenhagen, "Holy Desire to Serve."

8. This total includes the 1,074 women pilots who graduated from AAF training and the original 28 women in the Women's Auxiliary Ferrying Squadron, since the programs merged to form the WASP in July 1943. It does not include the 11 trainees

who lost their lives during the WASP training program. There were approximately 140,000 in the Women's Army Corps, 100,000 in the navy, 23,000 in the marines, 13,000 in the coast guard, 60,000 in the Army Nurse Corps, and 14,000 in the Navy Nurse Corps. Myers, "Women Airforce Service Pilots (WASP)"; and Hartmann, *Home Front and Beyond*, 31–32.

9. Florence Shutsy Reynolds, interview by the author, August 27, 2017, digital recording, The Keirn Family World War II Museum at Saint Francis University, Loretto, PA.

10. Shutsy was in class 44-W-5. Reynolds, interview.

11. A small number of WASP flew outside the United States' borders, to destinations including Canada, Puerto Rico, and Cuba. These overseas locations remained hidden from the American public, and historians have not mentioned them in previous histories of the WASP.

12. Jacqueline Cochran's "Final Report on Women Pilot Program," TWU WASP Collection.

13. The use of the term "militarization" throughout this book references military status that provides veterans or military benefits. It also refers to cultural militarization that the WASP experienced, as many claimed the title "veteran" in the 1960s and 1970s. O'Connell's *Underdogs* examines the progression of the US Marine Corps' culture, its importance in the survival of this military branch in the post–World War II era, and its participation in the militarization of American society. This examination of the WASP is in conversation with O'Connell's study. However, this work is less about identity formation as a branch and instead focuses on a specific unit's identity and the work culture of the Army Air Force. O'Connell, *Underdogs*.

14. There has only been one peer-reviewed book written on the WASP, Molly Merryman's *Clipped Wings*. Historian Katherine Sharp Landdeck recently published a manuscript on the WASP that is based on extensive primary source research, but it is not a peer-reviewed study. Merryman's is an institutional history that focuses on the 1940s and 1970s congressional bills rather than on the female pilots' perspectives, arguing that "the issue [of failed 1940s militarization] was very clearly not about the WASPs as pilots, but about women who were going beyond culturally constructed normative boundaries of how women were expected to behave, and who were serving in what were constructed to be male roles." However, this assertion dismisses the fact that top AAF officials strongly supported the WASP, although Congress ignored those voices. Furthermore, the fact that the WASP were pilots and constructed an identity is central to the program's history. The WASP continually asserted their place as professional pilots when roles in the military were in a state of fluidity and redefinition. Merryman, *Clipped Wings*, 175; Landdeck, *Women with Silver Wings*.

15. Early historians of World War II, including William Chafe, Leila Rupp, Karen Anderson, D'Ann Campbell, Susan Hartmann, Sherna Berger Gluck, Margaret R. Higonnet, and Patrice L.-R. Higonnet have debated the long-term impact of the war on women and gender roles. Many argue that World War II led to increased political consciousness among women. For a brief historiographical essay on

gender and World War II in the United States, see Myers, "Women behind the Men"; and Higonnet and Higonnet, "Double Helix."

16. Cobb, *Hello Girls*.

17. Huebner, "Gee! I Wish I Were a Man."

18. Eleanor Roosevelt, "My Day" column, September 1, 1942, TWU WASP Collection.

19. Medical studies conducted on the WASP showed that women pilots performed on the same level as male pilots. Jacqueline Cochran's "Final Report on Women Pilot Program," TWU WASP Collection. Also, some of the WASP remember reading Roosevelt's article. For example, Carl, *WASP among Eagles*, 36.

20. The AAF officially used the acronym "WASP" to reference an individual and the entire unit. For consistency, this book adopts the same usage.

21. Philosopher Kelly Oliver recently published a study describing the connections between descriptions of women and female sexuality in metaphors of weapons. Other historians (i.e., Elaine Tyler May) have described ways the public and military perceived women's sexuality as dangerous. The military restricted women pilots' sexuality with additional rules and regulations. Oliver, *Women as Weapons of War*; May, *Homeward Bound*.

22. Leisa Meyer, *Creating GI Jane*, 39–47.

23. Historian Lucy Noakes examines the emotional economy of Britain and how Britons "valued stoicism and self-control over emotional expressiveness," which "shaped" cultural representations and "the ways in which individuals and families discussed death and grief." She builds on medieval historian Barbara Rosenwein's work on emotional communities and feminist theorist Sara Ahmed's *The Cultural Politics of Emotion*. Noakes, *Dying for the Nation*, 4; Noakes, Langhamer, and Siebrecht, *Total War*.

24. This discussion of the sensory experience is shaped by historian Mary Louise Roberts's work on World War II soldiers' combat experiences. Roberts, *Sheer Misery*.

25. It is impossible to fully understand the experience of war, including its "existence, definition, causes, practices, and consequences," without examining gender. This quote is from Corinna Peniston-Bird and Emma Vickers, although numerous scholars have made this same argument. Peniston-Bird and Vickers, *Gender and the Second World War*, 1; Joshua S. Goldstein, *War and Gender*, 251; Sjoberg, *Gender, War, and Conflict*, 12; Vuic, *Routledge History*, 2.

26. Describing the WASP as "professionals" signifies that they received special training and worked assignments that required high levels of skill, while their competence qualified them for careers as military pilots.

27. The concept of altitude as contested space builds on themes in Phil Tiemeyer's and Kathleen Barry's works. They examined flight attendants' struggles within their work environment of airplanes. This book pushes this discussion further by arguing for the consideration of altitude as contested space. Tiemeyer, *Plane Queer*; Barry, *Femininity in Flight*.

28. For a historiography of oral history, see Thomason, "Four Paradigm Transformations."

29. For a brief background on life history, see Larson, "Research Design and Strategies." While I conducted interviews with WASP at air shows, their reunions, and in their homes, I also read and watched oral histories from TWU, the Veterans History Project at the Library of Congress, and the Flying Heritage and Combat Armor Museum in Washington. For interview techniques, see the following sources: Anderson and Jack, "Learning to Listen," 11–25; Morrissey, "Two-Sentence Format"; Frisch, *Shared Authority*; and Slim and Thompson, "Ways of Listening."

30. Summerfield, "Oral History."

31. For a study of communities via shared identity formation and the ways individuals' memories are "rooted in places," as Sweetwater, Texas, is foundational for the memories of the WASP, see Shopes, "Oral History."

32. For the issue of memory, see Cándida-Smith, "Analytic Strategies"; and Summerfield, "Oral History."

33. My intention was to avoid romanticizing the WASP. Yow, "Do I Like Them." For the "Greatest Generation" myth, see Adams, *Best War Ever*; Piehler, *Remembering War the American Way*.

34. For the United States during World War II, the home front was defined as the mainland where battles and combat fighting did not occur. For countries that experienced total war, such as those in Europe, the lines between "battlefront" and "home front" were blurred. In both the United States and Europe, "home" was often a constructed image that motivated men to fight. Summerfield and Peniston-Bird, *Contesting Home Defense*, 11, 15. For further discussion of these blurred lines, see Higonnet, Jensen, Michel, and Weitz, *Behind the Lines*.

35. Kerber, *No Constitutional Right*, xxiv. Cynthia Enloe makes similar arguments in her work, as she explains that men need to serve overseas or in combat to justify dominant positions of power in society. Enloe, *Globalization and Militarism*.

36. As Steve Estes explains, "Citizen-soldiers must protect and defend the state in return for the right to have a say in how the state is run." Estes, *I Am a Man!*, 13.

37. Cynthia Enloe defines militarization as the "step-by-step social, political, and psychological process by which any person, any group, or any society absorbs the ideas and resultant practices of militarism." Her definition is broad, and she finds that militarization can occur in any life situation, including "a school's history lessons; the role of the 'good wife,' a father's aspirations for his son." Mathers, "Women and State Military Forces," 135; Enloe, *Globalization and Militarism*, 11; Enloe, *Maneuvers*, 2–4.

38. This quote is from historian Richard H. Kohn. His definition fits with the work of anthropologist Catherine Lutz and historian Michael S. Sherry. Lutz argues that in US history, militarization "accelerated in three major bursts," with World War II, "the establishment of the national security state in 1947," and with September 11, 2001. Michael Sherry defines militarization as "the contradictory and tense social process in which civil society organizes itself for the production of violence." Kohn, "Danger of Militarization," 182; Lutz, "Making War at Home"; Sherry, *In the Shadow of War*, x–xi.

39. Internationally, militarized cultures idealize patriarchal values and heteronormative gender roles. Enloe, *Maneuvers*, 46; González, Gusterson, and Houtman, *Militarization*, 4.

40. Their efforts influenced the racial integration of the US military after the war, although that did not mean the end of discrimination. In the post–World War II era, many Black and Latinx Americans became disillusioned with the concept of military service equating to full citizenship, and they saw the military as imperialist. Bristol and Stur, *Integrating the US Military*; Lentz-Smith, *Freedom Struggles*; Moore, *To Serve My Country*; Kieran and Martini, *At War*, 3; Bérubé, *Coming Out Under Fire*, 2, 7, 176, 183.

41. For women, third-wave feminists during the Persian Gulf War thought that "feminism and military service in war were mutually exclusive" and that a path to full citizenship was not possible through military service. Stur, "Men's and Women's Liberation," 158–59. For men of color, see the previous footnote.

42. Phillips, *War!*, 16, 22.

43. Estes, *I Am a Man!*, 13.

44. Leisa Meyer, *Creating GI Jane*, 12.

45. Matthews, *Smoke Jumping*, 51.

46. Pitt, "Ceasing to Be of Value."

47. Margaret Weitekamp discusses how as America entered the jet age in the postwar period, women's exclusion from space flight was due to lack of access to flying military aircraft, since NASA made jet experience mandatory. Weitekamp, *Right Stuff, Wrong Sex*.

48. A 2016 National Endowment for the Humanities Summer Institute at Virginia Tech University, "Veterans in Society: Ambiguities & Representations," discussed the creation of veterans studies as an official field of academic study: http://www.veteransinsociety.org/. Furthermore, Marten's *America's Corporal* and Ortiz's *Beyond the Bonus March* laid the foundation for the discussion of veterans, social welfare, and homecoming.

49. Historian Jessica Adler's work on the development of the modern veteran health care system after World War I reveals how "the nation and its veterans struggled to define" care. Adler, *Burdens of War*, 263.

50. Boulton examines how Vietnam veterans thought that the GI Bills of 1966, 1972, and 1974 failed them, as well as the "limits of social obligation." Boulton, "Price on Patriotism," 243.

51. Boulton, "Price on Patriotism," 243–44.

52. Thomas Andrews's *Killing for Coal* offers theoretical insights into this camaraderie, as his labor history study of the "Great Coalfield War" evokes images of war through the sense of brotherhood that developed amid dangerous work experiences. Several published memoirs and personal accounts also offer insights into the ways military men and women experience war. Andrews, *Killing for Coal*.

53. For people's motivations for fighting, see Kindsvatter, *American Soldiers*; McPherson, *For Cause and Comrades*. For men's reluctance to engage in combat, see Marshall, *Men against Fire*; and Grossman, *On Killing*. The memory of war has

often been gendered male, as evidenced in works such as Little, *Abraham in Arms*; Purcell, *Sealed with Blood*; Alfred Young, *Masquerade*; and Zagarri, *Revolutionary Backlash*. Sarah Purcell's study of the memory of the American Revolution offers perspectives into how the memory of war became gendered and racialized, and into the influence of memory on national identity. Alfred Young and Rosemarie Zagarri explain the relationship between the emerging American government and the establishment of citizens as white and male as coinciding with the memory of war centering on male veterans.

54. Philosopher Kelly Oliver argues that Private Jessica Lynch was an "ideal hero" in the US media: "She is a woman who suffers, [according to] the ideal of feminine self-sacrifice and suffering." Furthermore, Lynch was simultaneously a "victim and hero." Her portrayal in the media was as a woman both "fighting to the death" and "young, pretty, and vulnerable." Oliver, *Women as Weapons of War*, 41–42.

55. During World War II, British men and women's service in the Home Guard also confronted the idea of men as protectors and women as protected. Summerfield and Peniston-Bird, *Contesting Home Defence*, 16–20.

56. Pfau, *Miss Yourlovin*.

57. Similar motivations of patriotism and a sense of adventure drove women to serve in entertainment work (i.e., with the USO) during World War II. Vuic, *Girls Next Door*, 77–80.

58. Kara Dixon Vuic's study of women nurses in Vietnam is one of the first to discuss women's desire to make nursing a career. Vuic, *Officer, Nurse, Woman*.

59. Blanton and Cook, *They Fought like Demons*.

60. Hankins, *Flying Camelot*, 2–4.

61. There were only a few women of color admitted to the program, but none of them identified as Black or African American.

62. According to Dominick Pisano, this was a federal government–sponsored program that offered free private pilot's license training to both women and men. The CPTP admitted one woman for every ten men. Approximately 2,500 women received training. Only a small section of this book explains women pilots in the CPTP, so there is a need for additional study. Pisano, *To Fill the Skies with Pilots*, 77.

63. According to Robert Westbrook, pinup images served as symbols of soldiers' motivations for fighting. Westbrook, "I Want a Girl."

64. Maureen Honey's study of World War II propaganda argues that propaganda campaigns portrayed women's wartime work as temporary, domestic, feminine, and self-sacrificial. Honey, *Creating Rosie the Riveter*.

65. German female pilots "did not identify themselves primarily as women, but as citizens and patriots, they were not striving for the emancipation of their gender, but for the emancipation" of Germany, wanting to "restore" the nation's status in the world. Zegenhagen, "Holy Desire to Serve," 479–80.

66. Knaff, *Beyond Rosie the Riveter*, 20–21.

67. Walck and Walter, "Soaring Out of the Private Sphere."

68. This emphasis on traditional femininity fulfilled heterosexual men's fantasies of fighting for women awaiting their return on the home front. McEuen, *Making War, Making Women*, 2.

69. Elizabeth M. Norman argues that men called women "angels" in wartime "to remind women to sacrifice, to work long hours for low pay and not complain." She continues, "It [the angel image] is meant to idealize women, to push them to be perfect, because that is the kind of woman, the kind of nurse, men want." Norman, *We Band of Angels*, xii.

70. In her analysis of wartime print culture, Marilyn Hegarty also addresses the idea of women's sexuality as dangerous and necessary to the war effort. Hegarty, *Victory Girls*.

71. In addition, as Margot Canaday argues, the federal government created military regulations to enforce and control sexuality. Therefore, sexuality, race, and gender all influenced government policies and definitions of citizenship. Canaday contends that the federal government defined homosexuality as a problem and actively sought to restrict citizenship to heterosexuals in the first half of the twentieth century. Canaday, *Straight State*.

72. McManus, *Deadly Sky*; Truxal, "Politics of Operational Planning"; Sambaluk, *Other Space Race*.

73. Letter, Franklin D. Roosevelt to Amelia Earhart, January 18, 1935, The Ninety-Nines Inc. History Books Collection, Box 1, Ninety-Nine History, Sept 1, 1934 to Sept 1, 1935 Folder, NASM.

74. Van Vleck, *Empire of the Air*.

75. Female pilots complained that media coverage focused predominantly on their role as surprising oddities, since there were fewer of them than of male pilots. As Ninety-Nines president Opal Kunz explained in a 1929 letter, the organization sought to generate "a different attitude toward the girl in aviation, whereby, she is accepted as an equal rather than spoiled as something rare and very precious." Furthermore, Kunz described her wishes for the future: "[I long for the day when] it will no longer be news of first page interest when a woman takes to the air." Letter, Ninety-Nines acting president Opal Kunz to Mrs. Kenny, December 31, 1929, The Ninety-Nines Inc. History Books Collection, Box 1, Sept 1, 1929 to Sept 1, 1930 [Photographs and Correspondence] Folder, NASM.

76. Weinbaum et al., *Modern Girl around the World*; Scharff, *Taking the Wheel*.

77. Corn, *Winged Gospel*.

78. Recent historians, including Phil Tiemeyer and Kathleen Barry, have examined the work culture in aviation history, including that of astronauts and flight attendants, but not the work culture of military pilots. Tiemeyer's *Plane Queer* explains how male flight attendants faced opposition from the American public and airlines who viewed women as more suitable for their work positions. While men could expand their civil rights, there were also "moments of retreat, when sexism and homophobia prevailed over queer equality." Barry's examination of female flight attendants highlights their decades-long struggle against these sexist requirements and a glamorous public image as they attempted to earn

respect and recognition as professionals. Tiemeyer, *Plane Queer*, 3; Barry, *Femininity in Flight*.

79. Van Vleck, *Empire of the Air*, 4–7.

80. Sherry, *Rise of American Air Power*, 41.

81. Susan Porter Benson's and Barbara Melosh's studies of work culture offer theoretical frameworks for this study by articulating the development of worker solidarity through working conditions and experiences. Melosh defines work culture as the "adaptations or resistance to constraints imposed by managers, employers or the work itself." For Melosh, nurses worked in an all-female environment, and it is this sexual division of labor that fostered their camaraderie through their shared employment experiences and an appreciation for their abilities as workers. Melosh argues that nurses could not be professionals because they were forever subordinate to doctors and lacked autonomy. Saleswomen, whom Benson describes as a "clerking sisterhood," were seen as professionals, unlike the nurses in Melosh's study, because of their subordination to doctors. Benson discusses the class-based culture of department stores where negotiations occurred between customers, managers, and saleswomen. Saleswomen exercised control over their labor, engaged in shared acts of resistance, and identified as workers, women, and consumers. Benson, *Counter Cultures*, 227; Melosh, *"Physician's Hand,"* 5.

82. This book responds to Barton Hacker's call for an analysis of the sexual division of labor in the military, a call that is still largely unexplored by scholars. Hacker was one of the first scholars to discuss the inseparability of women and war through his study of women's supportive roles in Western armies from the fifteenth through the nineteenth centuries. His work focuses on women's roles in the military similar to those they were already performing in society (i.e., laundresses and nurses). He argues these roles are evidence of the sexual division of labor within the military, since previous historians had only analyzed this division of labor within society. Hacker, "Where Have All the Women Gone?," 107–48. One recent exception is in an edited collection of essays on new working-class studies. Historian Kimberley L. Phillips argues for further analyses of work in the military, particularly as a form of employment. Phillips's study is one of the few that combines the fields of labor and military history. Phillips, "All I Wanted Was a Steady Job," 42–54.

83. Aaron O'Connell examines the progression of the US Marine Corps' culture, its importance in the survival of this branch of the military in the post–World War II era, and its participation in the militarization of American society. He traces how the marines defined themselves as a group, including through stories and shared beliefs that became their identity. Using the scholarship of Benedict Anderson, O'Connell illuminates the ways organizations besides the nation-state also have imagined communities. For O'Connell's study, it was the marines who possessed a military brotherhood. Furthermore, officer culture was distinct from enlisted culture. O'Connell, *Underdogs*; Anderson, *Imagined Communities*, 5–7, 15–18.

84. Smith, *Wrong Stuff*; Tibbets, *The Tibbets Story*.

85. Milkman, *Gender at Work*.

86. Scharff, *Taking the Wheel*.

87. Weber, "Manufacturing Gender," 235–53.

88. Similarly, Ruth Oldenziel argues that from 1870 to 1945, technology became established as a masculine field. She examines the ways the field of engineering became a white, middle-class male profession. Oldenziel, *Making Technology Masculine*.

89. DeGrott and Peniston-Bird, *Soldier and a Woman*.

90. In the all-volunteer force ideas shifted, as the army and most Americans decided not to embrace military service as an obligation of citizenship. Instead, they embraced "two major assumptions: individual liberty is the most essential American value, and the free market is the best means to preserve it." Bailey, *America's Army*, 5, 33.

91. For a comprehensive and engaging history about the fight for inurnment at Arlington, see Miller, *Final Flight, Final Fight*. Laurel Wamsley, "Pentagon Releases New Policies Enabling Transgender People to Serve in the Military," NPR, March 31, 2021, https://www.npr.org/2021/03/31/983118029/pentagon-releases-new-policies-enabling-transgender-people-to-serve-in-the-milit. US president Donald Trump's 2017 decision to ban transgender people from enlisting in the American military banned them from all military spaces. Heather Marie Stur, "Donald Trump's 'Trans Ban' Reverses More Than 70 Years of Military Integration," *Washington Post*, January 29, 2019.

Chapter 1

1. Simbeck, *Daughter of the Air*, 2–3.

2. She made fifty dollars a weekend doing stunts, and the air shows charged two dollars per passenger. Teresa James, interview by Dawn Letson, June 16, 1998, TWU MSS 300.

3. The CPTP trained over 400,000 pilots from 1939 to 1944. Johnson, *Taking Flight*, 191.

4. Corn, *Winged Gospel*, 88.

5. Alan Meyer, *Weekend Pilots*, 5.

6. Corn, *Winged Gospel*, 8–9.

7. The first American women were Harriet Quimby and Matilde Moisant. Lady Heath, "Women Who Fly," *Popular Aviation and Aeronautics*, May 1929, 34; John Goldstrom, "Modern Valkyries," *Flying Magazine*, June 1929, 29; Planck, *Women with Wings*, 303.

8. In 1928, there were an estimated 34 women with pilot's licenses. By 1929, the year of the Ninety-Nines organization's formation, there were 99. By the end of 1929, there were around 117 women pilots. By 1930, there were 182 women pilots and over 8,000 male pilots. Amelia Earhart said there were 472 licensed women pilots out of a total of 17,226 pilots in 1932. Charles Planck noted that around 675 women held their pilot's licenses in 1939 prior to the start of the CPTP program. It is estimated that 2,145 women held pilot's licenses in 1941 and 3,206 in 1942. There were 5,112 women pilots by 1945. Amelia Earhart, "The Feminine Touch:

Woman's Influence on Air Transport Luxury," *Aero News and Mechanics*, April–May 1930, The Ninety-Nines Inc. History Books Collection, Box 1, Sept 1, 1929 to Sept 1, 1930 [Photographs and Correspondence] Folder, NASM; Louise Thaden, "Women's Activities," *Popular Aviation*, March 1931, 50, Louise McPhetridge Thaden Collection, NASM; Earhart, *Fun of It*, 146; Planck, *Women with Wings*, 150; Jacqueline Cochran, "Auxiliary Air Corps for Women Urged," *Dixie Air News*, June 1941, 23, 28, The Ninety-Nines Inc. History Books Collection, Box 2, Sept 1, 1940 to Sept 1, 1941 Folder, NASM; Civil Aeronautics Administration "Information and Statistics Service" data in "Aviation Facts and Figures, 1945," 76, https://www.aia-aerospace.org/wp-content/uploads/aviation-facts-and-figures-1945.pdf; Deborah Douglas, *American Women and Flight since 1940*, appendix 1.

9. For example, men's Cold War adventure magazines shaped American GIs' "expectations and perceptions of war in Vietnam," and had dangerous implications in violence against Vietnamese people. Daddis, *Pulp Vietnam*, 5 and 24.

10. Unfortunately, she died in a plane crash a year later. Marjorie Selfridge Dresbach, Scrapbook, Marjorie Selfridge Dresbach Papers, MSS 861x, Box 3 of 3, TWU; Corn, *Winged Gospel*, 35.

11. Margery Brown, "Flying Is Changing Women," *Pictorial Review*, June 1930, 30.

12. Brown, "Flying Is Changing Women," 30.

13. Heath, "Women Who Fly," 34; Margery Brown, "What Aviation Means to Women," *Flying Magazine*, September 1928, 52.

14. Brown, "Flying Is Changing Women," 30.

15. For more on women's suffrage, forms of protest, and the political climate, see Lemay, *Votes for Women*; and Dumenil, *Second Line of Defense*.

16. Corn, *Winged Gospel*.

17. Corn, *Winged Gospel*, vii.

18. Corn, *Winged Gospel*, 34.

19. This quote was a part of a Smithsonian traveling exhibit entitled *Black Wings: American Dreams of Flight*. "Smithsonian Traveling Exhibition Tells the Story of African American Pioneers of Flight," Smithsonian Institution, May 20, 2011, www.si.edu/newsdesk/releases/smithsonian-traveling-exhibition-tells-story-african-american-pioneers-flight.

20. Ralph Eliot, "Bessie Coleman Says Good Will Come from Hurt," *Chicago Defender*, March 10, 1923, 3; Haynesworth and Toomey, *Amelia Earhart's Daughters*, 10–12; Evangeline Roberts, "Chicago Pays Parting Tribute to 'Brave Bessie' Coleman," *Chicago Defender*, May 15, 1926, 2.

21. These activists described their service in the Red Cross as military nurses and in the Young Women's Christian Association as tied to citizenship, and they "framed their war work in the context of their long-standing agenda for racial uplift and community service." Dumenil, *Second Line of Defense*, 94.

22. Powell, *Black Wings*, xi–xii, 143, 195–215.

23. Powell, *Black Wings*, 195.

24. Corn, *Winged Gospel*, 36.

25. The emphasis is in the original text. Powell, *Black Wings*, xi.

26. Corn, *Winged Gospel*, 12.

27. Ware, *Still Missing*, 63.

28. Brown, "What Aviation Means to Women," 52.

29. Brown, "What Aviation Means to Women," 54.

30. Corn, *Winged Gospel*, 73; Haynesworth and Toomey, *Amelia Earhart's Daughters*, 9; Planck, *Women with Wings*, 305.

31. Planck, *Women with Wings*, 304; Haynesworth and Toomey, *Amelia Earhart's Daughters*, 9.

32. James H. Winchester, "Leading Ladies," *Flying Magazine*, January 1961, 88.

33. Haynesworth and Toomey, *Amelia Earhart's Daughters*, 9.

34. Goldstrom, "Modern Valkyries," 100.

35. Haynesworth and Toomey, *Amelia Earhart's Daughters*, 10.

36. Heath, "Women Who Fly," 34.

37. As in the example of Bessie Coleman, who tragically died during a stunt performance in 1926. Goldstrom, "Modern Valkyries," 101; Haynesworth and Toomey, *Amelia Earhart's Daughters*, 11-12.

38. Haynesworth and Toomey, *Amelia Earhart's Daughters*, 11.

39. Haynesworth and Toomey, *Amelia Earhart's Daughters*, 10.

40. Bogdan, *Freak Show*, 60.

41. Kasson, *Houdini, Tarzan, and the Perfect Man*, 147.

42. Weinbaum et al., *Modern Girl around the World*.

43. Gibson, "Flag," 5, 23-24.

44. The same was true of German female pilots in the 1920s and 1930s. Historian Evelyn Zegenhagen argues that they flew "because of the athletic, technical or mental challenges [flying] provided," as well as the "general climate of airmindedness." Zegenhagen, "Holy Desire to Serve," 585.

45. Turner, *Out of the Blue and into History*, 482.

46. Corn, *Winged Gospel*, 9.

47. Brooks-Pazmany, *United States Women in Aviation*, 46.

48. Teresa James, interview by Dawn Letson, June 16, 1998, TWU MSS 300.

49. Corn, *Winged Gospel*.

50. The author of the quoted article, Frank Copeland, was the National Women's Air Derby director. Frank T. Copeland, "The Women's Air Derby and Why," *Aeronautics*, May 1930, 412.

51. Copeland, "Women's Air Derby and Why," 412.

52. Copeland, "Women's Air Derby and Why," 412.

53. Corn, *Winged Gospel*, 88.

54. Scharff, *Taking the Wheel*.

55. Goldstrom, "Modern Valkyries," 29.

56. Dorothy Swain Lewis, interview by Dawn Letson and Elizabeth Snapp, September 12, 1992, TWU MSS 300.

57. Helen Wyatt Snapp saw a parade with Charles Lindbergh. Turner, *Out of the Blue*, 89. Ann B. Carl heard Earhart speak at her school. Carl, *WASP among Eagles*, 31.

58. Brown, "What Aviation Means to Women," 52.

59. Turner, *Out of the Blue*, 33.

60. WASP Marjorie Selfridge Dresbach kept an article in her scrapbook that aviator Harriet Quimby wrote. In this article, Quimby said that airplanes should "open up a fruitful occupation for women." Marjorie Selfridge Dresbach Papers, MSS 861x, Box 3 of 3, TWU. WASP Hazel Stamper Hohn collected photos of Amelia Earhart in a scrapbook of her time as a WASP and at WASP reunions. Hazel Stamper Hohn Papers, MSS 863, Box 3 of 3, TWU.

61. Corn, *Winged Gospel*, 87.

62. Thaden, "Women's Activities," 50.

63. As of March 1931, the organization had over 275 members, so there were at least that many women pilots in the United States then. Thaden, "Women's Activities," 50.

64. Ware, *Still Missing*, 25.

65. Historian Nancy Cott argues that there was a "tension between feminism and professional identity . . . There was lively debate among the few women lawyers in the 1880s whether a woman should pursue her profession because of her sex (to vindicate women's capacities or to help her sisters) or must forget her sex in order to pursue her profession." Cott, *Grounding of Modern Feminism*, 232.

66. This viewpoint is similar to Joseph Corn's concept of "air-mindedness." Ware, *Still Missing*, 25.

67. Ware, *Still Missing*, 63.

68. Ware, *Still Missing*, 99.

69. Corn, *Winged Gospel*, 73.

70. Pilot Lenora McElroy was scared when she went for her first ride in an airplane over Niagara Falls. She wanted to overcome her fear of flying, so she got lessons at the local airport. Turner, *Out of the Blue*, 25–26.

71. Teresa James, interview by Dawn Letson, June 16, 1998, TWU MSS 300.

72. WASP Barbara Erickson London said that flying sounded "fun" because she was "pretty adventurous." Barbara "BJ" Erickson London, interview by Sarah Rickman, March 17 and 19, 2004, TWU MSS 300. WASP Marie Mountain Clark described herself as an "adventuresome youth." Clark, *Dear Mother and Daddy*, 19.

73. Carl, *WASP among Eagles*, 23.

74. While WASP Mary Catherine Johnson McKay was growing up, her father and brother became pilots. While at the University of Michigan, McKay heard about a Glider Club, and, when someone told her that it was "very dangerous," her interest was piqued, and she joined it. Mary Catherine "Jary" Johnson McKay, interview by Dawn Letson, October 14, 1944, TWU MSS 300. WASP Catherine Vail Bridge was the only woman on the University of California Flying Team. Team members competed against students at other universities in flying competitions. Catherine Vail Bridge, interview by Dawn Letson, October 27, 2003, TWU MSS 300.

75. Florene Miller Watson, interview by Dawn Letson, September 7, 2006, TWU MSS 300.

76. Catherine Vail Bridge, interview by Dawn Letson, October 27, 2003, TWU MSS 300.

77. Ethel Meyer Finley, interview by Nancy Durr, September 25, 1998, TWU MSS 300.

78. Haydu, *Letters Home, 1944–1945*, 4.

79. To qualify for the WASP program, women had to be between the ages of 21 and 35. Since the programs that became the WASP started in 1942 and ended in 1944, the earliest year a woman could be born would be 1907, and the latest year would be 1923. Those pilots in the first women's pilot program, the Women's Auxiliary Ferrying Squadron (WAFS), required 500 flying hours, and the second women's pilot program that became the WASP required 200 flying hours, although later reduced to 35 hours. Therefore, at the very least, women possessed 35 hours of flying time.

80. Helen Wyatt Snapp had three different classmates who held these jobs. Group interview of WASPs (Helen Wyatt Snapp, Marjorie Popell Sizemore, Doris Elkington Hamaker, Mary Ann Baldner Gordon, Mary Anna "Marty" Martin Wyall) and WAFS Teresa James, interview by Rebecca Wright on behalf of NASA, July 18, 1999, NASA Headquarters Oral History Project, https://historycollection.jsc.nasa .gov/JSCHistoryPortal/history/oral_histories/NASA_HQ/Aviatrix/WASP/WASP _7-18-99.htm.

81. Some examples follow: Nancy Love went to Vassar College. Rickman, *Nancy Love*, 17. Catherine Vail Bridge went to the University of California, Berkeley. Catherine Vail Bridge, interview by Dawn Letson, October 27, 2003, TWU MSS 300. Violet "Vi" Cowden grew up in a lower-income family and went to a teachers college. Violet "Vi" Cowden, interview by Dawn Letson, December 4, 2003, TWU MSS 300.

82. Teresa James never went to college, unlike most of her WAFS peers. Teresa James, interview by Dawn Letson, June 16, 1998, TWU MSS 300.

83. V. Scott Bradley Gough, interview by Thomas Healy, video recording, Experiencing War: Stories from the Veterans History Project, Library of Congress, Washington, DC, https://www.loc.gov/collections/veterans-history-project -collection/serving-our-voices/diverse-experiences-in-service/the-wasp-first-in -flight/.

84. WASP Geri Lamphere Nyman experience in Turner, *Out of the Blue*, 37; Dorothy Allen, interview by Dawn Letson, December 3, 1997, TWU MSS 300.

85. WASP Brooks Lois E. Hailey experience in Turner, *Out of the Blue*, 70.

86. Ethel Meyer Finley, interview by Nancy Durr, September 25, 1998, TWU MSS 300.

87. WASP Marion Carlstrom Trick seized this opportunity and became the second woman in Peru to receive her pilot's license. Turner, *Out of the Blue*, 162.

88. Spector, *Eagle against the Sun*.

89. Douhet, *Command of the Air*; Hurley, *Billy Mitchell*.

90. Schrader, *Sisters in Arms*.

91. Although few records remain on these women pilots, at least five worked as ferry pilots and two—Hanna Reitsch and Melitta Schiller-von Stauffenberg—as experimental test pilots. At least sixty women were glider instructors. Zegenhagen, "German Women Pilots at War," 12. The most famous German female pilot was Hanna Reitsch, a friend of Adolf Hitler's who worked as a test pilot and received the Iron Cross for her service. Reitsch, *Sky My Kingdom*.

92. Pennington, *Wings, Women, and War*.

93. Pisano, *To Fill the Skies*, 76.

94. Pisano, *To Fill the Skies*, 3–4.

95. The first classes of women needed 200 hours of flying time, but this was later reduced to 35 hours of flying time, as the number of women pilots with 200 hours or more was hard to find.

96. Historian Dominick Pisano estimates that around 2,500 women received their pilot's licenses from 1939 to 1941 with the Civilian Pilot Training Program. Civil Aeronautics Administration "Information and Statistics Service" data in "Aviation Facts and Figures, 1945," 76, https://www.aia-aerospace.org/wp-content /uploads/aviation-facts-and-figures-1945.pdf; and Pisano, *To Fill the Skies*, 77.

97. The name of the CPTP changed to the War Training Service (WTS) with this 1942 transition to designate its new focus on training men for combat. Pisano, *To Fill the Skies with Pilots*, 76–77.

98. Clark first applied to Drake University, which was her alma mater. After rejection, she applied at Dowling College and was accepted. Clark, *Dear Mother and Daddy*, 20.

99. Elaine Danforth Harmon, interview by the author, September 1, 2012, digital recording.

100. Each university or college that hosted a CPT program houses the records from CPT programs, so going through all of these records would be a time-consuming and painstaking task. Betty Turner's *Out of the Blue* has stories of 673 WASP, but the majority of these accounts do not mention how the women obtained their licenses. According to historian Dominick Pisano, "Literature on women's participation in the CPTP is sketchy." Pisano's study of the CPTP has one paragraph about women. Pisano, *To Fill the Skies*, 170.

101. Historian John McCullough interviewed Maria Oliva, who participated in this wartime program. McCullough, "Oliva Built Models for WWII Aviators," *Plainview (TX) Herald*, 8A; "Air Cadets: A.T.C.A. Trains Air-Minded Youth for Future Careers in Aviation," *Life*, August 31, 1942, 86–89.

102. At least twenty-five of the WASP, including six who died during the war, were members of the Civil Air Patrol. Jane Dolores Champlin, Frances Fortune Grimes, Beverly Jean Moses, Mabel Virginia Rawlinson, Margaret June "Peggy" Seip, and Helen Jo Anderson Severson are examples of WASP who joined the Civil Air Patrol. Dawn Seymour, Clarice Bergemann, Jeanette Jenkins, Mary Ellen Keil, "In Memoriam: Thirty-Eight American Women Pilots," pamphlet (Denton, TX: Texas Woman's University Press), 6, https://texashistory.unt.edu/ark:/67531 /metapth908179/. The other nineteen are listed in the Women Airforce Service Pilots Official Archive, Denton, TX.

103. Deborah Douglas, *American Women and Flight since 1940*, 26.

104. Deborah Douglas, *American Women and Flight since 1940*, 27.

105. "Civil Air Patrol Does the 'Impossible' in Illinois," *Chicago Defender*, March 7, 1942; Frank Blazich, "Civil Air Patrol's Unsung Civil Rights Milestone," *Civil Air Patrol Volunteer*, Spring 2020, 46–49.

106. Founded after the Betsy Ross Corps by women who had different opinions was the Women's Air Reserve. According to its preamble, the Women's Air Reserve sought to teach women mechanics as well as flying in order to prepare them for a "national or civil emergency." "Betsy Ross Corps Off to a Good Start," *Airway Age*, 1931, Manila Davis Talley Scrapbook, Manila Davis Talley Collection, NASM; "Women's Air Reserve Preamble," The Ninety-Nines Inc. History Books Collection, Box 1, Sept 1, 1932 to Sept 1, 1933 Folder, NASM.

107. Rickman, *Nancy Love*, 27-29.

108. She eventually developed a cosmetics line, which she named "Wings to Beauty."

109. Cochran and Odlum, *Stars at Noon*; Rich, *Jackie Cochran*.

110. Rickman, *Nancy Love*, 210.

111. Barbara "BJ" Erickson London, interview by Sarah Rickman, March 17 and 19, 2004, TWU MSS 300; Rickman, *Nancy Love*, 25.

112. She suggested women's use as pilots of ambulance planes, courier planes, and commercial/transport planes. Letter, Jacqueline Cochran to Mrs. Eleanor Roosevelt, September 28, 1939, Record Group 80, General Correspondence of the Office of the Secretary of the Navy, 1930-1942, Microfilm 1067, MV1/P14-4 (391012) c, NARA-DC.

113. Although Roosevelt mentioned that women would soon be flying in France, the French never used women pilots during the war. Letter, Cochran to Roosevelt, September 28, 1939, Record Group 80, General Correspondence of the Office of the Secretary of the Navy, 1930-1942, Microfilm 1067, MV1/P14-4 (391012) c, NARA-DC.

114. Letter, Malvina C. Thompson, secretary to Mrs. Roosevelt, to Charles Edison, acting secretary of the navy, October 12, 1939, Record Group 80, General Correspondence of the Office of the Secretary of the Navy, 1930-1942, Microfilm 1067, MV1/P14-4 (391012)c, NARA-DC.

115. Eleanor Roosevelt, "My Day" column, November 22, 1939, *Washington Daily News*.

116. In May 1940, Nancy Love wrote a letter to Lieutenant Colonel Robert Olds with a list of women pilots with around 1,000 hours of flying experience who could join the war effort. "Women Pilots with the AAF, 1941-1944," *AAF Historical Studies*, March 1946, 3, AFHRA, https://www.afhra.af.mil/Portals/16/documents/Studies/51-100/AFD-090529-109.pdf.

117. "Women Pilots with the AAF," 2.

118. "Women Pilots with the AAF," 5.

119. Eleanor Roosevelt, "My Day" column, August 5, 1941, *Washington Daily News*.

120. "Arnold and Jackie Cochran—Women Pilots for the AAF," MICFILM 43806, IRIS #1102998, Henry H. Arnold Collection, AFHRA.

121. The media announced that Cochran was recruiting women. After this announcement, several women pilots wrote letters to Cochran asking for more information about this opportunity. "Jacqueline Cochran to Recruit U.S. Women

to Fly in Britain," *New York Herald Tribune*, January 24, 1942, Emily Chapin Scrapbook, MSS 828, Box 1 of 2, Women Airforce Service Pilots Official Archive, TWU.

122. "Jacqueline Cochran to Recruit U.S. Women."

123. Arnold said this in July 1942. "Women Pilots with the AAF."

124. The qualifications for the WAFS included being twenty-one to thirty-five years old, possessing a commercial pilot's license, clocking 500 hours of flying time, and having a CAA rating for 200 horsepower.

125. "Women Pilots with the AAF," 13.

126. "Women Pilots with the AAF," 18.

127. Ralph Habas, "Women Pilots Here Anxious to Join WAFS," September 13, 1942, *Chicago Sunday Times*, TWU WASP Collection.

128. More on Love's personality is available in the first chapter of this book. Rickman, *Nancy Love*, 28.

129. Kate Massee, *Chicago Daily Tribune*, December 3, 1942; Henry Ward, "Women Take Leading Role in Pittsburgh Aviation and Prove Their Ability as Men Go to War Posts," *Pittsburgh Press*, February 27, 1942; Ann France Wilson, "WAFS to Wear Trousers While Flying Army Planes," newspaper clipping, September 15, 1942, TWU WASP Collection; "First of the WAFS Pass Ground Tests," *New York Times*, September 12, 1942; Margaret Kernodle, "Flying Mothers: Hands That Rock the Cradle Now Wield WAF Control Sticks," *Wilmington (DE) Morning News*, October 23, 1942; Edith M. Hutchinson, "N.J.C. Girls and Graduates Play Their Part in the War Effort," *Newark Evening News*, November 30, 1942, TWU WASP Collection; Granger, *On Final Approach*, 58–59.

130. Memo, WDBPR to Colonel Ennis, October 26, 1942, WASP News Releases and Correspondence Collection, Microfilm Reel 4033, Frame 1703, AFHRA.

131. This slander campaign accused WACs of serving as prostitutes for male soldiers and engaging in lesbian relationships.

132. "WASP Accidents" Memo, Jacqueline Cochran to Captain H. H. Ford, December 13, 1943, WASP News Releases and Correspondence Collection, Microfilm Reel 4033, Frames 286–87, AFHRA.

133. "Flying Regulations Revised," December 11, 1943, TWU WASP Collection.

134. Memo, "Subject: Policy for WASP," December 3, 1943, Henry H. Arnold Collection, Microfilm Reel 43803, Frame 30, AFHRA.

135. Memo, Hazel Taylor to Major Gordon Rust and Lieutenant William Geddings, April 29, 1943, WASP News Releases and Correspondence Collection, Microfilm Reel 4032, Frame 1910, AFHRA.

136. For example, see WDBPR memo, "Public Relations Policy for WASP," December 3, 1943, WASP News Releases and Correspondence Collection, Microfilm Reel 4033, Frames 477–78, AFHRA.

137. Rich, *Jackie Cochran*, 39, 41, 64.

138. Hugh Williamson, "'Lipstick Squadron' Trains in West Texas to Ferry Warplanes," *Houston Post*, April 26, 1943, TWU WASP Collection; Hugh Williamson, "Hundreds of Women Training for Service as Ferry Pilots," *Colorado Springs Evening Telegraph*, April 28, 1943, WASP Collection, MSS 240c, TWU; "Women

Train in West Texas for Army Ferry Flying," *Christian Science Monitor*, May 8, 1943, TWU WASP Collection.

139. Letter, Marjorie Ludwigsen to Ninety-Niners having more than 200 hours, July 7, 1941, Jacqueline Cochran Papers, WASP Series, Box 2, EPL.

140. Jacqueline Cochran, "Final Report on Women Pilot Program," June 1, 1945, Jacqueline Cochran Papers, WASP Series, Box 12, EPL.

141. Twenty-eight women pilots were a part of the original Women's Auxiliary Ferrying Squadron, which eventually merged with the Women's Flying Training Detachment to form the WASP in July 1943. Myers, "Women Airforce Service Pilots (WASP)."

142. Historian Kara Dixon Vuic argues that American women primarily volunteered for the Army Nurse Corps during the Vietnam War because of the equal opportunities through benefits, pay, rank, and career advancements that were not available in the civilian world. Vuic, *Officer, Nurse, Woman*.

143. Dora Dougherty Strother, lieutenant colonel USAF Reserve, Air Force Museum Research Division, "The W.A.S.P. Program: An Historical Synopsis," TWU WASP Collection.

144. Dorothy Allen, interview by Dawn Letson, December 3, 1997, TWU MSS 300.

145. Strother, "W.A.S.P. Program."

146. WASP Marie Pederson experiences in Evidence in Militarization Box, Byrd Howell Granger Papers, MSS 265, TWU.

147. For example, Bernice Falk Haydu's brother joined the Army Air Force. Haydu, *Letters Home, 1944–1945*, 5.

148. Cornelia Fort, "At Twilight's Last Gleaming," *Woman's Home Companion*, July 1943, 19, TWU WASP Collection.

149. Landdeck, *Women with Silver Wings*, 114.

150. Marine Shirley Allen and WAVES Mardell Bushaw joined because most men they knew were drafted or enlisted. Mardell Bushaw, interview by Holly Sinco, February 23, 2004, Coll #05.0038, The Institute on World War II and the Human Experience, Florida State University, Tallahassee. WAVES Gloria Sullivan stated, "There was a great deal of patriotism at the time. It—the country was involved, and it really spurred most of us who were young, I believe, to be part of it in some way, and this is what I just wanted to do." Gloria Sullivan, interview by Holly Sinco, November 19, 2004, Coll #04.0303, The Institute on World War II and the Human Experience, Florida State University, Tallahassee. Marine Martha Timanus mentioned that Pearl Harbor "was very emotional in a variety of ways" and persuaded people to join the war effort. Martha Timanus, interview by Stacy Tanner, April 20, 2005, Coll #07.0138, Reichelt Program for Oral History, Institute on World War II and the Human Experience, Florida State University, Tallahassee.

151. As WASP Margaret Ray Ringenberg explained, "I could serve my country and fly. . . . WOW!" Parrish, *WASP in Their Own Words*, 13.

152. Barbara "BJ" Erickson London, interview by Sarah Rickman, March 17 and 19, 2004, TWU MSS 300.

153. WASP Pearl Brumett Judd experiences in Turner, *Out of the Blue*, 482.

154. Catherine Vail Bridge, interview by Dawn Letson, October 27, 2003, TWU MSS 300.

155. Mary Catherine "Jary" Johnson McKay, interview by Dawn Letson, October 14, 1944, TWU MSS 300.

156. Hartmann, *Home Front and Beyond*, 37.

157. When inquiring about the latter two programs, she thought, "Oh, no, another typewriter." Parrish, *WASP in Their Own Words*, 12.

158. Since Watson was a part of the original WAFS program, she preferred the title "WAFS" rather than "WASP."

159. Florene Miller Watson, interview by Dawn Letson, September 7, 2006, TWU MSS 300.

160. Dorothy Swain Lewis, interview by Dawn Letson and Elizabeth Snapp, September 12, 1992, TWU MSS 300.

161. Elaine Danforth Harmon, interview by the author, September 1, 2012, digital recording.

162. Harmon, interview.

163. Group interview of WASP (Helen Wyatt Snapp, Marjorie Popell Sizemore, Doris Elkington Hamaker, Mary Ann Baldner Gordon, Mary Anna "Marty" Martin Wyall) and WAFS Teresa James, interview by Rebecca Wright on behalf of NASA, July 18, 1999, https://historycollection.jsc.nasa.gov/JSCHistoryPortal/history/oral_histories/NASA_HQ/Aviatrix/WASP/WASP_7-18-99.htm.

164. Group interview of WASP and WAFS Teresa James.

165. Catherine Vail Bridge, interview by Dawn Letson, October 27, 2003, TWU MSS 300.

166. Teresa James, interview by Dawn Letson, June 16, 1998, TWU MSS 300.

167. This data was collected in case the WASP would be incorporated with the Women's Army Corps sometime in the future. Telegram, Leoti Deaton to Jacqueline Cochran, June 1943, Jacqueline Cochran Papers, WASP Series, Box 5, Establishment of the WASP, EPL.

168. WASP Vi Cowden said of her outlook on life, "I don't think of myself as a woman. I think of myself as a competitor more. I mean equal grounds." Violet "Vi" Cowden, interview by Dawn Letson, December 4, 2003, TWU MSS 300.

169. "Memo Regarding Hiring Civilian Women Pilots," September 15, 1942, Jacqueline Cochran Papers, WASP Series, Box 12, Establishment of WASP, EPL; and "Director of Women Pilots Asks Military Status for WASPs," War Department Bureau of Public Relations, August 8, 1944, TWU WASP Collection.

170. "Jacqueline Cochran Established Program: Convinced Air Heads That Women Can Fly," *Avenger*, May 11, 1943, TWU WASP Collection.

171. "Air heads" was a military term that originated during World War II. According to the *Merriam-Webster Dictionary*, it did not become a slang term for being mindless until the 1970s. "Jacqueline Cochran Established Program." For "rough and uncouth," see *Avenger*, June 28, 1943, TWU WASP Collection.

172. Leisa Meyer, *Creating GI Jane*.

173. One example: Letter, Jacqueline Cochran to Miss Sadie Lee Johnson, August 19, 1943, TWU WASP Collection.

174. The WASP and Women Marines did not accept African American women into their programs. Honey, *Bitter Fruit*. Reference to Tuskegee Airmen: Takaki, *Double Victory*.

175. Hartmann, *Home Front and Beyond*, 33, 40–41; Stremlow, *Free a Marine to Fight*, 5.

176. One of the WASP, for example, had a Croatian background. Alberta Paskvan Kinney used Croatian phrases in her letters home to her family. Letter, Alberta Paskvan Kinney to her family, February 21, 1943, TWU. Another WASP, Anne Chisholm Dessert Oliver, was born in Canada and held dual citizenship until she was twenty-two and chose to be an American citizen. Anne Chisholm Dessert Oliver, interview by Dawn Letson, December 4, 1997, TWU MSS 300.

177. Memo Regarding Hiring Civilian Women Pilots, September 15, 1942, Jacqueline Cochran Papers, WASP Series, Box 12, Establishment of WASP, EPL.

178. Takaki, *Double Victory*, 7.

179. Moore, *Serving Our Country*.

180. In addition to these almost 1,000 male pilots, around 14,000 men and women served in support roles, including flight instructors, mechanics, and nurses. Moye, *Freedom Flyers*, 12.

181. According to Air Mobility Command Museum and National Air and Space Museum records, no African American pilots flew with the Air Transport Command during the war. The Tuskegee Airmen served in the 99th Pursuit Squadron (later renamed the 99th Fighter Squadron), the 332nd Fighter Group (including the 301st, 302nd, and 100th Fighter Squadrons), and the 447th Bombardment Group, which was an all-Black bomber unit. The 447th never saw combat due to racial discrimination. Moye, *Freedom Flyers*, 30, 49, 77–84, 132–44.

182. He discussed this in a conversation with Nancy Love. Brigadier General Noel F. Parrish, interview by Vivian M. White, August 6–10, 1980, N. F. Parrish Collection, Call #K239.0512-1276, AFHRA.

183. After visits to the archives at EPL, AFHRA, NARA, and TWU, as well as extensive searches online and in book bibliographies, this appears to be the only letter still in existence.

184. Letter, Jacqueline Cochran to Miss Sadie Lee Johnson, August 19, 1943, TWU WASP Collection.

185. The Civilian Pilot Training Program was a US government–sponsored program that offered free classes for civilians to earn their pilot's licenses. The CPTP admitted one woman for every ten men. Pisano, *To Fill the Skies with Pilots*.

186. Vivian White, "Born in Georgia in 1912, She Never Stopped Dreaming," TWU WASP Collection. See also Bragg, *Soaring above Setbacks*, 40.

187. Jeff Hardy, "Grounded by Race," *Sunday Magazine*, January 31, 1999, 12–14, TWU WASP Collection.

188. Mary Rodd Furbee, "Rose Rolls Cousins," *American Visions*, August–September 1998, TWU WASP Collection; and M. Cargill, "Dorothy McIntyre Paved the Way for Women Pilots," newspaper clipping, TWU WASP Collection.

189. Dorothy Lane McIntyre, interview by the History Makers, June 18, 2004, https://www.thehistorymakers.org/biography/dorothy-mcintyre-38.

190. Gubert, Sawyer, and Fannin, *Distinguished African Americans*, 51.

191. Cochran and Odlum, *Stars at Noon*, 127–28.

192. Takaki, *Double Victory*.

193. Jeff Hardy, "Grounded by Race," *Sunday Magazine*, January 31, 1999, 14, TWU WASP Collection.

194. For anti-Asian sentiment, see Dower, *War without Mercy*.

195. Moore, *Serving Our Country*, 151.

196. Furthermore, the 1943 Magnuson Act repealed the Chinese Exclusion Act of 1882.

197. Ola Rexroat, interview by Pat Jernigan, September 8, 2006, TWU MSS 300; and Katherine Landdeck, "Pushing the Envelope: The Women Airforce Service Pilots and American Society," (PhD diss., University of Tennessee, Knoxville, 2003), 41.

198. Bruce H. Wolk's work identifies nine Jewish WASP and lists three of them: Bernice Falk Haydu, Florence Elion Mascott, and Elizabeth Haas Pfister. Wolk, *Jewish Aviators*, 8, 203. In her study of the WASP, historian Kate Landdeck identifies Julie Jenner Stege. Landdeck, *Women with Silver Wings*, 132.

199. Wolk, *Jewish Aviators*, 20, 24.

200. Lee went by the nickname "Ah Ying." When she married Major Yin Cheung Louie of the Chinese Air Force on October 9, 1943, she sent a telegram announcement to some of her WASP friends from training: "Knot tied today 1400 SNAFU CAVU for Cliff and Me = Ah Ying." A copy of the telegram is in the Dorothea Johnson Moorman Papers, MSS 358c, TWU. Letter, Madge Rutherford to Mother and Dad, June 5, 1943, TWU MSS 300.

201. Rosenberg, *"A Brief Flight."*

202. Roediger, *Wages of Whiteness*.

203. Maggie Gee, interview by Leah McGarrigle, Robin Li, and Kathryn Stine, April 10, April 29, and May 20, 2003, for the Rosie the Riveter World War II American Homefront Oral History Project, Regional Oral History Office, University of California, Berkeley, http://digitalassets.lib.berkeley.edu/roho/ucb/text/gee _maggie.pdf.

204. Years after the war, some of these Tuskegee Airmen attended the annual EAA AirVenture Oshkosh air show, and they met up with four of the WASP who were also at Mather Field during the war. They sat in a restored B-25 and took a picture together. Nell Stevenson Bright, interview by Jolene Pierson, Nell S. Stevenson Bright Collection (AFC/2001/001/60871), Veterans History Project, American Folklife Center, Library of Congress, Washington, DC. WASP Madeline Allaire Bennett also remembered sitting with the Tuskegee Airmen in the mess hall. Madeline Allaire Bennett, interview by Dawn Letson, September 30, 1995, TWU MSS 300.

Chapter 2

1. Lillian Lorraine Yonally, interview by Wayne Clarke, for the New York State Military Museum in Saratoga Springs, August 27, 2009, New Bedford, MA, https://museum.dmna.ny.gov/application/files/3215/9464/6639/Yonally_Lillian_Lorraine .pdf.

2. These words are attributed to French author and pilot Antoine de St. Exupery in the *Avenger*, May 11, 1943, TWU WASP Collection.

3. It appeared in their classbooks and later in their newsletter, the *Avenger*, on May 11, 1943, TWU WASP Collection.

4. Hugh Williamson, "'Lipstick Squadron' Trains in West Texas to Ferry Warplanes," April 27, 1943, *Houston Post*, section 1, p. 10, TWU WASP Collection.

5. This sisterhood is similar to the military brotherhood in O'Connell, *Underdogs*.

6. During training, the WASP learned basic or primary aerobatics. Cole, *Women Pilots of World War II*, 61.

7. Craven and Cate, *Army Air Forces*, 6:xxxiii.

8. Approximately 25,000 women pilots applied to the program, 1,830 women were accepted, and 1,074 graduated. The washout rate for these check rides was the same for both men and women trainees, because it was the job of the instructors to eliminate pilots who were not of the highest caliber.

9. Leisa Meyer, *Creating GI Jane*, 14–15.

10. The first WFTD class of twenty-three women pilots graduated on April 24, 1943. Their class designation was 43-W-1, based on the year they graduated and their status as the first class of 1943. In the meantime, three other WFTD classes (43-W-2, 43-W-3, and 43-W-4) had started training.

11. 44-W-2 Classbook, TWU WASP Collection.

12. The first two classes graduated from Houston, but the third class moved to Sweetwater.

13. Cochran and Odlum, *Stars at Noon*, 120–21.

14. Sweetwater resident Grace Faver won a local contest to name the field when her entry of Avenger Field won. 43-W-4 through 43-W-5 Classbook, TWU WASP Collection.

15. Cochran and Odlum, *Stars at Noon*, 120–21.

16. Aviation Enterprises, the contractors who ran the field at Houston, bought out the previous contractors at Avenger Field and took over training. 43-W-4 through 43-W-5 Classbook.

17. Cochran and Odlum, *Stars at Noon*, 122; Group interview of WASP (Helen Wyatt Snapp, Marjorie Popell Sizemore, Doris Elkington Hamaker, Mary Ann Baldner Gordon, Mary Anna "Marty" Martin Wyall) and WAFS Teresa James, interview by Rebecca Wright on behalf of NASA, July 18, 1999, https:// historycollection.jsc.nasa.gov/JSCHistoryPortal/history/oral_histories/NASA_HQ /Aviatrix/WASP/WASP_7-18-99.htm.

18. Maureen Honey's study of wartime women's magazines illuminates the evidence of propaganda crafted by the US Office of War Information (OWI). The OWI offered magazines guides to encourage them to perpetuate patriotism and motivate women to participate in the war effort. Honey, *Creating Rosie the Riveter*.

19. Marilyn Hegarty also addresses the issue of women's sexuality as dangerous. Hegarty, *Victory Girls*.

20. "Medical Consideration of WASPS," Jacqueline Cochran Papers, WASP Series, Box 15, EPL.

21. In a 700-plus-page volume on the history of pilots in the AAF during the war, only one page cites men's instruction in sex hygiene. There are no other mentions of rules imposed on men to control their social conduct or sexuality. Craven and Cate, *Army Air Forces*, 6:532.

22. Canaday, *Straight State*.

23. Pfau, *Miss Yourlovin*.

24. Leisa Meyer, *Creating GI Jane*, 157.

25. Leisa Meyer, *Creating GI Jane*, 10.

26. The three places explicitly mentioned were the Rock Inn, Blue Grill Café, and Airport Tavern. "Article 14" of "Supplementary Rules and Regulations," September 22, 1943, TWU WASP Collection.

27. Letter, Adaline Blank to "Sis" Edwina Blank, July 8, 1943, Adaline Blank Correspondence, July 1943–December 1943, TWU MSS 300. For regulations, see Major Robert K. Urban, "Woman Pilot Trainee Regulations," June 14, 1943, Record Group 18, Army Air Forces, Central Decimal Files, Oct 1942–May 1944, Box No. 918, Folder 353, Women's Flying Training, NARA.

28. Delano, "Making Up for War," 33–68.

29. Delano, "Making Up for War," 33.

30. Delano, "Making Up for War," 35.

31. "General Military Regulations," #6, #17, 318th Army Air Forces Flying Training Detachment at Avenger Field, Sweetwater, Texas, June 14, 1943, TWU WASP Collection.

32. Cole, *Women Pilots of World War II*, xvii.

33. Group interview of WASP (Helen Wyatt Snapp, Marjorie Popell Sizemore, Doris Elkington Hamaker, Mary Ann Baldner Gordon, Mary Anna "Marty" Martin Wyall) and WAFS Teresa James, interview by Rebecca Wright on behalf of NASA, July 18, 1999, https://historycollection.jsc.nasa.gov/JSCHistoryPortal/history/oral _histories/NASA_HQ/Aviatrix/WASP/WASP_7-18-99.htm.

34. Harmon's response to being a teacher: "Gosh, I couldn't do that!" Elaine Danforth Harmon, interview by the author, September 1, 2012, digital recording.

35. Harmon, interview.

36. Maggie Gee, interview by Leah McGarrigle, Robin Li, and Kathryn Stine, April 10, April 29, and May 20, 2003, for the Rosie the Riveter World War II American Homefront Oral History Project, Regional Oral History Office, University of California, Berkeley, http://digitalassets.lib.berkeley.edu/roho/ucb/text/gee _maggie.pdf. For more on the experiences of gay men and women during the war: Bérubé, *Coming Out Under Fire*; Chauncey, *Gay New York*.

37. "Girl Pilots," *Life*, July 19, 1943, WASP Collection, MSS 240c, TWU.

38. "Girl Pilots."

39. Wood, *We Were WASPS*, 71–73.

40. Cole, *Women Pilots of World War II*, 32; Dedi L. Deaton, "Supplementary History of the Women's Airforce Service Pilot Training Program," TWU WASP Collection.

41. *WASP WWII News Report*, #1 c.1, #2, & #3, *Army-Navy Screen Magazine* #16, produced by the Army Information Branch, Signal Corps, Air Forces, and Navy Department, 1943–1944, TWU WASP Collection.

42. Two of the WASP who remember are Winifred Wood and Jean Hascall Cole. Wood, *We Were WASPS*, 104; Cole, *Women Pilots of World War II*, 32.

43. Captain Gilbert Warrenton of the Eighteenth Army Air Force Base Unit Motion Picture Unit wrote this narration. *WASP WWII News Report*, #1 c.1, #2, & #3, *Army-Navy Screen Magazine* #16, produced by the Army Information Branch, Signal Corps, Air Forces, and Navy Department, 1943–1944, TWU WASP Collection; Dedi L. Deaton, "Supplementary History of the Women's Airforce Service Pilot Training Program," TWU WASP Collection.

44. Constance Luft Huhn, ad for Tangee lipsticks, *Ladies Home Journal*, August 1943, TWU WASP Collection.

45. *McCall's*, February 1943, TWU WASP Collection.

46. "America's Smart Flying Women," "More Women Choose Cutex Than Any Other Nail Polish in the World," 1943, TWU WASP Collection.

47. Letter, Hazel Taylor to Miss Elaine M. Conway, October 29, 1943, WASP Public Relations Material, Call #220.0721-12 V. 7, IRIS #145362, USAF Collection, AFHRA.

48. In this ad, Cutex featured military-themed colors with such names as "Honor Bright," "On Duty," "Off Duty," and "At Ease." "Best Dressed Women Choose Favorite Cutex Shade," Cutex ad, TWU WASP Collection.

49. The Department of Defense supported the WASP receiving veteran status in 1977 due to these characteristics of the program. "Summary of Historical Review (WASPs)" located in the congressional record: "To Provide Recognition to the Women's Air Force Service Pilots for Their Service during World War II by Deeming Such Service to Have Been Active Duty in the Armed Forces of the United States for Purposes of Laws Administered by the Veterans Administration," Hearing before a Subcommittee of the Committee on Veterans' Affairs, House of Representatives, 95th Congress, 1st sess., *Congressional Record*, September 20, 1977, H453.

50. Telegram, Jackie Cochran and General Arnold to Lorraine Zillner, September 1, 1943. This telegram is located in the congressional record: "To Provide Recognition," H455.

51. Letter, Commanding Officer Chester R. Keown to Lucile Doll Wise, April 26, 1943, Lucile Doll Wise Papers, MSS 271, TWU.

52. The $1.65 room and board included $0.35 for breakfast, $0.40 for dinner, $0.50 for supper, and $0.40 a day for room rent. "Salary," "Pay Grades," and "Expenses" sections of "A Handbook for Women Student Pilot Trainees," Headquarters of the Army Air Forces and Director of Women Pilots, TWU WASP Collection; Granger, *On Final Approach*, 70; Clark, *Dear Mother and Daddy*, 24.

53. Jacqueline Cochran Papers, WASP Series, Box 14, Folder, Cochran: Reports and Correspondence (1), EPL.

54. "Director of Women Pilots Asks Military Status for WASPs," War Department Bureau of Public Relations, August 8, 1944, TWU WASP Collection.

55. An insurance agent from Fort Worth, Texas, contacted Jacqueline Cochran several times, negotiating with her to provide insurance to all the trainees via AAF funding. He said he thought the WASP were "neglected by the Government and those in authority" because they were not provided with insurance. Letter, Russell H. Pearson, CLU general agent, to Jacqueline Cochran, April 28, 1944, Jacqueline Cochran Papers, WASP Series, Box 6, EPL. For an explanation of civil service insurance, see "A Handbook for Women Student Pilot Trainees," Headquarters of the Army Air Forces and Director of Women Pilots, TWU WASP Collection.

56. By removing their work clothes and donning zoot suits, these men participated in "infrapolitics" as they "represented a subversive refusal to be subservient." Kelley, *Race Rebels*; Peiss, *Zoot Suit*.

57. Major Robert K. Urban, "Woman Pilot Trainee Regulations," June 14, 1943, Record Group 18, Army Air Forces, Central Decimal Files, Oct 1942–May 1944, Box No. 918, Folder 353, Women's Flying Training, NARA.

58. Minton's instructor reacted to her braids by telling her that she looked like she was "about twelve years old." Letter, Madge Rutherford Minton to Mother and Dad, March 17, 1943, TWU MSS 300.

59. There are, of course, political and racial undercurrents of their use of the term, and it is worth noting that the WASP were a group of predominantly white women. I was unable to find evidence in primary sources that indicates there was a purposeful racist undertone to their language. It is also likely that the WASP were not aware of their white privilege, so they would not have thought about how their use of the term was racially insensitive or cultural appropriation. Their white privilege includes the "wages of whiteness," as referenced in Roediger, *Wages of Whiteness*.

60. Urban, "Woman Pilot Trainee Regulations." See also: Sloan Taylor, "Girl Pilots Train Like Cadets," undated, TWU WASP Collection.

61. The WAFS uniforms were a shade of green. Teresa James, interview by Dawn Letson, June 16, 1998, TWU MSS 300.

62. Report, Jacqueline Cochran to AAF commanding general through assistant chief of Air Staff, August 1, 1944, Jacqueline Cochran Papers, WASP Series, Box 14, Folder, Cochran: Reports and Correspondence (1), EPL.

63. Cochran said that she personally paid designer Bergdorf Goodman to design the WASP uniform and that she then received approval from General Arnold's office to have the uniforms produced. In this interview she made no reference to the other companies that contributed to the design, as mentioned in her 1944 report. See Jacqueline Cochran, interview by Major John F. Shiner and Captain Robert S. Bartanowicz, March 11–12, 1976, Department of History, USAF Academy, Colorado, magnetic tape recording, Oral Histories, EPL.

64. The AAF paid $176.82 per WASP. It paid an additional $149.24 per WASP for "functional clothing" needed by all pilots. This same $149.24 was the amount the AAF paid for the men's "functional clothing." See Report, Jacqueline Cochran

to AAF commanding general through assistant chief of Air Staff, August 1, 1944, Jacqueline Cochran Papers, WASP Series, Box 14, Folder, Cochran: Reports and Correspondence (1), EPL.

65. An estimation is that these items together cost around $100. Report, Jacqueline Cochran to AAF commanding general through assistant chief of Air Staff.

66. Uniform Regulations, Record Group 18 Army Air Forces, Central Decimal Files, Oct 1942–May 1944, Box No. 918, Folder 353, Women's Flying Training, NARA.

67. For more on the media's discussion, see Honey, *Creating Rosie the Riveter*. Studying the media's portrayal of women working during the war, Honey concludes that these images supported traditional roles for women. She illuminates how American magazines distributed propagandized ideas of temporary wartime work and self-sacrifice through fiction plots. By mid-1944, advertisements in these magazines encouraged women to think about returning home after the war.

68. "How a Woman Should Wear a Uniform," *Good Housekeeping*, August 1942, in Walker, *Women's Magazines, 1940–1960*.

69. Roberta Smith, "Uniforms Pro and Con," 19, Jacqueline Cochran Papers, Air Transport Auxiliary Series, Box 5, Folder, Magazine Articles and Clippings (1), EPL.

70. Michaela Hampf argues that women in the WAC found "donning the uniform . . . to be a liberating experience." Hampf, *Release a Man for Combat*, 7, 62, 176, 281.

71. "Songs of Class 44-W-8" to the tune of "Swinging on a Star," *WASP Songbook*, 16, TWU WASP Collection.

72. "Correct Wear of the WASP Uniform," *Avenger*, March 3, 1944, TWU WASP Collection.

73. "Correct Wear of the WASP Uniform."

74. Letter, Adaline Blank to "Sis" Edwina Blank, July 15, 1943, Adaline Blank Correspondence, July 1943–December 1943, TWU MSS 300; Letter, Mary Anna "Marty" Martin Wyall to her family, June 30, 1944, TWU MSS 300; Letter, Alberta Kinney to her family, August 3, 1943, TWU MSS 300.

75. Letter, Adaline Blank to "Sis" Edwina Blank, August 26, 1943, Adaline Blank Correspondence, July 1943–December 1943, TWU MSS 300.

76. 44-W-9 Classbook, TWU WASP Collection.

77. Jean Hascall Cole, self-interview for TWU, December 9, 1997, TWU MSS 300.

78. Mary Anna "Marty" Martin Wyall, interview by the author, December 28, 2009, digital recording, Fort Wayne, IN.

79. Letter, Adaline Blank to "Sis" Edwina Blank, September 10, 1943, Adaline Blank Correspondence, July 1943–December 1943, TWU MSS 300.

80. Ruth Adams, interview by Jean Hascall Cole, 1989, TWU MSS 300.

81. This documentary features only the voice of WASP Vi Cowden. Bonn and Bonn, *Wings of Silver*.

82. Letter, Adaline Alma Blank to her sister Edwina, July 8, 1943, and July 15, 1943, Adaline Blank Correspondence, July 1943–December 1943, TWU MSS 300.

83. WASP Vi Cowden in Bonn and Bonn, *Wings of Silver*.

84. Letter, Betty June Overman Brown to "Dearest Family," April 27, 1944, Betty Overman Brown Personal Letters, Papers, and News Clippings, 1944–2002, TWU MSS 300.

85. Betty Williamson Shipley, interview by Dawn Letson, August 20, 1997, TWU MSS 300. Others used the language of "freedom," like WASP Anna Mae Petteys Pattee. Anna Mae Petteys Pattee, interview by Jean Hascall Cole, 1989, TWU MSS 300.

86. WASP Vi Cowden in Bonn and Bonn, *Wings of Silver*.

87. Letter, Betty June Overman Brown to Bonnie, August 12, 1944, Betty Overman Brown Personal Letters, Papers, and News Clippings, 1944–2002, TWU MSS 300. The story about the game in the clouds was from Florene Miller Watson. Florene Miller Watson, interview by Dawn Letson, June 23, 1994, TWU MSS 300.

88. Letter, Adaline Blank to "Sis" Edwina Blank, July 21, 1943, Adaline Blank Correspondence, July 1943–December 1943, TWU MSS 300.

89. Letter, Adaline Blank to "Sis" Edwina Blank, August 18, 1943, Adaline Blank Correspondence, July 1943–December 1943, TWU MSS 300.

90. Memo, "Military Training, Program of Instruction for WASP Trainees," AAF Training Command Headquarters, Record Group 18, Army Air Forces, Central Decimal Files, Oct 1942–May 1944, Box No. 918, Folder 353, Women's Flying Training, NARA.

91. Major Robert K. Urban, "Woman Pilot Trainee Regulations," June 14, 1943, Record Group 18 Army Air Forces, Central Decimal Files, Oct 1942–May 1944, Box No. 918, Folder 353, Women's Flying Training, NARA.

92. "Bay Arrangement" memo to "All women pilot trainees" from Chief Establishment Officer Leni L. Deaton, July 27, 1943, Record Group 18, Army Air Forces, Central Decimal Files, Oct 1942–May 1944, Box No. 918, Folder 353, Women's Flying Training, NARA.

93. Letter, Adaline Blank to "Sis" Edwina Blank, August 10, 1943, Adaline Blank Correspondence, July 1943–December 1943, TWU MSS 300.

94. The other WASP listening to this story laughed in response. WASP homecoming reunion, Sweetwater, Texas, May 2011.

95. "Editorial," *Avenger*, May 11, 1943, TWU WASP Collection.

96. "Songs of Class 44-W-9" to the tune of "Aviation Air Cadet March," *WASP Songbook*, 22, TWU WASP Collection.

97. *Avenger*, June 28, 1943, TWU WASP Collection.

98. "Prisoners of Japan," *Avenger*, February 4, 1944, TWU WASP Collection.

99. The women trainees wrote and edited newsletters during the war from February 1943 to the end of 1944. In 1989, WASP Doris Brinker Tanner suggested that their publication probably ended because deactivation was coming and the number of trainees had diminished. Aviation Enterprises, the company that ran the airfield at Houston and later the *Sweetwater Daily Reporter*, published these newsletters. The *Sweetwater Daily Reporter* supported the publication of the *Avenger* with numerous advertisements for Sweetwater businesses. See "Fifinella's Underwriters," *Fifinella Gazette*, February 10, 1943, TWU WASP Collection; Tanner, *Who Were the WASP?*; and "The Avenger Survives," *Avenger*, August 24, 1944, TWU WASP Collection.

100. "Class News," *Fifinella Gazette*, February 10, 1943, TWU WASP Collection. The trainees received permission from Disney to use the Fifinella image.

101. Local newspapers published the newsletters for the WASP each month.

102. Cochran offered to pay for the publication of these newsletters, but it is unclear whether the trainees accepted her offer. Letter, Jacqueline Cochran to Byrd Granger, February 16, 1943, Jacqueline Cochran Papers, WASP Series, Box 7, EPL.

103. The heading "All the News Is Safe to Print" appeared under the newsletter's title. See "Note from the Editor," *Fifinella Gazette*; April 23, 1943, TWU WASP Collection. In the *Avenger*, the editors explained the publisher association: "*The Avenger* is published by the *Sweetwater Daily Reporter* in the interests of personnel of Avenger Field and does not constitute an official Army publication."

104. Yount was the commanding general of the AAF Training Command. Others who received newsletters were officers in the Individual Training Branch of the AAF, AAF officers at Randolph Field in San Antonio, Texas, AAF officers at Ellington Field, Texas, and others whose names were mentioned in the newsletter. Letter, Jacqueline Cochran to Byrd Granger, February 16, 1943, Jacqueline Cochran Papers, WASP Series, Box 7, EPL; letter, B. K. Yount, major general, to Jacqueline Cochran, March 2, 1943, Jacqueline Cochran Papers, WASP Series, Box 7, EPL.

105. For example, "Ah Men," *Avenger*, March 17, 1944, TWU WASP Collection.

106. The first number in the class represented the year, followed by a "W," and then the number of classes created that year. For example, class 44-W-10 was the tenth class in 1944. This book uses these same AAF designations. Letter, Mary Anna "Marty" Martin Wyall to her family, June 30, 1944, TWU MSS 300.

107. According to pilot and retired USAF lieutenant colonel C. W. "Bill" Getz, most male pilots' songs were humorous. Getz, *Wild Blue Yonder*.

108. One example of a World War II male pilot's classbook is available in Mary R. Jones Papers, MSS 362, TWU.

109. Letter, Mary Anna "Marty" Martin Wyall to her family, October 12, 1944, TWU MSS 300.

110. 44-W-5 Classbook, TWU WASP Collection.

111. For one example, see 44-W-2 Classbook, TWU WASP Collection.

112. See historian Mary Louise Roberts on male soldiers in World War II: "Bonds of solidarity were forged around sense perceptions and bodily events." Roberts, *Sheer Misery*, 6.

113. Letter, Adaline Blank to "Sis" Edwina Blank, July 8, 1943, Adaline Blank Correspondence, July 1943–December 1943, TWU MSS 300.

114. Anne Chisholm Dessert Oliver, interview by Dawn Letson, December 4, 1997, TWU MSS 300.

115. Historian Thomas Andrews's *Killing for Coal* offers theoretical insights into this camaraderie, as his history of the "Great Coalfield War" identifies a sense of brotherhood that developed amid common dangerous work experiences. In addition to the treacherous conditions of the mines, workers bonded over their relationships with rodents and mules. The workers made "mice into pets," which "brightened" their workday. Andrews, *Killing for Coal*, 130.

116. Mackin, *Suddenly We Didn't Want to Die*, 57.

117. Milam, *Not a Gentleman's War*, 143–44.

118. "The Captain Says—," *Fifinella Gazette* no. 1 (February 10, 1943); "Songs of Class 44-W-9" to the tune of "Home on the Range," *WASP Songbook*, 22, both in TWU WASP Collection.

119. Group interview of WASP (Helen Wyatt Snapp, Marjorie Popell Sizemore, Doris Elkington Hamaker, Mary Ann Baldner Gordon, Mary Anna "Marty" Martin Wyall) and WAFS Teresa James, interview by Rebecca Wright on behalf of NASA, July 18, 1999, https://historycollection.jsc.nasa.gov/JSCHistoryPortal/history/oral _histories/NASA_HQ/Aviatrix/WASP/WASP_7-18-99.htm.

120. "Sky Happy," *Fifinella Gazette*, February 10, 1943; Associated Press, "Texas Weather," *Fifinella Gazette*, February 10, 1943, both in TWU WASP Collection.

121. Margaret Hurlburt, "A Letter Home," *Avenger*, June 28, 1943, TWU WASP Collection.

122. *Avenger*, October 22, 1943, TWU WASP Collection.

123. "Cockpit Cackle," *Avenger*, July 26, 1943, TWU WASP Collection.

124. Cole, *Women Pilots of World War II*, 34, 46.

125. Clark, *Dear Mother and Daddy*, 34.

126. Haydu, *Letters Home, 1944–1945*, 44.

127. Major Robert K. Urban, "Woman Pilot Trainee Regulations," June 14, 1943, Record Group 18, Army Air Forces, Central Decimal Files Oct 1942–May 1944, Box No. 918, Folder 353, Women's Flying Training, NARA.

128. Margaret Hurlburt, "A Letter Home," *Avenger* 1, no. 2 (June 28, 1943), TWU WASP Collection.

129. McPherson, *For Cause and Comrades*, 37.

130. While serving in the army, Ruby Henderson Humer kept *Bombsight* magazines from Kirtland Field in Alburquerque, New Mexico, where she served for thirteen months. Ruby J. Henderson Humer Papers, Coll #02.0133, The Institute on World War II and the Human Experience, Florida State University, Tallahassee.

131. Evelyn Norton and Sue Toce, *Fifinella Gazette*, April 23, 1943, TWU WASP Collection.

132. "Sky Happy," *Fifinella Gazette*, April 23, 1943, TWU WASP Collection.

133. "Sky Happy," *Fifinella Gazette*, May 24, 1943, TWU WASP Collection.

134. "Fifinella Insignia Makes Debut," *Fifinella Gazette*, March 1, 1943, TWU WASP Collection.

135. Dahl, *Gremlins*.

136. "Future of Fifinella Insignia and Gazette," *Fifinella Gazette*, April 23, 1943, TWU WASP Collection. In 1943, there were even Christmas cards featuring Fifinella for the trainees to send to their friends and family. See Clark, *Dear Mother and Daddy*, 82. Examples of songs: "Songs of Class 44-W-7" to the tune "Wishing," *WASP Songbook*, 12, 13; "Confidential!," *Fifinella Gazette*, May 24, 1943, both in TWU WASP Collection.

137. "The Fifinella," *Avenger*, May 3, 1944, TWU WASP Collection.

138. MacKenzie, *Flying against Fate*; Smith, *Wrong Stuff*.

139. Sloan Taylor, "Girl Pilots Train Like Cadets," undated, TWU WASP Collection. Decades later, when women again flew military planes for the

air force, another aviator followed this same superstition. At the 2013 WASP homecoming reunion in Sweetwater, Texas, Thunderbirds pilot Caroline Jensen spoke at the luncheon and told the audience, including many WASP, that she stopped in Sweetwater on her way to pilot training at the USAF Academy in Colorado so that she could throw a coin into the wishing well, just as the WASP had done so many years before her. She said it brought her luck, as she also graduated from training.

140. This dedication is mentioned in classbooks for classes 43-W-1 through 44-W-4. Classbooks are in TWU WASP Collection.

141. This tradition was mentioned frequently. See, for example, *Avenger*, June 28, 1943, TWU WASP Collection.

142. Tony Coonley, "Simple Rules for that 'Pro' Touch in Emergency Landing," *Avenger*, October 8, 1943, TWU WASP Collection.

143. Jean Moore Soard, interview by Jean Hascall Cole, March 6, 1989, TWU MSS 300.

144. For example, they provided the acronym "GARB" for green, amber, red, and blue. See *Fifinella Gazette,* February 10, 1943, TWU WASP Collection.

145. Example: "Consolidated B-24," *Fifinella Gazette,* February 10, 1943, TWU WASP Collection.

146. "Some Tips on Cross-Country," *Avenger*, June 28, 1943, TWU WASP Collection.

147. Jacqueline Cochran, "Final Report on Women Pilot Program," June 1, 1945, Jacqueline Cochran Papers, WASP Series, Box 12, EPL.

148. Orr was describing Susan Clarke's death. Joanne Wallace Orr, interview by Jean Hascall Cole, September 16, 1991, TWU MSS 300.

149. These benefits were for trainee Margie Davis, who died in an accident in Sweetwater on October 6, 1944. WASP Accident Reports, TWU WASP Collection.

150. Jacqueline Cochran Papers, WASP Series, Box 6, Fatalities (2) Folder, EPL.

151. In some letters, General Arnold included personal comments about the women. For example, see letter, H. H. Arnold to Mrs. Chang, December 4, 1944, Jacqueline Cochran Papers, WASP Series, Box 6, EPL.

152. For example, see letter, Jacqueline Cochran to Mrs. Mabel G. Nichols, June 12, 1944, Jacqueline Cochran Papers, WASP Series, Box 6, EPL.

153. Letter, Nora Rawlinson to Jacqueline Cochran, September 13, 1943, Jacqueline Cochran Papers, WASP Series, Box 6, EPL.

154. Pam Pohly, "Mabel Virginia Rawlinson," Wings across America, accessed March 8, 2023, http://wingsacrossamerica.us/web/obits/rawlinsom_mabel.htm.

155. Pohly, "Mabel Virginia Rawlinson."

156. "Dorothy Mae 'Dottie' Nichols," *CAF Rise Above*, September 21, 2021, https://cafriseabove.org/dorothy-mae-dottie-nichols/. "Military Funeral Held for Wasp Betty Stine," Jacqueline Cochran Papers, WASP Series, Box 6, Folder Fatalities (4), EPL.

157. As a trainee, WASP Marjorie Osborne Nicol told her family that there were no memorial services for her classmate at Sweetwater because there had been a memorial service for a previous WASP, which turned out to be "very demoralizing"

for the rest of the trainees. Letter, Marjorie Osborne Nicol to her family, June 21, 1944, TWU WASP Collection.

158. Letter, Adaline Blank to "Sis" Edwina Blank, August 15, 1943, Adaline Blank Correspondence, July 1943–December 1943, TWU MSS 300.

159. For example, 43-W-8 and 44-W-1 Classbooks, TWU WASP Collection.

160. Interview in Ladvich, *Fly Girls*.

161. "In Memoriam" for Jane Champlin, *Avenger*, June 28, 1943, TWU WASP Collection. The author called Champlin's death "a sacrifice." "In Memoriam" for Margaret Oldenburg, *Fifinella Gazette*, April 1, 1943, TWU WASP Collection. The author said of Oldenburg, "She had a smile for everyone." For memorial service announcements of Mary Howson, Elizabeth Erickson, and Kay Lawrence, see *Avenger*, April 21, 1944, and *Avenger*, September 2, 1943, TWU WASP Collection.

162. Frances Smith Tuchband, interview by Jean Hascall Cole, 1989, TWU MSS 300.

163. Letter, Jacqueline Cochran to Reverend T. M. Johnston, August 21, 1943, Jacqueline Cochran Papers, WASP Series, Box 6, EPL.

164. Examples in a scrapbook in the Dorothea Johnson Moorman Papers, MSS 358c, TWU.

165. Letter, Adaline Blank to "Sis" Edwina Blank, August 15, 1943, Adaline Blank Correspondence, July 1943–December 1943, TWU MSS 300.

166. Mildred Darlene Tuttle Axton interview by Patricia Kuentz, Mildred Darlene Tuttle Axton Collection (AFC/2001/001/10290), Veterans History Project, American Folklife Center, Library of Congress.

167. Magid, *Women of Courage*; Ladvich, *Fly Girls*.

168. Wood, *We Were WASPs*, 66.

169. Melosh, *"Physician's Hand."*

170. Jacqueline Cochran, "Final Report on Women Pilot Program," June 1, 1945, Jacqueline Cochran Papers, WASP Series, Box 12, EPL.

171. Granger, *On Final Approach*, 385.

172. "Here Come the WAFS," *Time*, June 7, 1943, TWU WASP Collection.

173. Keil, *Those Wonderful Women*, 175.

174. Letter, Adaline Blank to "Sis" Edwina Blank, July 21, 1943, Adaline Blank Correspondence, July 1943–December 1943, TWU MSS 300.

175. Weber, "Manufacturing Gender," 235–53.

176. Weber, "Manufacturing Gender," 137.

177. Cole, *Women Pilots of World War II*, 126; Wood, *We Were WASPs*, 60; Magid, *Women of Courage*.

178. "Director of Women Pilots Asks Military Status for WASPs," War Department Bureau of Public Relations, August 8, 1944, TWU WASP Collection; Jacqueline Cochran, "Final Report on Women Pilot Program," June 1, 1945, Jacqueline Cochran Papers, WASP Series, Box 12, EPL.

179. Virginia Dulaney Campbell, interview by Jean Hascall Cole, 1989, TWU MSS 300. Other women pilots encountered similar situations. See Teresa James, interview by Dawn Letson, June 16, 1998, TWU MSS 300.

180. "Medical Consideration of WASPS," Jacqueline Cochran Papers, WASP Series, Box 15, EPL.

181. In 2019, the navy was working on new equipment for in-flight relief since flight suits were initially created for the male body. Female pilots have had the option of wearing a diaper or practicing "tactical dehydration." Hope Hodge Seck, "The Navy Is Buying Equipment That Makes It Easier for Female Pilots to Pee," Military.com, December 19, 2019, https://www.military.com/daily-news/2019/12/19/navy-buying-equipment-makes-it-easier-female-pilots-pee.html. In 2020, the air force offered a cash reward of $100,000 for a new bladder system for female pilots to "relieve themselves during flight without interfering with operations or compromising flight safety." Jennifer H. Svan, "Air Force Offers Cash for Better System Allowing Female Pilots to Relieve Themselves in Flight," *Stars and Stripes*, August 26, 2020, https://www.stripes.com/branches/air_force/air-force-offers-cash-for-better-system-allowing-female-pilots-to-relieve-themselves-in-flight-1.642670.

182. Sociologist Melissa S. Herbert argues that the questioning of military women's abilities and bodily capabilities is similar to earlier historical fears of women receiving a college education or participating in sports. Nineteenth-century medical professionals like Dr. Edward H. Clarke argued these activities could lead to infertility, damaged female reproductive organs, or even insanity. Herbert, *Camouflage Isn't Only for Combat*, 1–2.

183. "Medical Consideration of WASPS," Jacqueline Cochran Papers, WASP Series, Box 15, EPL. See also Clark, *Dear Mother and Daddy*, 21.

184. Mary Douglas, *Purity and Danger*.

185. WAFS Teresa James thought the men acted as if women came out of nowhere because they continually asked about menstrual cycles, despite a history of women flying for over two decades. Teresa James, interview by Dawn Letson, June 16, 1998, TWU MSS 300.

186. Jacqueline Cochran, "Final Report on Women Pilot Program," June 1, 1945, Jacqueline Cochran Papers, WASP Series, Box 12, EPL.

187. Carl, *WASP among Eagles*, 83; Letter, "Physical Standards and Stamina of WASPs," by Bryan Army Airfield in Bryan, TX, in "History of the WASP Program: Central Flying Training Command," December 1944, Call #223.072 V.1, IRIS #00146288, USAF Collection, AFHRA.

188. Jacqueline Cochran, "Final Report on Women Pilot Program," June 1, 1945, Jacqueline Cochran Papers, WASP Series, Box 12, EPL.

189. "Director of Women Pilots Asks Military Status for WASPs," War Department Bureau of Public Relations, August 8, 1944, TWU WASP Collection.

190. The review was based on statements via letters and interviews from "AAF surgeons, commanding officers, flight safety officers, and other interested personnel at fields where WASPs were trained or stationed," as well as medical records, statistical data from the air surgeon's office, and other sources. Jacqueline Cochran, "Final Report on Women Pilot Program," June 1, 1945, Jacqueline Cochran Papers, WASP Series, Box 12, EPL.

191. "Medical Consideration of WASPS," Jacqueline Cochran Papers, WASP Series, Box 15, EPL.

192. Letter, Edward Leefer, senior flight surgeon at Childress Army Airfield (TX) to commanding general at Randolph Field, December 12, 1944, in "History of the WASP Program: Central Flying Training Command," December 1944, Call #223.072 V.1, IRIS #00146288, USAF Collection, AFHRA.

193. Jacqueline Cochran, "Final Report on Women Pilot Program," June 1, 1945, Jacqueline Cochran Papers, WASP Series, Box 12, EPL.

194. "Director of Women Pilots"; "Suggested Report to Be Released in Response to Unfavorable Reports to Proposed Militarization of the WASPs, 1943," Jacqueline Cochran Papers, WASP Series, Box 5, Militarization, EPL.

195. This number includes men listed as civilian instructors, flight instructors, ground-school instructors, guards, and other personnel positions in the WASP classbooks. For one example of a list of male personnel, see 43-W-4 and 43-W-5 Classbooks, TWU WASP Collection.

196. There were 1,830 women accepted as trainees and 18 classes, which means there were approximately 100 trainees on base per class. Although there were slightly fewer in early WASP classes and slightly more in later classes, the average was 100 women trainees per class.

197. "Your Personal Relationship" section of "A Handbook for Women Student Pilot Trainees," Headquarters of the Army Air Forces and Director of Women Pilots, TWU WASP Collection; Clark, *Dear Mother and Daddy*, 116.

198. Clark, *Dear Mother and Daddy*, 116.

199. Joanne Wallace Orr, interview by Jean Hascall Cole, September 16, 1991, TWU MSS 300.

200. Group interview of WASP (Helen Wyatt Snapp, Marjorie Popell Sizemore, Doris Elkington Hamaker, Mary Ann Baldner Gordon, Mary Anna "Marty" Martin Wyall) and WAFS Teresa James, interview by Rebecca Wright on behalf of NASA, July 18, 1999, https://historycollection.jsc.nasa.gov/JSCHistoryPortal/history/oral_histories/NASA_HQ/Aviatrix/WASP/WASP_7-18-99.htm.

201. Maggie Gee, interview by Leah McGarrigle, Robin Li, and Kathryn Stine, April 10, April 29, and May 20, 2003, for the Rosie the Riveter World War II American Homefront Oral History Project, Regional Oral History Office, University of California, Berkeley, http://digitalassets.lib.berkeley.edu/roho/ucb/text/gee_maggie.pdf.

202. Letter, Marjorie Osborne Nicol to her parents, August 30, 1944, and September 11, 1944, TWU MSS 300.

203. Carl, *WASP among Eagles*, 53.

204. "Zoot-Suits and Parachutes" to the tune of "Bell Bottom Trousers," *WASP Songbook*, 8, TWU WASP Collection. The WASP sang this song together at their 2010 reunion in Sweetwater, Texas.

205. Wood, *We Were WASPs*, 43–45.

206. Jean Hascall Cole, self-interview for TWU, December 9, 1997, TWU MSS 300.

207. Malvina Stephenson, "WASPS—Heroines of Air War," undated, TWU WASP Collection; Granger, *On Final Approach*, 151–52, 398.

208. Dedi L. Deaton, "Supplementary History of the Women's Airforce Service Pilot Training Program," 37, TWU WASP Collection; Ladvich, *Fly Girls*.

209. Cole, *Women Pilots of World War II*, 52.

210. Cole, *Women Pilots of World War II*, 75.

211. This example certainly seemed to be the experience of many WASP, as evidenced in their oral history interviews and published personal accounts. Carl, *WASP among Eagles*, 42.

212. "Director of Women Pilots Asks Military Status for WASPs," War Department Bureau of Public Relations, August 8, 1944, TWU WASP Collection.

213. "319th AAFFTD Alphabetical Listing of Delinquencies and Demerits," TWU WASP Collection.

214. Jean Hascall Cole, self-interview for TWU, December 9, 1997, TWU MSS 300.

215. Cole, *Women Pilots of World War II*, 56–57, 26–28.

216. Letter, Adaline Blank to "Sis" Edwina Blank, August 10, 1943, Adaline Blank Correspondence, July 1943–December 1943, TWU MSS 300.

217. Letter, Marjorie Osborne Nicol to her parents, August 3, 1944, TWU MSS 300.

218. Letter, Marjorie Osborne Nicol to her parents, June 24, 1944, TWU MSS 300.

219. Letter, Marjorie Osborne Nicol to her parents, May 11, 1944, TWU MSS 300.

220. Cole, *Women Pilots of World War II*, 56.

221. "Life under the Hood," *Fifinella Gazette*, March 1, 1943, TWU WASP Collection.

222. Malvina Stephenson, "WASPS—Heroines of Air War," undated, TWU WASP Collection; Granger, *On Final Approach*, 151–52, 398.

223. Lucile Wise, email interview by the author, February 2008.

224. Jean Hascall Cole, self-interview December 9, 1997, TWU MSS 300.

225. Adaline Alma Blank Scrapbook, 1943–1986, MSS 668c, TWU.

226. At the 2013 WASP reunion in Sweetwater, Texas, a panel of WASP answered questions about their experiences as women pilots during the war. WASP Elizabeth Strohfus told this story and mentioned that she was a "goody-goody" and did not participate. The other WASP on the panel laughed at this story but did not elaborate on it.

227. For example, there is an invitation in the Adaline Alma Blank Scrapbook, 1943–1986, MSS 668c, TWU.

228. Letter, R. E. McKaughan, president of Aviation Enterprises, to Mr. R. T. Rance, October 5, 1943, Mary Ruth Rance Papers, MSS 746, TWU.

229. "With Sympathetic Guidance," *Avenger*, June 28, 1943, TWU WASP Collection.

230. "Songs of Class 44-W-9" to the tune of "Put on Your Old Gray Bonnet," *WASP Songbook*, 19, 21; "Songs of Class 44-W- (I) 3" to the tune of "You Wanted Wings," *WASP Songbook*, 27, both in TWU WASP Collection.

231. Letter, Mary Anna "Marty" Martin Wyall to her family, June 30, 1944, TWU MSS 300.

232. "Hello, 43-W-4," *Fifinella Gazette*, March 1, 1943, TWU WASP Collection.

233. "Songs of Class 44-W-8" to the tune of "Swinging on a Star," *WASP Songbook*, 18, TWU WASP Collection.

234. "Songs of Class 44-W-7" to the tune of "Casey Jones," *WASP Songbook*, 14; "Songs of Class 44-W-9" to the tune of "Elmer's Tune," *WASP Songbook*, 19, both in TWU WASP Collection.

Chapter 3

1. They accused previous WASP stationed there of wrecking airplanes and of sleeping with AAF officers. While both are possible and would fit with wartime stereotypes of women as sexually tempting to men, there is no mention of either offense in the official history of the WASP program from the Western Flying Training Command. Merced Army Airfield was in the Western Flying Training Command. "History of the WASP Program, Western Flying Training Command, Nov 15, 1943–December 20, 1944," Call #224.072, IRIS #00146374, USAF Collection, AFHRA.

2. Virginia Dulaney Campbell, interview by Jean Hascall Cole, 1989, TWU MSS 300.

3. Before World War II, according to historian Joseph Corn, women pilots worked selling the safety of aviation to the American public. The WASP offer a continuation of this story, as they demonstrated the safety of particular aircraft to male air force pilots and used their femininity to accomplish this assignment. Corn, *Winged Gospel*. The Central Flying Training Command concluded that "the WASPs were novelties." "History of the WASP Program: Central Flying Training Command," December 1944, Call #223.072 V.1, IRIS #00146288, USAF Collection, AFHRA.

4. "History of the WASP Program: Central Flying Training Command."

5. Jacqueline Cochran, "Final Report on Women Pilot Program," June 1, 1945, Jacqueline Cochran Papers, WASP Series, Box 12, EPL.

6. "In the event that a similar program may be activated in the future," as one such history of the WASP program explains. "History of the WASP Program: Central Flying Training Command," December 1944, Call #223.072 V.1, IRIS #00146288, USAF Collection, AFHRA.

7. As explained previously, the WAFS was the first women's pilot program during World War II, and in 1943, the WAFS merged with the WFTD to become the WASP. The WAFS were highly experienced pilots who had logged hundreds of flying hours before the war.

8. For example, women pilots were allowed to check out in classes of aircraft higher than Class III, which consisted of twin-engine cargo and transport planes, and in higher classes, including Class P. Series I—USAF Historical Studies, Jacqueline Cochran Papers, Box 15, EPL.

9. "History of the WASP Program, Western Flying Training Command, Nov 15, 1943–December 20, 1944," Call #224.072, IRIS #00146374, USAF Collection, AFHRA.

10. WASP Vi Cowden in Bonn and Bonn, *Wings of Silver*.

11. Jacqueline Cochran, "Final Report on Women Pilot Program," June 1, 1945, Jacqueline Cochran Papers, WASP Series, Box 12, EPL.

12. Teresa James, interview by Dawn Letson, June 16, 1998, TWU MSS 300.

13. These pranks occurred at New Castle Army Air Base. Teresa James, interview by Dawn Letson, June 16, 1998, TWU MSS 300.

14. Teresa James, interview by Dawn Letson, June 16, 1998, TWU MSS 300.

15. Scharr, *Sisters in the Sky*, 2:200; Granger, *On Final Approach*, 70, 200, 325; Magid, *Women of Courage of World War II*.

16. Clark, *Dear Mother and Daddy*, 150–51.

17. The emphasized "ARE" is in the transcript of this interview. Florine Phillips Maloney Papers, Coll #05.0141, The Institute on World War II and the Human Experience, Florida State University, Tallahassee.

18. Florine Phillips Maloney Papers. Virginia Dulaney Campbell provided another example of a male officer who was surprised at women in uniform. When she presented her orders at Stockton Army Air Base, the officer at the gate responded, "What do you mean orders? You're a woman." Virginia Dulaney Campbell, interview by Jean Hascall Cole, 1989, TWU MSS 300.

19. Joanne Wallace Orr, interview by Jean Hascall Cole, September 16, 1991, TWU MSS 300.

20. Dorothy Allen, interview by Dawn Letson, December 3, 1997, TWU MSS 300.

21. Letter, Alyce Stevens Rohrer to "Mother and Daddy," July 24, 1944, MSS 475c, TWU.

22. Male pilots emphasized gendered assumptions about the WASP instead of acknowledging their actual abilities, similar to the ways male drivers in Virginia Scharff's study dismissed women's technological skills as luck. Scharff, *Taking the Wheel*.

23. Series I—USAF Historical Studies, Jacqueline Cochran Papers, Box 15, EPL.

24. Even in letters home, the WASP could not mention target towing. Instead, they described the work, for example, as "secret" work at antiaircraft school. Letter, Betty Budde to her parents, July 21, 1943, and August 9, 1943, TWU.

25. They towed targets at the following airfields: Biggs Army Airfield (El Paso, TX), Buckingham Army Airfield (Fort Myers, FL), Camp Davis Army Airfield (Camp Davis, NC), Dodge City Army Air Base (Dodge City, KS), Eglin Army Air Base (Niceville, FL), Harlingen Army Airfield (Harlingen, TX), Laredo Army Air Base (Laredo, TX), Las Vegas Army Airfield (Las Vegas, NV), Liberty Field (Fort Stewart, GA), March Army Air Base (Riverside, CA), Moore Army Air Base (Mission, TX), Peterson Army Air Base (Colorado Springs, CO), Pratt Army Air Base (Pratt, KS), Tyndall Army Air Base (Panama City, FL), and Yuma Army Airfield (Yuma, AZ).

26. Towing-target display including a DVD of WASP Bev Beesemyer explaining her experiences at the Sweetwater Museum in Sweetwater, TX.

27. William "Bill" Bauer, interview by G. Kurt Piehler and Linda E. Lasko, October 7, 1994, Rutgers Oral History Archives, https://oralhistory.rutgers.edu /rutgers-history/30-interviewees/interview-html-text/731-bauer-william.

28. Jacqueline Cochran, "Final Report on Women Pilot Program," June 1, 1945, Jacqueline Cochran Papers, WASP Series, Box 12, EPL.

29. Letter, Betty Budde to her parents, August 21, 1945, TWU.

30. Stallman, *Women in the Wild Blue*, 48, 93.

31. The same is true for women in other lines of work. Cooper, *Once a Cigar Maker*.

32. Some of the WASP described male pilots with the term "chauvinism." For example, WASP Dorothy Allen said that when six to seven more WASP were assigned to the Foster Army Airfield where she was stationed, Colonel Taute "was very upset about it. He was one of these male chauvinists. He didn't want these women pilots. He didn't ask for them and he doesn't know why he has to have them." Dorothy Allen, interview by Dawn Letson, December 3, 1997, TWU MSS 300.

33. William "Bill" Bauer, interview by G. Kurt Piehler and Linda E. Lasko, October 7, 1994, Rutgers Oral History Archives, https://oralhistory.rutgers.edu/rutgers-history/30-interviewees/interview-html-text/731-bauer-william.

34. Magid, *Women of Courage*.

35. Stallman, *Women in the Wild Blue*, 106, 132.

36. Alice Rogers Hager, "Service Pilots," *Skyways Magazine*, February 1944, WASP Collection, MSS 240c, TWU; Carl, *WASP among Eagles*, 51–54.

37. Letter, Betty Budde to her parents, August 27, 1943, TWU.

38. Jacqueline Cochran, "Final Report on Women Pilot Program," June 1, 1945, Jacqueline Cochran Papers, WASP Series, Box 12, EPL.

39. Most of the newspaper coverage of the WASP towing targets appeared in regional, not national, newspapers. Articles about this assignment appeared several pages into the newspaper; the lede to the story was often buried several paragraphs into the article.

40. "Women Pilots Tow Targets and Fly Tracking Missions," *Milwaukee (WI) Journal*, October 26, 1943.

41. Ann Stevick, "Girl Flyers Who Tow Targets May Be Real 'Soldiers' before Very Long," *Tuscaloosa News*, November 2, 1943; Honey, *Creating Rosie the Riveter*.

42. This is a rare example of national-level media coverage of the WASP. The story appears on page twenty of the newspaper and does not allude to the dangerous aspects of the work. Bess Furman, "Army Status Asked for Women Pilots," *New York Times*, August 8, 1944.

43. They performed spotlight-tracking missions first at Camp Davis. Jacqueline Cochran, "Final Report on Women Pilot Program," June 1, 1945, Jacqueline Cochran Papers, WASP Series, Box 12, EPL.

44. "Wasps' Nest," *Charm*, March 1944, 72–73, 122, WASP Collection, MSS 240c, TWU; Carl, *WASP among Eagles*, 52.

45. Jacqueline Cochran, "Final Report on Women Pilot Program," June 1, 1945, Jacqueline Cochran Papers, WASP Series, Box 12, EPL.

46. The telephone conversation between Cochran and McNaughton took place in September 1944. Series I—USAF Historical Studies, Jacqueline Cochran Papers, Box 15, EPL.

47. Several WASP dubbed these planes "war-weary" because they came from overseas theaters of war. Joanne Wallace Orr, interview by Jean Hascall Cole, September 16, 1991, TWU MSS 300; Magid, *Women of Courage*.

48. When WASP Virginia Dulaney Campbell was stationed at Stockton Army Air Base in California, there were fifteen male test pilots, but by the end of her assignment there, she and another WASP were the only ones remaining, as the men had left for overseas duty. Virginia Dulaney Campbell, interview by Jean Hascall Cole, 1989, TWU MSS 300.

49. Ethel Meyer Finley, interview by Nancy Durr, September 25, 1998, TWU MSS 300.

50. Campbell, interview.

51. Campbell, interview.

52. Joanne Wallace Orr, interview by Jean Hascall Cole, September 16, 1991, TWU MSS 300.

53. Campbell, interview.

54. Orr, interview. This response is similar to the one female cigar makers and firefighters encountered in Cooper, *Once a Cigar Maker*, and MacLean, "Hidden History of Affirmative Action," 356–78.

55. Virginia Dulaney Campbell, interview by Jean Hascall Cole, 1989, TWU MSS 300.

56. Corn argues, "This demeaning lady-flier stereotype . . . was pervasive." Corn, *Winged Gospel*, 76. Even Jacqueline Cochran participated in this charade. When she had mechanical problems and had to drop out of air races, she claimed to be simply too tired to fly, rather than concern the public about the safety of her aircraft. Rich, *Jackie Cochran*.

57. "Arnold and B-26 Crashes," Henry H. Arnold Collection, Call #MICFILM 28106, IRIS #2052789, AFHRA; Virginia Dulaney Campbell, interview by Jean Hascall Cole, 1989, TWU MSS 300.

58. Joanne Wallace Orr, interview by Jean Hascall Cole, September 16, 1991, TWU MSS 300. Male pilots also called the B-26 a flying prostitute. World War II veteran pilot Lawrence Hunter used this term as the title of his memoir. Hunter, *Flying Prostitute*, 103.

59. General Patrick Timberlake, interview, San Antonio, TX, May 7, 1970, Call #43828, IRIS #01103243, USAF Collection, AFHRA.

60. "Sugar and Spice! B-26 Gentle as Lamb in Hands of WASPS," *Martin Star*, February 1944, TWU WASP Collection.

61. Bess Furman, "Army Status Asked for Women Pilots," *New York Times*, August 8, 1944.

62. Tunner, *Over the Hump*, 37.

63. Barry, *Femininity in Flight*.

64. Granger, *On Final Approach*, 410–11; Ladvich, *Fly Girls*; photograph of Dorothea Moorman Johnson, Colonel Paul Tibbets, and Dora Dougherty Strother McKeown with the B-29 Superfortress "Ladybird," MSS 255.7.47, TWU.

65. Paul Tibbets, interview by Dawn Letson, February 24, 1977, TWU MSS 300.

66. General Patrick Timberlake, interview, San Antonio, TX, May 7, 1970, Call #43828, IRIS #01103243, USAF Collection, AFHRA.

67. Corn, *Winged Gospel*, 76.

68. When learning of the B-26's reputation among male pilots, Cochran had 150 WASP fly the plane, and "they flew 175,000 hours of tow work alone, without a single fatality." "Jackie Cochran Helps Out with the B-26," Henry H. Arnold Collection, Call #MICFILM 28106, IRIS #2052789, AFHRA.

69. Jean Hascall Cole discussed this in an interview she was conducting with Virginia Dulaney Campbell. Virginia Dulaney Campbell, interview by Jean Hascall Cole, 1989, TWU MSS 300.

70. "History of Women Airforce Service Pilots Army Air Forces, Eastern Flying Training Command, Inception to Conclusion, Sept 1943–1944," TWU WASP Collection.

71. Series I—USAF Historical Studies, Jacqueline Cochran Papers, Box 15, EPL.

72. "History of Women Airforce Service Pilots Army Air Forces."

73. For example, Ethel Meyer Finley attended flight-instructor school at Randolph Field. Ethel Meyer Finley, interview by Nancy Durr, September 25, 1998, TWU MSS 300. One of the original WAFS, Teresa James, also received additional instructor ratings to teach acrobatics to pilots. Teresa James, interview by Dawn Letson, June 16, 1998, TWU MSS 300. During training at Sweetwater, the WASP learned how to do chandelles and lazy eights, primary-level acrobatics. For examples, see the following: letter, Sara Chapin to Mom, June 21, 1943, TWU; letter, Mary Anna "Marty" Martin Wyall to her family, June 30, 1944, TWU MSS 300; letter, Marjorie Osborne Nicol to her family, June 5, 1944, TWU MSS 300; letter, Madge Rutherford Minton to Mother & Dad, April 3, 1943, TWU MSS 300.

74. There are two WASP, Betty Williamson Shipley and Dorothy Allen, who mentioned performing this role in two oral history interviews, although they did not give specific details about the experience. There is also a photograph of WASP Jane Shirley "explaining instrument panel of AT-6 to Mexican officers" at Foster Army Airfield in Victoria, Texas, on August 10, 1944. This photograph seems staged, and there is no mention of the WASP performing the role of instructing these officers in the AAF history of the WASP at the field in the "duties performed" section. Dorothy Allen, interview by Dawn Letson, December 3, 1997, TWU MSS 300; Betty Williamson Shipley, interview by Dawn Letson, May 11, 2000, TWU; "History of Womans Airforce Service Pilots, Foster Field Texas, June 6–Dec 20, 1944," Foster Field TX Collection, Call #283.21-5, IRIS #172230, AFHRA.

75. Only two WASP (Gloria W. Heath and Mildred W. Grossman) were stationed at Pocatello during the duration of the war, and they towed targets. According to the official AAF history of the WASP at this field, this was their only assignment at this base. In an interview with a journalist, Lieutenant Colonel Joaquín Ramírez Vilchis of the 201st Mexican Squadron said that the WASP ferried P-47 planes to Pocatello Army Airfield. "History of WASP at Pocatello Army Air Field (23 Sept 1944 to 12 Oct 1944)," USAF Collection, Call #287.61-14, IRIS #176626, AFHRA; Kim Anglesey, "Pocatello and Mexico History Meet Again," *Idaho State Journal*, December 14, 2014, C1.

76. "History of Women Airforce Service Pilots Army Air Forces, Eastern Flying Training Command, Inception to Conclusion, Sept 1943-1944," TWU WASP Collection.

77. Elizabeth Strofus as told to Cheryl J. Young, *Love at First Flight,* 41–45.

78. Clark, *Dear Mother and Daddy,* 132–35; and Ethel Meyer Finley, interview by Nancy Durr, September 25, 1998, TWU MSS 300.

79. Finley, interview.

80. It also should be noted that Harmon only had one month of active duty before the WASP program disbanded. Elaine Danforth Harmon, interview by the author, September 1, 2012, digital recording.

81. Cole, *Women Pilots of World War II,* 113.

82. Jacqueline Cochran, interview, February 25, 1970, Call #168.7326-60, IRIS #1102998, USAF Collection, AFHRA.

83. Lorraine Zillner Rodgers told this story to classmate Jean Hascall Cole during an interview in 1989. Cole, *Women Pilots of World War II,* 45.

84. Mary Ellen Keil, interview by Jean Hascall Cole, September 24, 1989, TWU MSS 300.

85. She believed this was due to inadequate monitoring, as base personnel were "lax." Leona Golbinec Zimmer, interview by Jean Hascall Cole, September 23, 1989, TWU MSS 300.

86. "History of the WASP Program: Western Flying Training Command, Nov 15, 1943-December 20, 1944," Call #224.072, IRIS #00146374, USAF Collection, AFHRA.

87. "AAF School of Applied Tactics Student Handbook," KK141.33-20 to K141.33-38, Box 19, IRIS #01097925, USAF Collection, AFHRA.

88. Numerous WASP explained that they ignored the pay difference, difficulties of flying, and problems with other male pilots because they were so excited about the opportunity to fly. For brief examples, see Mary Helen Foster, interview by the author, October 10, 2009, digital recording; Virginia Dulaney Campbell, interview by Jean Hascall Cole, 1989, TWU MSS 300; and Ethel Meyer Finley, interview by Nancy Durr, September 25, 1998, TWU MSS 300.

89. Hugh Williamson, "'Lipstick Squadron' Trains in West Texas to Ferry Warplanes," *Houston Post,* April 27, 1943, Section 1, p 10, TWU WASP Collection; Clark, *Dear Mother and Daddy,* 181. For WASP uniform costs, see Byrd Granger's "Evidence Supporting Military Service," WASP Collection, MSS 245, Box 8, Folder 2, TWU.

90. "Director of Women Pilots Asks Military Status for WASPs," War Department Bureau of Public Relations, August 8, 1944, TWU WASP Collection; Carl, *WASP among Eagles,* 37.

91. Scharr, *Sisters in the Sky,* 2:538.

92. "Director of Women Pilots."

93. "Supplementary Rules and Regulations," September 22, 1943, TWU WASP Collection.

94. "Insurance" section of "A Handbook for Women Student Pilot Trainees," Headquarters of the Army Air Forces and Director of Women Pilots, TWU WASP Collection.

95. Leoti Deaton, WASP staff executive, "Brief History of the WASPs," 1976, TWU WASP Collection.

96. Kerber, *No Constitutional Right*, xxiv.

97. Hugh Williamson, "Hundreds of Women Training for Service as Ferry Pilots," *Colorado Springs Evening Telegraph*, April 28, 1943, WASP Collection, MSS 240c, TWU; Scharr, *Sisters in the Sky*, 2:414; "Director of Women Pilots."

98. Pennington, *Wings, Women, and War*.

99. Series I—USAF Historical Studies, Jacqueline Cochran Papers, Box 15, EPL; Committee on the Civil Service House of Representatives, *Investigation of Civilian Employment*, 78th Cong., 2nd sess., June 16, 1944, H.R. 16, A3306.

100. The three were WASP Hazel Stamper Hohn, WASP Elinor Fairchild, and WASP Lorraine R. Lasswell. This trip took place in December 1944, and numerous AAF male pilots also ferried planes on this same flight. A copy of this wartime order is in Hazel Stamper Hohn Papers, MSS 863, Box 3 of 3, TWU. A copy is also in Byrd Howell Granger, "Evidence Supporting Military Service by WASP World War II," 1977, Call #K141.33–45, IRIS #01097935, USAF Collection, AFHRA.

101. WASP Gloria DeVore Schwager gave this statement about her assignment during the 1970s WASP quest for militarization. Dora Strother also made a statement about flying over the ocean near the coasts of the United States. "Statement from WASP Gloria DeVore Schwager re Flying B-26s to Cuba for Target-Towing Missions" and "Statement from Dora Strother re Target Towing Missions Carried Out over the Ocean outside the Continental US," in Granger, "Evidence Supporting Military Service by WASP World War II."

102. Mary Belle Ahlstrom Smith described her experiences flying to Canada with other WASP: "We'd pick up the Taylorcrafts right in Ohio and take them to different training fields. I took one up to Canada—several of them to Canada. One out to Desert Center in California . . . I covered five Canadian provinces. . . . I took one [plane] out to Alberta, and that was about as far as I got. But the Canadian version of the AT-6 was made in Montreal and we enjoyed getting to Montreal." Mary Belle Ahlstrom Smith, interview by Dawn Letson, March 2, 1996, TWU MSS 300. During training, WASP Inez Woodward Woods wrote a letter to her mother telling her not to worry because the WASP were not receiving assignments outside of the United States. Letter, Pilot [Inez Woodward Woods] to Mamma Dea, April 26, 1943, TWU MSS 300.

103. Rickman, *Nancy Love*, 220–29; "Heavenly Flight: Nancy Harkness Love," *WASP Newsletter*, December 1976, TWU WASP Collection. This obituary includes a copy of the article "Mrs. Robert M. Love, Prominent Aviatrix," *Vineyard Gazette*, October 26, 1976, TWU WASP Collection.

104. "Address by General H. H. Arnold, Commanding General, Army Air Forces, before WASP Ceremony," Press Release, December 7, 1944, TWU WASP Collection.

105. Craven and Cate, *Army Air Forces in World War II*, vol. 6, *Men and Planes*.

106. Rupp, *Mobilizing Women for War*; Honey, *Creating Rosie the Riveter*.

107. For example, in Ruth Milkman's analysis of the auto industry and electrical manufacturing in World War II, male employers created a new sexual division

of labor to identify some of the jobs as female that had previously all been male. Milkman, *Gender at Work*.

108. For people's motivations for fighting, see Kindsvatter, *American Soldiers*; McPherson, *For Cause and Comrades*. For men's reluctance to engage in combat, see Marshall, *Men against Fire*; Grossman, *On Killing*. The memory of war has often been gendered male, as evidenced in works such as Little, *Abraham in Arms*; Purcell, *Sealed with Blood*; Alfred Young, *Masquerade*; and Zagarri, *Revolutionary Backlash*. Sarah Purcell's study of the American Revolution offers perspectives into how the memory of war became gendered and racialized and how memory influences national identity. Alfred Young and Rosemarie Zagarri explain the relationship between the emerging American government and the establishment of citizens as White and male as coinciding with the memory of war as centering on male veterans.

109. Honey, *Creating Rosie the Riveter*. Nurses who served overseas, even those who were POWs under the Japanese on the island of Bataan, were described as caring "angels," not part of the military. Norman, *We Band of Angels*.

110. One example is the story of Private Jessica Lynch. Philosopher Kelly Oliver argues that Lynch was an "ideal hero" in the US media, stating, "She is a woman who suffers, [according to] the ideal of feminine self-sacrifice and suffering." During Operation Iraqi Freedom, Lynch's Humvee crashed, and Iraqi doctors took her to a hospital and treated her injuries. American forces later rescued her. At first, the American media falsely described Lynch as fighting with the enemy via a firefight and hand-to-hand combat with a knife when, in reality, she was unable to fight. Later, the media emphasized her rescue, making her simultaneously a "victim and hero" through portrayals of her as a woman "fighting to the death" and as a "young, pretty" white woman. Few media sources mentioned fellow soldier and POW Shoshana Johnson, an African American woman captured simultaneously but held in prison and abused. Oliver, *Women as Weapons of War*, 41–42.

111. As in Milkman's *Gender at Work*, men justified the new sexual division of labor with gendered terms.

112. For one example, see "The Girls Make Good: Women Pilots Overcome Both Masculine Tradition and a Tough Flying Chore," *National Aeronautics*, November 1943, TWU WASP Collection.

113. Phyllis Battelle, "Veteran Pilot Says Women Make Better Fliers Than Men," WASP Collection, MSS 240c, TWU.

114. "Director of Women Pilots Asks Military Status for WASPs," War Department Bureau of Public Relations, August 8, 1944, TWU WASP Collection; "Words from a WASP," editorial, *New York World-Telegram*, April 17, 1944, WASP Collection, Gray Collection, TWU. Information about men's overseas preference taken from Carl, *WASP among Eagles*; Cole, *Women Pilots of World War II*; and Granger, *On Final Approach*. A discussion about women being more suitable for tedious, repetitive work is found in Light, "Programming," 299, 306.

115. "Statement by Miss Jacqueline Cochran on Accomplishments of WASP Program," War Department Bureau of Public Relations, December 19, 1944, TWU

WASP Collection; Jacqueline Cochran, "Final Report on Women Pilot Program," June 1, 1945, Jacqueline Cochran Papers, WASP Series, Box 12, EPL.

116. "Address by General H. H. Arnold, Commanding General, Army Air Forces, before WASP Ceremony, Sweetwater, Texas," December 7, 1944, TWU WASP Collection.

117. "History of Women Pilots with the AAF," Jacqueline Cochran Papers, WASP Series, Box 15, EPL.

118. "History of the WASP Program: Central Flying Training Command," December 1944, Call #223.072 V.1, IRIS #00146288, USAF Collection, AFHRA.

119. Ruth Oldenziel argues that from 1870 to 1945, technology became established as a masculine field. She examines the ways the field of engineering became a white, middle-class male profession. Oldenziel, *Making Technology Masculine.*

120. The Western, Eastern, and Central Flying Training Commands, as well as Cochran and the Ferrying Division of the Air Transport Command, wrote histories on the WASP program at the request of the AAF Headquarters.

121. "History of the WASP Program: Central Flying Training Command," December 1944, Call #223.072 V.1, IRIS #00146288, USAF Collection, AFHRA.

122. "History of the WASP Program: Western Flying Training Command, Nov 15, 1943–December 20, 1944," Call #224.072, IRIS #00146374, USAF Collection, AFHRA.

123. "History of the WASP Program: Central Flying Training Command." The Eastern Flying Training Command also reported on this habit: "WASP had evidently not been well indoctrinated in Army methods, and their informal methods of communicating out of channels with higher headquarters to obtain transfers or for personal reasons was a recurrent source of trouble." See "History of Women Airforce Service Pilots Army Air Forces, Eastern Flying Training Command, Inception to Conclusion, Sept 1943–1944," TWU WASP Collection.

124. "History of the WASP Program: Western Flying Training Command, Nov 15, 1943–December 20, 1944," Call #24.072, IRIS #00146374, USAF Collection, AFHRA.

125. Jacqueline Cochran, "Final Report on Women Pilot Program," June 1, 1945, Jacqueline Cochran Papers, WASP Series, Box 12, EPL.

126. According to Caro Bosca, Cochran told the WASP going through OCS in Orlando the following: "We were absolutely no use to the Air Corps—they had to keep the manpower on hand anyway—just in case we wanted to resign." As a result, 25 percent of the WASP stationed at Biggs Field resigned. Letter, Caro Bosca to CGB and Capt, August 22, 1944, TWU.

127. Here are a few examples: Inez Woods's and Hazel Ying Lee's friend resigned to get married. Letter, Hazel Ying Lee to Inez Woodward Woods, September 2, 1944, TWU. WASP Anne Chisholm Dessert Oliver resigned to get married. Anne Chisholm Dessert Oliver, interview by Dawn Letson, December 4, 1997, TWU MSS 300. Caro Bosca's friend Sam resigned to get married since the program was ending regardless. Letter, Caro Bosca to Dodie, June 22, 1944, TWU MSS 300.

128. Jacqueline Cochran, "Final Report on Women Pilot Program," June 1, 1945, Jacqueline Cochran Papers, WASP Series, Box 12, EPL. Dorothy Allen had to resign

when her mother became ill. Dorothy Allen, interview by Dawn Letson, December 3, 1997, TWU MSS 300. Inez Woods went home to care for her mother when she heard of the program's disbandment. Inez Woods Papers, TWU.

129. Marjorie Osborne Nicol discussed some WASP she knew who resigned for this reason. Letter, Marjorie Osborne Nicol to her parents, August 11, 1944, TWU.

130. Furthermore, some WASP regretted resigning when asked about it decades after the war. WASP Joanne Wallace Orr felt "childish" that she resigned to get married. She said just thinking about it made her feel "sick," declaring, "[I could have] had a few more hours of flying if I just waited." Joanne Wallace Orr, interview by Jean Hascall Cole, September 16, 1991, TWU MSS 300.

131. Virginia Dulaney Campbell, interview by Jean Hascall Cole, 1989, TWU MSS 300.

132. Series I—USAF Historical Studies, Jacqueline Cochran Papers, Box 15, EPL.

133. Series I—USAF Historical Studies, Jacqueline Cochran Papers, Box 15, EPL.

134. A total of nine WASP were disciplined by being brought in front of an AAF board for a hearing. Jacqueline Cochran, "Final Report on Women Pilot Program," June 1, 1945, Jacqueline Cochran Papers, WASP Series, Box 12, EPL.

135. Cochran mentioned these issues in a 1970 interview, but there is 1940s evidence of one WASP eliminated for drinking as well. Jacqueline Cochran, interview by Lieutenant Colonel Ann R. Johnson, aerospace historian, February 25, 1970, Call #43819, IRIS #01103072, USAF Collection, AFHRA; and Memo, Office of Assistant Secretary for Air to the assistant chief of Air Staff, March 30, 1944, Record Group 18, Army Air Forces, Central Decimal Files Oct 1942–May 1944, Box No. 506, Folder 231.21, Women Pilots, NARA, College Park, MD.

136. Jacqueline Cochran, "Final Report on Women Pilot Program," June 1, 1945, Jacqueline Cochran Papers, WASP Series, Box 12, EPL.

137. Series I—USAF Historical Studies, Jacqueline Cochran Papers, Box 15, EPL.

138. There is some truth to this conclusion, as evidenced by the failed militarization bill in Congress.

139. There are numerous examples of interservice rivalries during the war. For some examples, see Spector, *Eagle against the Sun*; Keegan, *Second World War*; Weigley, *Eisenhower's Lieutenants*; Weigley, *American Way of War*; Atkinson, *Army at Dawn*; Atkinson, *Day at Battle*; Atkinson, *Guns at Last Light*.

140. "History of the WASP Program: Western Flying Training Command, Nov 15, 1943–December 20, 1944," Call #224.072, IRIS #00146374, USAF Collection, AFHRA.

141. "History of Women Airforce Service Pilots Army Air Forces, Eastern Flying Training Command, Inception to Conclusion, Sept 1943–1944," TWU WASP Collection.

142. Florine Phillips Maloney Papers, Coll #05.0141, The Institute on World War II and the Human Experience, Florida State University, Tallahassee.

143. "History of the WASP Program: Western Flying Training Command, Nov 15, 1943–December 20, 1944," Call #224.072, IRIS #00146374, USAF Collection, AFHRA.

144. Series I—USAF Historical Studies, Jacqueline Cochran Papers, Box 15, EPL.

145. "History of the WASP Program: Western Flying Training Command."

146. "History of Women Airforce Service Pilots Army Air Forces, Eastern Flying Training Command, Inception to Conclusion, Sept 1943–1944," TWU WASP Collection.

147. "History of the WASP Program: Western Flying Training Command, Nov 15, 1943–December 20, 1944," Call #224.072, IRIS #00146374, USAF Collection, AFHRA.

148. "History of Women Airforce Service Pilots Army Air Forces, Eastern Flying Training Command."

149. "History of Women Airforce Service Pilots Army Air Forces, Eastern Flying Training Command."

150. "History of the WASP Program: Western Flying Training Command, Nov 15, 1943–December 20, 1944," Call #224.072, IRIS #00146374, USAF Collection, AFHRA.

151. "History of the WASP Program: Western Flying Training Command."

152. This WASP was stationed at Bryan Army Airfield in Bryan, Texas. "History of the WASP Program: Central Flying Training Command," December 1944, Call #223.072 V.1, IRIS #00146288, USAF Collection, AFHRA.

153. Letter, Edward Leefer, senior flight surgeon at Childress Army Airfield (TX) to commanding general at Randolph Field, December 12, 1944, in "History of the WASP Program: Central Flying Training Command."

154. "History of Women Airforce Service Pilots Army Air Forces, Eastern Flying Training Command, Inception to Conclusion, Sept 1943–1944," TWU WASP Collection.

155. Letter, Betty Budde to her parents, July 26, 1943, TWU MSS 300.

156. Dorothy Allen, interview by Dawn Letson, December 3, 1997, TWU MSS 300. There are other instances of male hostility toward the WASP for their relationships with the officers on base. For another example, see Virginia Dulaney Campbell, interview by Jean Hascall Cole, 1989, TWU MSS 300.

157. Teresa James, interview by Dawn Letson, June 16, 1998, TWU MSS 300.

158. "History of the WASP Program: Central Flying Training Command," December 1944, Call #223.072 V.1, IRIS #00146288, USAF Collection, AFHRA.

Chapter 4

1. Catherine Vail Bridge, interview by Dawn Letson, October 27, 2003, TWU MSS 300.

2. Leisa Meyer, *Creating GI Jane*, 14–15.

3. Congress listened to the voices of male CAA-WTS pilots who accused the WASP of holding jobs that they wanted. However, these male War Training Service pilots inaccurately accused the WASP of taking their jobs. Most of the WTS pilots did not qualify.

4. "Songs of Class 44-W-10" to the tune of "Ivan Skavinsky Skavar," *WASP Songbook*, 24, TWU WASP Collection.

5. Cochran and Brinley, *Jackie Cochran*, 204–7.

6. Cochran and Brinley, *Jackie Cochran*, 204–7.

7. Memo, "Appointment of WASP Pilots as AAF Officers," Henry Arnold to George Marshall, January 17, 1944, Henry H. Arnold Collection, Call #MICFILM 43806, IRIS #1102998, USAF Collection, AFHRA.

8. Rickman, *Nancy Love*, 216.

9. Bess Furman, "Army Status Asked for Women Pilots," *New York Times*, August 8, 1944.

10. "Women Fliers Will Seek Benefits Given Veterans," *Dallas Morning News*, February 4, 1946, TWU WASP Collection.

11. Report, Jacqueline Cochran to Commanding General Henry Arnold, August 1, 1944, Jacqueline Cochran Papers, Box 14, EPL.

12. Report, Jacqueline Cochran to Commanding General Henry Arnold, August 1, 1944.

13. Merryman, *Clipped Wings*, 77-78.

14. Report, Jacqueline Cochran to Commanding General Henry Arnold, August 1, 1944.

15. Pisano, *To Fill the Skies with Pilots*, 109.

16. For more on men's draft deferments during World War II, see Rutenberg, *Rough Draft*.

17. Pisano, *To Fill the Skies with Pilots*, 111.

18. "WASP Militarization Favored by Stimson: Women Pilots Deserve Army Status, Secretary Asserts," *New York Times*, May 5, 1944; "Stimson Backs Plan to Place Wasps in Army: Says Putting Women Pilots in Air Forces Will Not Keep Out Qualified Men," *New York Herald Tribune*, Friday, May 5, 1944, WASP Collection, MSS 240c, TWU; "*Contact* Led in the Fight to Defeat the WASP Bill," *Contact*, June 1944, TWU WASP Collection; "House Defeats Bill to Put WASPs in Walking Army: Action Is Taken against Pleas of Military Leaders," *New York Times*, June 22, 1944, TWU WASP Collection.

19. This scenario is similar in some respects to the one Patricia Cooper describes in her study of cigar makers; she argues that divisions in the workplace resulted from gender. However, for the WASP, these male pilots were not ones that they had been working alongside. Many of them did not even meet the qualifications to be military pilots. Cooper, *Once a Cigar Maker*.

20. Committee on Civil Service, Interim Report No. 1600, "Concerning Inquiries Made of Certain Proposals for the Expansion and Change in Civil Service Status of the WASP," June 5, 1944, Jacqueline Cochran Papers, Box 19, EPL.

21. Report, Jacqueline Cochran to Commanding General Henry Arnold, August 1, 1944, Jacqueline Cochran Papers, Box 14, EPL.

22. "Suggested Report to Be Released in Response to Unfavorable Reports to Proposed Militarization of the WASPs, 1943," Jacqueline Cochran Papers, WASP Series, Box 5, Militarization, EPL; "Stimson Backs Plan to Place Wasps in Army: Says Putting Women Pilots in Air Forces Will Not Keep Out Qualified Men," *New York Herald Tribune*, Friday, May 5, 1944, WASP Collection, MSS 240c, TWU.

23. Letter, Henry Stimson to the Honorable Andrew J. May, February 16, 1944, Doris Brinker Tanner Papers, MSS 384, Series 17, TWU.

24. "Address by General H. H. Arnold, Commanding General, Army Air Forces, before WASP Ceremony, Sweetwater, Texas," December 7, 1944, TWU WASP Collection.

25. Jacqueline Cochran, "Final Report on Women Pilot Program," June 1, 1945, Cochran Papers, WASP Series, Box 12, EPL.

26. Hartmann, *Home Front and Beyond*, 37.

27. Leisa Meyer, *Creating GI Jane*, 77.

28. Leisa Meyer, *Creating GI Jane*, 17.

29. Norman, *We Band of Angels*, 272; Myers, "Women behind the Men," 91.

30. Mundy, *Code Girls*; Kiernan, *Girls of Atomic City*.

31. Leisa Meyer, *Creating GI Jane*, 44.

32. Leisa Meyer, *Creating GI Jane*, 38.

33. Hartmann, *Home Front and Beyond*, 175.

34. Merryman, *Clipped Wings*, 55, 62, 74.

35. Landdeck and Merryman emphasize that it was the "only" media attention the WASP received. Landdeck, *Women with Silver Wings*, 193; and Merryman, *Clipped Wings*, 55, 62, 74.

36. Leisa Meyer, *Creating GI Jane*, 17–19.

37. Representative John Costello, interview, June 1, 1971, Henry H. Arnold Collection, Call #MICFILM 43806, IRIS #1102998, USAF Collection, AFHRA.

38. *Congressional Record*, June 21, 1944, 6414.

39. *Congressional Record*, June 21, 1944, 6415.

40. Historian Dominick Pisano argues that when the CAA-WTS programs shut down in 1944, "it was obvious to insiders that the AAF was dissatisfied with the WTS, and that its dissatisfaction had a great deal to do with its decision to end the program." Pisano, *To Fill the Skies with Pilots*, 110.

41. Pisano, *To Fill the Skies with Pilots*, 111.

42. "D.C. Beauty Queen, 3 Others Win Ferry Command Wings," newspaper clipping, TWU WASP Collection.

43. Memo, Hazel Taylor to Colonel Westlake, November 25, 1942, WASP News Releases and Correspondence Collection, Microfilm Reel 4032, Frames 1886–87, AFHRA.

44. "WASP Pilot Proves Good Neighbor Policy," *Dallas Morning News*, Sunday, October 15, 1944; "Wings from a Queen," *Dallas Morning News*, June 12, 1943; "D.C. Beauty Queen, 3 Others Win Ferry Command Wings"; Ralph Habas, "Women Pilots Here Anxious to Join WAFS," *Chicago Sunday Times*, September 13, 1942; Hugh Williamson, "'Lipstick Squadron' Trains in West Texas to Ferry Warplanes," *Houston Post*, April 26, 1943. All in TWU WASP Collection.

45. References to Love included descriptions of her "large blue eyes," "slim, tall, and gracious" figure, and "prematurely-gray" hair. A *Liberty* journalist called Cochran a "chic and indomitable racing flyer." "New Wasps Arrive for Duty with 17th Wing: Four Lady Flyers Added to Bomb Wing Roster for Operational Duty," *Strictly GI* 1, no. 16 (August 26, 1944); Ann France Wilson, "WAFS to Wear Trousers While Ferrying Army Planes," newspaper clipping, September 15, 1942, TWU WASP Collection; Oscar Schisgall, "The Girls Deliver the Goods," newspaper clipping, 1943, TWU WASP Collection; Margaret Kernodle, "Flying Mothers: Hands That Rock the Cradle Now Wield WAF Control Sticks," *Wilmington (DE) Morning News*,

October 23, 1942; Frank J. Taylor, "Our Women Warbirds," *Liberty*, January 29, 1944; "Wings from a Queen," *Dallas Morning News*, June 12, 1943, TWU WASP Collection.

46. "WTS Pilots Also Vote" and "Bill to Commission WASPS as Army Officers Hits Plenty of Snags," *Contact*, May 1944; "Bill to Commission WASPS as Army Officers Killed in House," *Contact*, June 1944; "Some Back Door Breaks for WTS Instructors; WASPS Still Fly," *Contact*, September 1944; "WASPS to Disband on December 20, Says Arnold; Praises Work of Women Pilots," *Contact*, October 1944. All in TWU WASP Collection.

47. "*Contact* Led in the Fight to Defeat the WASP Bill," *Contact*, June 1944, TWU WASP Collection.

48. This political cartoon is similar to those discussing women's suffrage in the early twentieth century. There were fears that when women could vote, they would emasculate or dominate men.

49. "Pictures Male Fliers Doing Wasps' Chores," *New York Times*, June 20, 1944, TWU WASP Collection.

50. Mary Elizabeth McConnell, letter to the editor, "Voices from on High," *Contact*, October 1944, TWU WASP Collection.

51. Drew Pearson, "Washington Merry-Go-Round," *Dallas Morning News*, August 6, 1944, TWU WASP Collection; Granger, *On Final Approach*, 392; Scharr, *Sisters in the Sky*, 2:454, 541.

52. By 1969, Pearson's column was gaining incredible popularity in over 600 newspapers, and he had a readership of around 60 million. Hopkins, "Pearson"; Jim Heintze, "Biography of Drew Pearson," February 9, 2006, www.library .american.edu/pearson/biography.html (site discontinued).

53. Drew Pearson, "Washington Merry-Go-Round," *Dallas Morning News*, August 6, 1944, TWU WASP Collection.

54. Drew Pearson, "Washington Merry-Go-Round," *Dallas Morning News*, March 15, 1944, TWU WASP Collection.

55. Pearson, "Washington Merry-Go-Round," *Dallas Morning News*, March 15, 1944, TWU WASP Collection.

56. Drew Pearson, "Washington Merry-Go-Round," *Dallas Morning News*, August 6, 1944, TWU WASP Collection.

57. At least some WASP heard about his column, and they complained about his inaccurate depictions of their program. Granger, *On Final Approach*, 392; Scharr, *Sisters in the Sky*, 2:454, 541.

58. The CAA-WTS pilots were eligible to be drafted into the army if they did not meet the AAF's pilot qualifications.

59. Barbara E. Poole, "Requiem for the WASP," *Flying*, December 1944, WASP Collection, TWU.

60. "Keep 'Em Flying," *Fort Worth (TX) Star-Telegram*, December 20, 1944; Paul Hunter, "It's Not the Women Who Are Hysterical," *Liberty*, September 23, 1944, TWU WASP Collection.

61. "Recognition for the Wasps," *New York Times*, June 16, 1944, TWU WASP Collection.

62. The emphasis is in the original radio transcript. *Your Radio Hostess*, December 5, 1944; *America on the Air*, "Salute to the WASP," December 9, 1944; Robert St. John, NBC radio broadcast, December 20, 1944, TWU WASP Collection.

63. Scharr, *Sisters in the Sky*, 2:467; Granger, *On Final Approach*, 149; "Ladies Courageous (1944): At Loew's Criterion," *New York Times*, March 16, 1944, TWU WASP Collection.

64. In February 1944, Cochran requested the delay of the film's release for sixty days. WASP (1) note card, Call #222.06, IRIS #146168, USAF Collection, AFHRA.

65. "*New York Times* Reports WASP Shut-Down," *Avenger*, July 14, 1944, TWU WASP Collection.

66. *WASP WWII News Report*, #1 c.1, #2, & #3, *Army-Navy Screen Magazine* #16, produced by the Army Information Branch, Signal Corps, Air Forces, and Navy Department, 1943–44, TWU WASP Collection.

67. "Songs of Class 44-W- (I) 3" to the tune of "You Wanted Wings," *WASP Songbook*, 27, TWU WASP Collection.

68. "Songs of Class 44-W-10" to the tune of "Goin' Back to Where I Come From," *WASP Songbook*, 25, TWU WASP Collection.

69. Mardo Crane, "Just between Us," *WASP Newsletter*, February 1946, TWU WASP Collection.

70. Sherna Berger Gluck illustrates the lives of working-class women during the war through oral history interview excerpts and analysis. Gluck, *Rosie the Riveter Revisited*.

71. Letter, Alberta Paskvan Kinney to Flio, October 10, 1944, and October 12, 1944, TWU MSS 300.

72. Bernice "Bee" Falk Haydu, interview by Dawn Letson and Elizabeth Snapp, September 12, 1992, TWU MSS 300.

73. These are the experiences of WASP Gertrude Meserve Tubbs LeValley and WASP Betty Tackaberry "Tack" Blake, respectively. Turner, *Out of the Blue*, 30, 34.

74. Ethel Meyer Finley, interview by Nancy Durr, September 25, 1998, TWU MSS 300. A significant number of WASP expressed similar sentiments. For some additional examples, see Frances Laraway Smith, interview by Jean Hascall Cole, 1989; and Bonnie J. Dorsey Shinksi, interview by Dawn Letson, October 15, 1994, both in TWU MSS 300.

75. Frances Laraway Smith said, "I just was in quite a lull where I watched the sky and missed it very much." Laraway Smith, interview by Jean Hascall Cole.

76. Catherine Vail Bridge, interview by Dawn Letson, October 27, 2003, TWU MSS 300.

77. Sloan Taylor, "Girl Pilots Train Like Cadets," undated, TWU WASP Collection.

78. Weitekamp, *Right Stuff, Wrong Sex*.

79. Taylor, "Girl Pilots"; Magid, *Women of Courage*.

80. Lee wrote the letter as though Woods was interested in the plan, and although she did not list the names of other WASP who were interested, her wording suggests that there were at least a few others. Letter, Hazel Ying Lee to Inez Woodward Woods, October 27, 1944, TWU.

81. Letter, Lee to Woods, October 27, 1944.

82. Saylor, "Lee, Hazel Ying (1912–1944)."

83. Alan Meyer, *Weekend Pilots*.

84. Letter, Caro Bosca to CGB and Capt, August 9, 1944, TWU.

85. Letter, Transcontinental and Western Air (TWA) to Jeanette Jenkins, March 18, 1945, Jeanette Jenkins Papers, MSS 444, Box 4, TWU.

86. There were around 14,000 women in the CAP after World War II, some of whom were former WASP. Deborah Douglas, *American Women and Flight since 1940*, 137.

87. Juli Chase, "WASPs Demand Benefits," *Maui News*, June 15, 1977, (Virginia) Elaine Jones Papers, MSS 597, TWU.

88. Some of the WASP who were flight instructors are Jean Moore, Betty Thompson, Joan Tebtoske, Jackie Hughes, and Lois Dobbin. Faith Buckner worked in the United Airlines meteorology department and as a Link Trainer operator. Jean Landman was a writer for an aviation magazine. "Former Ferry Pilot in Britain Is Speaker at Fifinella Dinner," *Ponca City (OK) News*, August 26, 1947, Betty F. (Martin) Riddle Papers, MSS 767, TWU.

89. WASP Betty Petitt was a skywriter. Farwell Rhodes Jr., "WASPs, Wartime Women Fliers, Now Mobilizing to Teach Aviation to Girls," *Indianapolis Star*, March 14, 1948, TWU WASP Collection.

90. Nonie Horton held flight records. "Former Ferry Pilot in Britain Is Speaker at Fifinella Dinner."

91. WASP Betty F. Riddle was an aircraft inspector for Douglas. Dean Todd, "Flight Lines," *Rockford (NJ) Register*, November 28, 1959, Betty F. (Martin) Riddle Papers, MSS 767, TWU.

92. Farwell Rhodes Jr., "WASPs, Wartime Women Fliers, Now Mobilizing to Teach Aviation to Girls," *Indianapolis Star*, March 14, 1948, TWU WASP Collection.

93. Joe Park, "City Woman Scores First in Whirlybird," *Oklahoma City Times*, December 29, 1960, TWU WASP Collection.

94. Obituary for Dora Dougherty Strother McKeown, *Dallas Morning News*, November 23, 2013.

95. In Katherine Landdeck's study of over 150 of the WASP, she argues that "many more found other career paths rather than continuing to work in the expensive and male dominated world of aviation." Katherine Elizabeth Sharp Landdeck, "Pushing the Envelope: The Women Airforce Service Pilots and American Society" (PhD diss., University of Tennessee, Knoxville, 2003), vi. For one brief example of a career outside of aviation, WASP Mary Roby Anderson worked in ranching. "Former Ferry Pilot in Britain Is Speaker at Fifinella Dinner," *Ponca City (OK) News*, August 26, 1947, Betty F. (Martin) Riddle Papers, MSS 767, TWU.

96. In a letter home to her parents, WASP Betty Budde remarked that she wanted "to raise horses and have a family" after the war. Letter, Betty Budde to her parents, September 20, 1943, TWU.

97. In 1957, another woman flew in a jet (the Lockheed T-33) and assumed the controls for a portion of the flight. During World War II, Sister Mary Aquinas, a nun and flight instructor, was awarded the honor of flying a jet from the Air Force

Association due to her wartime service teaching at the Catholic University of America. Bob Considine, "'No Glamor Girl,' Flying Nun Says," *Milwaukee (WI) Sentinel,* September 8, 1957.

98. In the postwar period, Carl turned to marriage and a family. Carl, *WASP among Eagles.*

99. Rich, *Jackie Cochran,* and Weitekamp, *Right Stuff, Wrong Sex.*

100. Memo, "Integration of Ex-WASPS in the WAF Program," June 17, 1948, Jacqueline Cochran Papers, WASP Correspondence, Box 19, EPL.

101. The underlined "non-flying" is Cochran's emphasis.

102. Letter, Jaqueline Cochran to Mary Ruth Rance, January 4, 1949, Mary Ruth Rance Papers, MSS 746, TWU.

103. *WASP Newsletter,* April 1950, TWU.

104. Landdeck, *Women with Silver Wings,* 271; Elaine Danforth Harmon, interview by the author, September 1, 2012, digital recording; and Byrd Howell Granger Questionnaire, filled out by Margaret McGlinn Bergh, WASP Collection, Call # K141.33-39, Reel 43102, AFHRA.

105. Harmon, interview.

106. Leroy Ray, "Petticoat Pilot: A WWII Flyer Recalls Duty with the WASP," *Airman,* 1964, TWU WASP Collection.

107. Harmon, interview; Byrd Howell Granger Questionnaire, filled out by Margaret McGlinn Bergh, WASP Collection, Call # K141.33-39, Reel 43102, AFHRA.

Chapter 5

1. Bernice "Bee" Falk Haydu, interview by the Flying Heritage and Combat Armor Museum, September 7, 2006, Portland, OR; group interview of WASP (Helen Wyatt Snapp, Marjorie Popell Sizemore, Doris Elkington Hamaker, Mary Ann Baldner Gordon, Mary Anna "Marty" Martin Wyall) and WAFS Teresa James, interview by Rebecca Wright on behalf of NASA, July 18, 1999, https://historycollection.jsc.nasa.gov/JSCHistoryPortal/history/oral_histories/NASA_HQ/Aviatrix/WASP/WASP_7-18-99.htm.

2. Byrd Howell Granger Questionnaire, filled out by Gini Alleman Disney, Militarization 1977 Supporting Evidence folder, TWU WASP Collection.

3. Mary Anna "Marty" Martin Wyall, interview by the author, December 28, 2009, digital recording, Fort Wayne, IN.

4. Ann Chisholm Dessert Oliver, interview by Dawn Letson, December 4, 1997, TWU MSS 300.

5. Mary Ruth Rance Papers, MSS 746, TWU.

6. "Policy and Status Report of the Order of Fifinella," *WASP Newsletter,* December 20, 1944, TWU WASP Collection.

7. Adaline Alma Blank Scrapbook, 1943–1986, MSS 668c, TWU.

8. Scott, "Veterans and Veterans' Issues," 127.

9. Elaine Danforth Harmon, interview by the author, September 1, 2012, digital recording.

10. Ethel Meyer Finley, interview by Nancy Durr, September 25, 1998, TWU MSS 300.

11. Florene Miller Watson, interview by Dawn Letson, September 7, 2006, TWU MSS 300.

12. *WASP Newsletter*, December 1945, TWU WASP Collection.

13. *WASP Newsletter*, December 1945.

14. "Women Fliers Will Seek Benefits Given Veterans," *Dallas Morning News*, February 4, 1946, TWU WASP Collection.

15. Mary Ruth Rance Papers, MSS 746, TWU.

16. They include WASP Vyvian Williams and Mildred Davidson Dalrymple. *WASP Newsletter*, February 1946, TWU WASP Collection.

17. Maureen Honey's study of World War II propaganda argues that these campaigns portrayed women's wartime work as temporary, domestic, feminine, and self-sacrificial. Honey, *Creating Rosie the Riveter*.

18. Roth, *Her Cold War*, 6, 182–83.

19. Letter, Della Gremling Tissaw to WASP Congressional Hearings Committee, May 28, 1977, WASP Collection, Call #K141.33-39 to K141.33-51, AFHRA.

20. Joanne Wallace Orr, interview by Jean Hascall Cole, September 16, 1991, TWU MSS 300.

21. Karen S. Smith, "War Gave Her Wings," *Spectrum: La Jolla Light*, July 15, 1993, C1, Anne Chisholm Dessert Oliver Papers, TWU WASP Collection.

22. WASP Della Gremling Tissaw remarked that she joined the WASP to help the war effort. She clarified that the WASP program "was not a feminist movement or a Women's Liberation project, in any kind of way." Letter, Della Gremling Tissaw to WASP Congressional Hearings Committee, May 28, 1977, WASP Collection, Call #K141.33-39 to K141.33-51, AFHRA.

23. Enloe, *Does Khaki Become You?*, 220.

24. Charles Whited, "WASP Benefits Long Overdue," *Miami Herald*, April 10, 1977.

25. This statement was from WASP Elaine Jones. Juli Chase, "WASPs Demand Benefits," *Maui News*, June 15, 1977, (Virginia) Elaine Jones Papers, MSS 597, TWU.

26. Thomas J. Brazaitis, "Gates Mills Woman Seeks Veteran Status for WWII Flying Duty," *Plain Dealer* (Cleveland, OH), September 21, 1977, Mary R. Jones Papers, MSS 362, TWU.

27. Ruth Woods, interview by Jean Hascall Cole, 1989, TWU MSS 300; Dorothy Allen, interview by Dawn Letson, December 3, 1997, TWU MSS 300.

28. Roberta Boyd Sandoz Leveaux, interview by Rebecca Wright for the National Aeronautics and Space Administration, March 25, 2000, https://historycollection.jsc.nasa.gov/JSCHistoryPortal/history/oral_histories/NASA_HQ/Aviatrix/LeveauxRBS/LeveauxRBS_3-25-00.pdf.

29. Eileen Shanahan, "Equal Rights Amendment Is Approved by Congress," *New York Times*, March 23, 1972.

30. As he explained, "I have yet to admit my first girl to an academy. I may give in sometime before I am through, but I am not inclined that way." Moreover, Goldwater stated, "I do not think any man wants to see a woman go to combat, but they may be on the verge of it and we will have that fight when that comes along." Senator Barry Goldwater, speaking on S. 247, 95th Congress, 1st sess., *Congressional Record*, October 19, 1977, S34377-78.

31. Letter, Barry Goldwater to Elaine D. Harmon, September 10, 1981, in author's possession.

32. Senator Barry Goldwater, speaking on S. 247, 95th Congress, 1st sess., *Congressional Record*, January 14, 1977, S1183.

33. Senator Williams, speaking on S. 247, 95th Congress, 1st sess., *Congressional Record*, May 26, 1977, S16873.

34. The statement about volunteerism references the 1973 NOW goals. Mittelstadt, *Rise of the Military Welfare State*, 121–29, 133, 139–44.

35. Cobb, *Hello Girls*, 295; Theres, *Hello Girls*.

36. Among the positions listed in the article were a federal judge, an air force colonel, a federal aviation examiner, a golf champion, and a thoroughbred horse breeder. Among the WASP interviewed were Irene McLeahy, Lee Wheelwright, and Patricia Hughes. Paul Fanlund, "After 33 Years WASPs Toast a Victory," November 11, 1977, *Sentinel (Milwaukee, WI)*, in *Congressional Record—Extensions of Remarks*, November 15, 1977, E 6991, IRIS #01037023, USAF Collection, AFHRA.

37. Teresa James, interview by Dawn Letson, June 16, 1998, TWU MSS 300; and Lucile Wise, "Report of WASP Militarization Campaign," *WASP Newsletter*, March 2009, TWU WASP Collection.

38. Margaret McAleer et al., "Patsy T. Mink Papers: A Finding Aid to the Collection in the Library of Congress," Manuscript Division, Library of Congress website, 2007, https://findingaids.loc.gov/exist_collections/ead3pdf/mss/2010/ms010008.pdf; "Mink, Patsy Takemoto," U.S. House of Representatives: History, Art & Archives, accessed March 8, 2023, history.house.gov/People/detail/18329.

39. "Military Credit for WASP Reservists," *WASP Newsletter*, December 1972, TWU WASP Collection.

40. *WASP Newsletter*, December 1976, TWU WASP Collection.

41. The bill was written in 1973. *WASP Newsletter*, December 1973, TWU WASP Collection.

42. Lucile Wise, "Report of WASP Militarization Campaign," *WASP Newsletter*, March 2009, TWU WASP Collection.

43. The navy made this announcement in January 1973. Pat Hunter, "Women Military Pilots Not New to Nation," January 24, 1973, Mary R. Jones Papers, MSS 362, TWU. Hunter's article was published in an unnamed Hawaiian newspaper.

44. Wise, "Report of WASP Militarization Campaign."

45. *WASP Newsletter*, December 1974, TWU WASP Collection.

46. *WASP Newsletter*, November 1975, TWU WASP Collection.

47. *WASP Newsletter*, December 1976, TWU WASP Collection.

48. *WASP Newsletter*, August 1976, TWU WASP Collection.

49. Miller, *Final Flight, Final Fight*, 76–77.

50. *WASP Newsletter*, August 1976, TWU WASP Collection.

51. *WASP Newsletter*, December 1976, TWU WASP Collection.

52. Bernice "Bee" Falk Haydu, *WASP Newsletter*, April 1977, TWU WASP Collection.

53. Haydu, *WASP Newsletter*, April 1977.

54. Haydu, *WASP Newsletter*, April 1977; Associated Press, "Olin E. Teague: Texan in House over 3 Decades," *New York Times*, January 24, 1981, TWU WASP Collection.

55. Associated Press, "Olin E. Teague."

56. Bernice "Bee" Falk Haydu, *WASP Newsletter*, April 1977, TWU WASP Collection.

57. Teague referenced Red Cross workers and USO entertainers, although other groups like the merchant marines had tried unsuccessfully to receive veteran status.

58. Representative Hammerschmidt, speaking on H.R. 71, 94th Congress, 2nd sess., *Congressional Record*, September 14, 1976, H30215.

59. Other military men and women took an oath when they enlisted. For example, the WAVES took an oath. Marjorie Sue Green, USNR, "From Recruit to Salty Wave! The Ordeal of Seaman Green," 1944, Dorothy "Jane" Marshman Fredrickson Papers, Acc #07.0117, The Institute on World War II and the Human Experience, Florida State University, Tallahassee.

60. This regulation stated, "WASP personnel will wear the prescribed uniform at all times except: a. When on leave in excess of four days spent away from base, b. when in own home with not more than three guests present in addition to members of family, c. after duty hours within confines of quarters, d. when attending mixed social gatherings at which evening or dinner clothes are required, in which case evening or dinner clothes may be worn." U.S. Army Airforces Regulation 40-9, February 14, 1944, 3, http://www.wingsacrossamerica.us/wasp /documents/uniform_regulation.pdf.

61. 43-W-1 to 43-W-3 Classbook, TWU WASP Collection; Evidence in Militarization Box, Byrd Howell Granger Papers, MSS 265, TWU.

62. Senate Resolution 1810, House and Senate Resolutions and Other Reports folder, TWU WASP Collection.

63. Helen Fremd presented "Restricted Aircraft Delivery" memos with details about firearms that she was issued when delivering a P-40N and P-51B. "Restricted Aircraft Delivery Memorandums," Evidence in Militarization Box, Byrd Howell Granger Papers, MSS 265, TWU.

64. There was no organized plan for handing out these certificates to women pilots, so some bases issued them to the WASP when the program disbanded, and others did not. Patricia Hughes, "11 Bills Pending for Veterans Status," *Stars and Stripes*, September 1, 1977.

65. Numerous sources mention this story. Natalie Stewart-Smith wrote her master's thesis on the WASP program, and in the process of her research, she interviewed Colonel Bruce Arnold in September 1978. During that interview, Arnold explained that he and the other WASP were sitting in a place where they could see Teague pull out his certificate and express a look of "amazement." Stewart-Smith, "Women Airforce Service Pilots." Historian Deborah Douglas also briefly mentions this story in her book. Douglas, *American Women and Flight since 1940*, 193–94.

66. This was question seventeen on her questionnaire. Evidence in Militarization Box, Byrd Howell Granger Papers, MSS 265, TWU.

67. Kathryn Fine and Hazel Hohn used this exact quote: "I thought of myself as part of the military." Evidence in Militarization Box, Byrd Howell Granger Papers, MSS 2655, TWU. Others were issued a .45 automatic because they were delivering "classified equipment." Adela Riek Scharr had a memo receipt for the issue of a .45 automatic, holster, and extra magazines to her. "A. R. Scharr's Memo Receipt for Pistol—.45, Holster, and Magazine (Extra)," Evidence in Militarization Box, Byrd Howell Granger Papers, MSS 265, TWU.

68. Beryl Owens Paschich's questionnaire answer, Evidence in Militarization Box, Byrd Howell Granger Papers, MSS 265, TWU

69. These responses were all in the questionnaires that Granger sent. Evidence in Militarization Box, Byrd Howell Granger Papers, MSS 265, TWU

70. Boulton, "Price on Patriotism," 243–44.

71. Senator Barry Goldwater, speaking on S. 247, 95th Congress, 1st sess., *Congressional Record*, October 19, 1977, S34375; the Honorable Newton I. Steers Jr., 95th Congress, 1st sess., *Congressional Record*, October 5, 1977, H32581.

72. Historian John Kinder argues that "war's cost in money, bodies, minds, and memory is far more substantial than most would imagine." Kinder, *Paying with Their Bodies*, 11.

73. WASP Pearl Judd told a journalist that she had been thinking "for years" that she wanted a funeral service with an American flag draped on her casket. Sue Manning, "Former Lady Pilot Seeks Earned Veteran Status," *Daily Report*, June 12, 1977, Mary R. Jones Papers, MSS 362, TWU.

74. WASP Mary Jones had a copy of this pamphlet. Mary R. Jones Papers, MSS 362, TWU.

75. "Maggie Wilson's Album," *Arizona Women's Forum*, June 24, 1977, Mary R. Jones Papers, MSS 362, TWU.

76. Bernice "Bee" Falk Haydu, *WASP Newsletter*, April 1977, TWU WASP Collection; and Mary R. Jones Papers, MSS 362, TWU.

77. WASP Dorothy Davis gathered these signatures. Lucile Wise, "Report of WASP Militarization Campaign," *WASP Newsletter*, March 2009, TWU WASP Collection.

78. Turner, *Out of the Blue*.

79. These same veterans organizations also excluded Vietnam veterans.

80. Historian Stephen R. Ortiz argues that it is essential to remember that veterans are not a "monolithic power bloc" in their activism and politics. Ortiz, *Veterans' Policies, Veterans' Politics*, 3.

81. As male veterans returned from Vietnam, they found that some of their wives had participated in the women's liberation movement. Zaretsky, *No Direction Home*, 5, 25.

82. Statement of William B. Gardiner, national director of legislation, Disabled American Veterans before the Select Subcommittee on the WASPs of the House Committee on Veterans' Affairs, September 20, 1977, Series 5: Militarization/Legislation, Box 1, TWU WASP Collection.

83. *WASP Newsletter*, December 1976, TWU WASP Collection.

84. Statement of Dorothy L. Starbuck, chief benefits director, Department of Veterans Benefits, Veterans Administration, before the Senate Committee on Veterans' Affairs, May 25, 1977, Series 5: Militarization/Legislation, Box 1, TWU WASP Collection.

85. Statement of the American Legion by Edward Lord (assistant director, National Legislative Commission) and Robert Lynch (deputy director, National Veterans Affairs and Rehabilitation Commission) to the Committee on Veterans' Affairs, United States Senate, May 25, 1977, Doris Brinker Tanner Papers, MSS 384, Series 17, TWU; "To Provide Recognition to the Women's Air Force Service Pilots for Their Service during World War II by Deeming Such Service to Have Been Active Duty in the Armed Forces of the United States for Purposes of Laws Administered by the Veterans Administration," Hearing before a Subcommittee of the Committee on Veterans' Affairs, House of Representatives, 95th Congress, 1st sess., *Congressional Record*, September 20, 1977, H445.

86. Kerber, *No Constitutional Right*, xxiv.

87. Statement of the American Legion by Edward Lord and Robert Lynch to the Committee on Veterans' Affairs, United States Senate, May 25, 1977; "To Provide Recognition," H445.

88. The memory of war has often been gendered male, as evidenced in works such as Little, *Abraham in Arms*; Purcell, *Sealed with Blood*; Alfred Young, *Masquerade*; and Zagarri, *Revolutionary Backlash*.

89. "To Provide Recognition," H450.

90. Ortiz, *Beyond the Bonus March*.

91. Bernice "Bee" Falk Haydu, *WASP Newsletter*, April 1977, TWU WASP Collection.

92. Post Commander Sam C. Nailling Jr., Milton Talley Post No. 20 American Legion, Union City, Tennessee, Resolution No. 1, 1977, "Support for Women's Air Force Service Pilots (WASP) Benefits," Doris Brinker Tanner Papers, MSS 384, Series 17, TWU.

93. Letter, Colonel Bruce Arnold to Betty Jo Reed, B. J. Williams, Charlene Creger, and Doris Tanner, August 8, 1977, Doris Brinker Tanner Papers, MSS 384, Series 17, TWU.

94. For one example, see Patricia Hughes, "11 Bills Pending for Veterans Status," *Stars and Stripes*, September 1, 1977.

95. In the postwar period, the WASP were also allowed to join a veterans group, the American Veterans League, although this organization eventually dissolved. Doris Brinker Tanner Papers, MSS 384, Series 17, TWU; *WASP Newsletter*, December 1945, TWU WASP Collection.

96. Letter, Deputy Secretary of Defense Charles W. Duncan Jr. to acting director of Office of Management and Budget James T. McIntyre Jr., October 21, 1977. This letter is located in the congressional record: "To Provide Recognition to the Women's Air Force Service Pilots for Their Service during World War II by Deeming Such Service to Have Been Active Duty in the Armed Forces of the United States for Purposes of Laws Administered by the Veterans Administration," Hearing before

a Subcommittee of the Committee on Veterans' Affairs, House of Representatives, 95th Congress, 1st sess., *Congressional Record*, September 20, 1977, H453.

97. "To Provide Recognition," H451.

98. "To Provide Recognition," H452.

99. Senator Williams, speaking on S. 247, 95th Congress, 1st sess., *Congressional Record*, May 26, 1977, S16873.

100. His statements are part of a report on the Subcommittee on Priorities and Economy in Government of the Joint Economic Committee, which held hearings to discuss women in combat. Senator Proxmire, speaking on S. 247, 95th Congress, 1st sess., *Congressional Record*, September 24, 1977, S30776.

101. Senator Hathaway, speaking on S. 334, 94th Congress, 1st sess., *Congressional Record*, 1975, S 1021.

102. Letter, Colonel Bruce Arnold to Betty Jo Reed, B. J. Williams, Charlene Creger, and Doris Tanner, August 8, 1977, Doris Brinker Tanner Papers, MSS 384, Series 17, TWU.

103. Letter, Veterans Administration to Dorothy Ebersback, August 24, 1979, Dorothy Ebersback Papers, MSS 318c, TWU.

104. Betty Cross, *WASP Newsletter*, December 1977, TWU WASP Collection.

105. Dawn Seymour, interview by Rebecca Wright on behalf of NASA, July 19, 1999, https://historycollection.jsc.nasa.gov/JSCHistoryPortal/history/oral_histories/NASA_HQ/Aviatrix/WASP/WASP_7-18-99.htm.

106. Patricia Collins Hughes, "Hallelujah! WASPs Are Veterans at Last!" *Stars and Stripes*, December 1, 1977; Adaline Alma Blank Scrapbook, 1943–1986, MSS 668c, TWU.

107. Barbara "BJ" Erickson London, interview by Sarah Rickman, March 17 and 19, 2004, TWU MSS 300.

108. Juanita W. Cooke, interview by John Terreo, May 8, 1991, Montana Historical Society, Helena, MT, https://www.mtmemory.org/nodes/view/90318.

109. For the Women's Army Auxiliary Corps, veteran status applied to women who served in this unit and were honorably discharged before the updated Women's Army Corps received active-duty status from Congress in July 1943. These women did not receive overseas pay or equivalent pay and benefits to male officers of the same rank due to their auxiliary status. Vuic, "Gender, the Military, and War," 204; Leisa Meyer, *Creating GI Jane*, Hampf, *Release a Man for Combat*.

110. Adler calls Public Law 95-202 a "major public victory" and argues that additional "scholarly attention and analysis" is needed to understand its implications and ramifications fully. Adler, "To Recognize Those Who Served," 317.

111. G.I. Bill Improvement Act of 1977, Public Law 95-202, *U.S. Statutes at Large* 91 (1977): 1449–50.

112. Adler, "To Recognize Those Who Served," 307, 317. Historian and attorney Bruce Cohen argues that the Special Immigrant Visa program connected with the 2021 evacuation of Afghanistan is "a philosophical heir" to this decision based around the service of the WASP. Bruce Cohen, email message to the author, September 1, 2021.

113. Miller, *Final Flight, Final Fight*, 81.

114. Title IV: Women's Air Forces Service Pilots, Public Law 95-202, *U.S. Statutes at Large* 91 (1977): 1449.

115. When WASP Elaine Harmon testified before a congressional subcommittee about her issues with the OPM, she noted that other WASP were denied retirement. Harmon received multiple letters from the OPM, some stating that she was eligible and others stating the opposite. "Implementation of Title IV of Public Law 95-202, Relating to WASPS and Similarly Situated Groups: Hearing before the Subcommittee on Oversight and Investigations of the Committee on Veterans' Affairs," House of Representatives, 97th Congress, 1st sess., *Congressional Record*, September 29, 1981, H9–H10, H23–H25; Miller, *Final Flight, Final Fight*, 81–82.

116. Letter, Deputy Director of Personnel Dayle D. Marshall to Lieutenant Colonel Dora J. Strother, USAFR Retired, July 20, 1981; letter, Deputy Director of Personnel Dayle D. Marshall to Lieutenant Colone Jeanne L. McSheehy, USAFR Retired, September 24, 1979, "Implementation of Title IV of Public Law 95-202, Relating to WASPS and Similarly Situated Groups," H28–H29.

117. One of the materials submitted for the record was a statement by WASP Patricia Collins Hughes. She argued, "What has not been precise in the interpretation of the terminology of the word veteran . . . has led to continued discrimination" against them. Statement of WASP Patricia Collins Hughes before the House Committee on Veterans' Affairs Subcommittee on Oversight and Investigations, House of Representatives, 97th Congress, 1st sess., *Congressional Record*, September 29, 1981, H33, Series 5: Militarization/Legislation, Box 1, TWU WASP Collection.

Epilogue

1. F-35 pilot Lieutenant Colonel Christine Mau is the first woman attributed with saying "Flying is the ultimate equalizer." She made this comment in a statement released by the air force in 2015. Lieutenant Colonel Mau spoke at the 2016 WASP reunion. "Christine Mau Becomes First U.S. Female Pilot to Fly F-35 Lightning II Jet," *NBC News*, May 7, 2015, https://www.nbcnews.com/news/us-news/christine-mau-becomes-first-female-pilot-fly-f-35-lightning-n355101.

2. "Lockheed Martin's First Female F-35 Production and Training Pilot Takes Flight," *F-35 Lightning II*, June 28, 2021, https://www.f35.com/f35/news-and-features/lockheed-martins-first-female-f35-production-and-training-pilot-takes-flight.html.

3. Memorandum for assistant secretary of the army, "Military Honors at Arlington National Cemetery (ANC) for Active Duty Designees—Decision Memorandum," May 28, 2002, Fifinella.com, http://www.fifinella.com/2002memo.pdf; Julie I. Englund, "First-Rate, Second-Class," *Washington Post*, May 12, 2002.

4. Miller, *Final Flight, Final Fight*, 86.

5. Memorandum for executive director, army national military cemeteries, "Inurnment Eligibility of Active Duty Designees at Arlington National Cemetery (ANC)," March 23, 2015, Fifinella.com, http://www.fifinella.com/anc_mar23memo.pdf.

6. Miller, *Final Flight, Final Fight*, 87.

7. Miller, *Final Flight, Final Fight*, 112–18.

8. Andrea N. Goldstein, "No One Understands Us," 4.

9. Andrea N. Goldstein, "No One Understands Us," 3–4.

10. There are consequences for women who do not self-identify, as it can "hinder reintegration and have detrimental health outcomes, including high rates of suicide and homelessness among women veterans." Andrea N. Goldstein, "No One Understands Us," 14–17.

11. For one of the numerous examples of recent interviews, see transcript of "The WASPs: Women Pilots of WWII," produced by Joe Richman, Radio Diaries Inc., broadcast on *All Things Considered*, NPR, December 18, 2002, https://www .npr.org/2002/12/18/881741/from-radio-diaries-an-oral-history-of-the-wasps.

12. Author's audio recording of May 2010 reunion.

13. One of the programs from Cochran's funeral is in the Hazel Stamper Hohn Papers, MSS 863, TWU.

14. Caroline Jensen, WASP reunion luncheon, May 25, 2013, Sweetwater, TX.

15. Elaine Danforth Harmon, interview by the author, September 1, 2012, digital recording.

16. When asked at WASP reunions in Sweetwater, Texas, from 2009 to 2014, most say without hesitation that the AT-6 was their favorite plane to pilot.

17. Jean Hascall Cole discussed B-26 demonstrations in an interview she was conducting with Virginia Dulaney Campbell. Virginia Dulaney Campbell, interview by Jean Hascall Cole, 1989, TWU MSS 300.

18. The two women hired in 1973 were Emily Warner and Bonnie Tiburzi. Corn, *Winged Gospel*, 80; Deborah Douglas, *American Women and Flight since 1940*, 176, 217.

19. There were 26,854 women out of a total of 469,062 pilots with any license, including for private, commercial, or airline transportation. Federal Aviation Administration, "2020 Active Civil Airmen Statistics," Federal Aviation Administration website, https://www.faa.gov/data_research/aviation_data _statistics/civil_airmen_statistics/.

20. In 1985, 1.55 percent of all military pilots were women, and that number grew to 1.8 percent by 1990. Deborah Douglas, *American Women and Flight since 1940*, 205; Amy McCullough, "Erasing Artificial Barriers," *Air Force Magazine*, November 1, 2020, https://www.airforcemag.com/article/erasing-artificial -barriers/.

21. At the start of the all-volunteer force in 1973, women formed 2 percent of enlisted forces and 8 percent of the officer corps. Council on Foreign Relations, "Demographics of the U.S. Military," Council on Foreign Relations website, July 13, 2020, https://www.cfr.org/backgrounder/demographics-us-military.

22. "2020 Active Civil Airmen Statistics," Federal Aviation Administration website, https://www.faa.gov/data_research/aviation_data_statistics/civil_airmen _statistics/.

23. Kathy McCullough said this happened while flying flights from Korea to the United States. Francine Knowles, "Women with Wings: Female Pilots Still Rare in the Air," *Chicago Sun-Times*, August 15, 2014.

24. Knowles, "Women with Wings."

25. Weitekamp, *Right Stuff, Wrong Sex*, 2; Deborah Douglas, *American Women and Flight since 1940*, 201.

26. Michael Ryan, "A Ride in Space," *People Magazine*, June 20, 1983, 83.

27. Weitekamp argues that the first women's space program "reveals how aerospace medicine, cultural politics, and gender relations intersected" beginning in the 1960s and led to the "development of the United States' manned space program." Weitekamp, *Right Stuff, Wrong Sex*, 5.

28. In June 2021, the Supreme Court refused a case that would have challenged the constitutionality of women's exemption from registering for the selective service, an obligation of citizenship for men. Kara Dixon Vuic, "Registering Women for the Draft Wouldn't Be a Big Departure from the Past," *Washington Post*, April 14, 2021; Kara Dixon Vuic, "A Faulty Court Precedent on Selective Service Leaves the Last Legal Sex Discrimination in Place," History News Network, July 4, 2021, https://historynewsnetwork.org/article/180611.

29. Bristol and Stur, *Integrating the US Military*, 219.

30. Grohowski, "Moving Words, Words That Move," 121–30; Herbert, *Camouflage Isn't Only for Combat*, 5, 13, 22.

31. Williams, *Love My Rifle*.

32. Bailey, *America's Army*; Roth, "Attractive Career for Women."

33. *Report of the Fort Hood Independent Review Committee*, November 6, 2020, https://www.army.mil/e2/downloads/rv7/forthoodreview/2020-12-03_FHIRC _report_redacted.pdf.

34. Hope Hodge Seck, "After Outcry from Female Vets in Congress, Pentagon Revives Committee on Women in Service," Military.com, September 2, 2021, https://www.military.com/daily-news/2021/09/02/after-outcry-female-vets -congress-pentagon-revives-committee-women-service.html.

35. Over the last decades, 98 percent of recommendations from the DACOWITS have been "fully or partially implemented." Tanya L. Roth, "Axing the Committee That Studies and Advocates for Servicewomen Is a Mistake," *Washington Post*, July 16, 2021; Patricia Kime, "Female Vets in Congress Decry Proposal to Disband Pentagon's Advisory Panel on Women," Military.com, July 6, 2021, https://www .military.com/daily-news/2021/07/06/female-vets-congress-decry-proposal -disband-pentagons-advisory-panel-women.html.

36. Devon Suits, "Army Announces New Grooming Appearance Standards," *Army News Service*, January 27, 2021, https://www.army.mil/article/242536 /army_announces_new_grooming_appearance_standards; Defense Advisory Committee on Women in the Services, *2020 Annual Report*, https://dacowits .defense.gov/Portals/48/Documents/Reports/2020/Annual%20Report /DACOWITS%202020%20Annual%20Report%20WEB.pdf.

37. US Army Public Affairs, "Army Authorizes Female Soldiers Ponytails in All Uniforms," May 6, 2021,

38. https://www.army.mil/article/246037/army_authorizes_female_soldiers _ponytails_in_all_uniforms.

39. In 2010, the navy lifted its ban on women serving on submarines. Cameron

Stoner, "Women in Submarines: 10 Years Later," press release, America's Navy, June 25, 2021, https://www.navy.mil/Press-Office/News-Stories/Article/2671640/women-in-submarines-10-years-later/.

40. Combat pilot positions opened to women in 1994. Deborah Douglas, *American Women and Flight since 1940*, 233.

41. Lieutenant Colonel Kate Wilder graduated from Special Forces training when she was a captain in the army in August 1980. However, she did not join the Green Berets, likely due to discrimination from her superiors. Thomas Gibbons-Neff, "First Woman Joins Green Berets after Graduating from Special Forces Training," *New York Times*, July 9, 2020; James Sandy, "A War All Our Own: American Rangers and the Emergence of the American Martial Culture," PhD diss., (Texas Tech University, 2016), 250–51.

Bibliography

PRIMARY SOURCES
Archives
Air Force Historical Research Agency, Maxwell Air Force Base, Montgomery, AL
    Foster Field TX Collection
    Henry H. Arnold Collection
    N. F. Parrish Collection
    USAF Collection
    WASP Collection
    WASP News Releases and Correspondence Collection
Eisenhower Presidential Library, Abilene, KS
    Jacqueline Cochran Papers
    Oral Histories
The Institute on World War II and the Human Experience, Florida State University, Tallahassee
    Dorothy "Jane" Marshman Fredrickson Papers
    Florine Phillips Maloney Papers
    Ruby J. Henderson Humer Papers
Keirn Family World War II Museum, Saint Francis University, Loretto, PA
Library of Congress, Washington, DC
    Mildred Darlene Tuttle Axton Collection
    Nell S. Stevenson Bright Collection
    Veterans History Project
National Archives and Records Administration, College Park, MD
    Record Group 18, Army Air Forces
National Archives and Records Administration, Washington, DC
    Record Group 80, General Correspondence of the Office of the Secretary of the Navy
Smithsonian National Air and Space Museum Archives, Stephen F. Udvar-Hazy Center, Chantilly, VA
    Betty Skelton Collection
    Blanche Stuart Scott Collection
    Louise McPhetridge Thaden Collection
    Manila Davis Talley Collection
    Mary Charles Collection
    Moisant Family Scrapbooks
    The Ninety-Nines Inc. History Books Collection
    United States Women in Aviation through World War I Collection

Texas Woman's University, Denton
    Woman's Collection, Texas Woman's University Libraries
    Women Airforce Service Pilots Official Archive
    Adaline Blank Correspondence
    Anne Chisholm Dessert Oliver Papers
    Betty F. (Martin) Riddle Papers
    Byrd Howell Granger Papers
    Doris Brinker Tanner Papers
    Dorothea Johnson Moorman Papers
    Dorothy Ebersback Papers
    Hazel Stamper Hohn Papers
    Inez Woods Papers
    Jeanette Jenkins Papers
    Lucile Doll Wise Papers
    Marjorie Selfridge Dresbach Papers
    Mary R. Jones Papers
    Mary Ruth Rance Papers
    MSS 250: Women Airforce Service Pilots of World War II Collection
    MSS 300: Oral Histories and Letters
    Teresa D. James Papers
    (Virginia) Elaine Jones Papers

Books

Bragg, Janet Harmon. *Soaring above Setbacks: The Autobiography of Janet Harmon Bragg, African American Aviator, as told to Marjorie M. Kriz*. Washington, DC: Smithsonian Institution Press, 1996.

Carl, Ann B. *A WASP among Eagles: A Woman Military Test Pilot in World War II*. Washington, DC: Smithsonian Institution Press, 1999.

Clark, Marie Mountain. *Dear Mother and Daddy: World War II Letters Home from a WASP*. Livonia, MI: First Page, 2005.

Cochran, Jacqueline, and Floyd Odlum. *The Stars at Noon*. Boston: Little, Brown, 1954.

Cochran, Jacqueline, and Maryann Bucknum Brinley. *Jackie Cochran: The Autobiography of the Greatest Woman Pilot in Aviation History*. New York: Bantam, 1987.

Cole, Jean Hascall. *Women Pilots of World War II*. Salt Lake City: University of Utah Press, 1992.

Dahl, Roald. *The Gremlins*. Milwaukie, OR: Dark Horse Books, 1943.

Earhart, Amelia. *The Fun of It: Random Records of My Own Flying and of Women in Aviation*. Chicago: Academy Chicago Publishers, 1932.

Getz, C. W. "Bill," ed. *The Wild Blue Yonder: Songs of the Air Force*. San Mateo, CA: Redwood Press, 1981.

Granger, Byrd Howell. *On Final Approach: The Women Airforce Service Pilots of W.W.II*. Scottsdale, AZ: Falconer, 1991.

Haydu, Bernice "Bee" Falk. *Letters Home, 1944–1945*. Riviera Beach, FL: TopLine, 2003.

Hunter, Lawrence. *The Flying Prostitute*. Lincoln, NE: Writers Club Press, 2000.

Parrish, Nancy Allyson. *WASP in Their Own Words: An Illustrated History*. Waco, TX: Wings Across America, 2010.

Powell, William J. *Black Wings*. Los Angeles: Haynes Corporation, 1934.

Reitsch, Hanna. *The Sky My Kingdom: Memoirs of the Famous German World War II Test Pilot*. Drexel Hill, PA: Casemate, 2009.

Scharr, Adela Riek. *Sisters in the Sky*. Vol. 1, *The WAFS*. Gerald, MO: Patrice Press, 1986.

———. *Sisters in the Sky*. Vol. 2, *The WASP*. St. Louis, MO: Patrice Press, 1988.

Smith, Truman. *The Wrong Stuff: The Adventures and Misadventures of an 8th Air Force Aviator*. Norman: University of Oklahoma Press, 2002.

Strohfus, Elizabeth, and Cheryl Young. *Love at First Flight: One Woman's Experience as a WASP in World War II . . . and Fifty Years Later, She's Still Flying*. St. Cloud, MN: North Star Press, 1994.

Tanner, Doris Brinker. *Who Were the WASP? A World War II Record*. Sweetwater, TX: Sweetwater Reporter, 1989.

———. *Zoot-Suits and Parachutes and Wings of Silver, Too! The World War II Air Force Training of Women Pilots: 1942–1944*. Paducah, KY: Turner Publishing Company, 1996.

Tibbets, Paul. *The Tibbets Story*. New York: Stein and Day, 1978.

Tunner, William H. *Over the Hump*. New York: Duell, Sloan, and Pearce, 1964.

Turner, Betty Stagg. *Out of the Blue and into History: Women Airforce Service Pilots, WWII*. Arlington Heights, IL: Aviatrix Publishing, 2001.

Wood, Winifred. *We Were WASPs*. Coral Gables, FL: Glade House, 1945.

Government Documents

Congressional Record
Investigation of Civilian Employment
U.S. Statutes at Large

Newspapers/Magazines

Air Force
Atlanta Journal
Charm
Chicago Daily Tribune
Chicago Defender
Chicago Sunday Times
Christian Science Monitor
Civil Air Patrol Volunteer
Colorado Springs Evening Telegraph
Constitution Sunday Supplement
  (Atlanta, GA)
Contact
Curtiss Fly Leaf
Daily Report
Dallas Morning News
Fort Worth (TX) Star-Telegram
Flying Magazine
Great Falls (MT) Tribune
Harrisburg (PA) Telegraph
Houston Chronicle
Houston Post
Houston Press

Hudson (NJ) Dispatch
Independent Woman
Indianapolis Star
Ladies' Home Journal
Liberty
Life
Look
Martin Star
McCall's
Montgomery (AL) Advertiser
National Aeronautics
New York Herald Tribune
New York Post
New York Times
New York Times Magazine
New York World Telegraph
Newark Evening News
Newark Sunday Call
Oklahoma City Times
Pennsylvania Leader

Pictorial Review
Plainview (TX) Herald
Popular Aviation and Aeronautics
Rockford (NJ) Register
Saturday Evening Post
Sentinel (Milwaukee, WI)
Service Woman
Skyline
Skyways Magazine
Stars and Stripes
Strictly GI
Time
Tulsa (OK) World
Victory
Vox Prop
Washington Post
Wilmington (DE) Morning News
Witchita (KS) Daily Times
Woman's Home Companion

SECONDARY SOURCES
Books, Journal Articles, Essays, and Films

Adams, Michael C. C. *The Best War Ever: America and World War II*. Baltimore: Johns Hopkins University Press, 1994.

Adler, Jessica L. *Burdens of War: Creating the United States Veterans Health System*. Baltimore: Johns Hopkins University Press, 2017.

———. "To Recognize Those Who Served: Gendered Analyses of Veterans' Policies, Representations, and Experiences." In *The Routledge History of Gender, War, and the U.S. Military*, edited by Kara Dixon Vuic, 303-22. New York: Routledge, 2017.

Anderson, Benedict R. *Imagined Communities: Reflections on the Origin and Spread of Nationalism*. London: Verso, 1983.

Anderson, Kathryn, and Dana C. Jack. "Learning to Listen: Interview Techniques and Analyses." In *Women's Words: The Feminist Practice of Oral History*, edited by Sherna Berger Gluck and Daphne Patai, 11-25. Routledge: 1991.

Andrews, Thomas. *Killing for Coal: America's Deadliest Labor War*. Cambridge, MA: Harvard University Press, 2008.

Atkinson, Rick. *An Army at Dawn: The War in North Africa, 1942-1943*. New York: Henry Holt, 2002.

———. *The Day at Battle: The War in Sicily and Italy, 1943-1944*. New York: Henry Holt, 2007.

———. *The Guns at Last Light: The War in Western Europe, 1944-1945*. New York: Henry Holt, 2013.

Bailey, Beth. *America's Army: Making the All-Volunteer Force.* Cambridge, MA: Harvard University Press, 2009.

Barry, Kathleen. *Femininity in Flight: A History of Flight Attendants.* Durham, NC: Duke University Press, 2002.

Benson, Susan Porter. *Counter Cultures: Saleswomen, Managers, and Customers in American Department Stores, 1890-1940.* Urbana: University of Illinois Press, 1986.

Bérubé, Allan. *Coming Out Under Fire: Gay Men and Women in World War II.* New York: Free Press, 1990.

Blanton, DeAnne, and Lauren Cook. *They Fought like Demons: Women Soldiers in the American Civil War.* Baton Rouge: Louisiana State University Press, 2002.

Bogdan, Robert. *Freak Show: Presenting Human Oddities for Amusement and Profit.* Chicago: University of Chicago Press, 1988.

Bonn, Mark C., and Christine Seibert Bonn, dirs. *Wings of Silver: The Vi Cowden Story.* Hermosa Beach, CA: My Monkey House Productions, 2010.

Boulton, Mark. "A Price on Patriotism: The Politics and Unintended Consequences of the 1966 G.I. Bill." In *Veterans' Policies, Veterans' Politics: New Perspectives on Veterans in the Modern United States,* edited by Stephen R. Ortiz, 241-62. Gainesville: University Press of Florida, 2012.

Bristol, Douglas Walter, Jr., and Heather Marie Stur, ed. *Integrating the US Military: Race, Gender, and Sexual Orientation since World War II.* Baltimore: Johns Hopkins University Press, 2017.

Brooks-Pazmany, Kathleen. *United States Women in Aviation, 1919-1929.* Washington, DC: Smithsonian Institution Press, 1983.

Campbell, D'Ann. *Women at War with America: Private Lives in a Patriotic Era.* Cambridge, MA: Harvard University Press, 1984.

———. "Women in Combat: The World War II Experience in the United States, Great Britain, Germany, and the Soviet Union." *Journal of Military History* 57, no. 2 (April 1993): 301-23.

Canaday, Margot. *The Straight State: Sexuality and Citizenship in Twentieth-Century America.* Princeton, NJ: Princeton University Press, 2009.

Cándida-Smith, Richard. "Analytic Strategies for Oral History Interviews." In *Handbook of Interview Research,* edited by Jaber F. Gubrium and James A. Holstein, 711-31. Thousand Oaks, CA: SAGE, 2002.

Chafe, William. *The American Woman: Her Changing Social, Economic, and Political Roles, 1920-1970.* London: Oxford University Press, 1974.

Chauncey, George. *Gay New York: Gender, Urban Culture and the Makings of the Gay Male World, 1890-1940.* New York: Basic Books, 1994.

Cobb, Elizabeth. *The Hello Girls: America's First Women Soldiers.* Cambridge, MA: Harvard University Press, 2017.

Cooper, Patricia. *Once a Cigar Maker: Men, Women, and Work Culture in American Cigar Factories, 1900-1919.* Urbana: University of Illinois Press: 1992.

Corn, Joseph J. *The Winged Gospel: America's Romance with Aviation.* New York: Oxford University Press, 1983.

Cott, Nancy. *The Grounding of Modern Feminism*. New Haven, CT: Yale University Press, 1989.

Craven, Wesley Frank, and James Lea Cate. *The Army Air Forces in World War II*. Vol. 6, *Men and Planes*. Chicago: University of Chicago Press, 1955.

Daddis, Gregory A. *Pulp Vietnam: War and Gender in Cold War Men's Adventure Magazines*. New York: Cambridge University Press, 2020.

DeGrott, Gerard J., and Corinna Peniston-Bird, eds. *A Soldier and a Woman: Sexual Integration in the Military*. Harlow, UK: Pearson Education, 2000.

Delano, Page Dougherty. "Making Up for War: Sexuality and Citizenship in Wartime Culture." *Feminist Studies* 26, no. 1 (Spring 2000): 33–68.

Douglas, Deborah. *American Women and Flight since 1940*. Lexington: University Press of Kentucky, 2004.

Douglas, Mary. *Purity and Danger: An Analysis of Concepts of Pollution and Taboo*. London: Routledge, 1966.

Douhet, Guilio. *The Command of the Air*. Translated by Dino Ferrari. Washington, DC: Air Force History and Museums Program, 1998.

Dower, John. *War without Mercy: Race and Power in the Pacific War*. New York: Pantheon, 1987.

Dumenil, Lynn. *The Second Line of Defense: American Women and World War I*. Chapel Hill: University of North Carolina Press, 2017.

Enloe, Cynthia. *Does Khaki Become You? The Militarisation of Women's Lives*. Boston: South End Press, 1983.

——. *Globalization and Militarism: Feminists Make the Link*. Lanham, MD: Rowman and Littlefield, 2007.

——. *Maneuvers: The International Politics of Militarizing Women's Lives*. Berkeley: University of California Press, 2000.

Estes, Steve. *I Am a Man! Race, Manhood, and the Civil Rights Movement*. Chapel Hill: University of North Carolina Press, 2005.

Focşa, Daniel. "The White Squadron." Translated by Ancuţa Gălice. Bucharest Airports website, November 26, 2014. https://www.bucharestairports.ro/cnab/en//aviation-history/the-white-squadron.

Frisch, Michael. *A Shared Authority: Essays on the Craft and Meaning of Oral and Public History*. Albany: State University of New York Press, 1990.

Gluck, Sherna Berger. *Rosie the Riveter Revisited: Women, the War and Social Change*. New York: Meridian, 1987.

Goldstein, Andrea N. "No One Understands Us: Mapping Experiences of Women in the U.S. Military." In *Invisible Veterans: What Happens When Military Women Become Civilians Again*, edited by Kate Hendricks Thomas and Kyleanne Hunter, 3–21. Santa Barbara, CA: ABC-CLIO, 2019.

Goldstein, Joshua S. *War and Gender: How Gender Shapes the War System and Vice Versa*. New York: Cambridge University Press, 2001.

González, Roberto J., Hugh Gusterson, and Gustaff Houtman, eds. *Militarization: A Reader*. Durham, NC: Duke University Press: 2019.

Grohowski, Mariana. "Moving Words, Words That Move: Language Practices Plaguing U.S. Servicewomen." *Women and Language* 37, no. 1 (2014): 121–30.

Grossman, David. *On Killing: The Psychological Cost of Learning to Kill in War and Society*. Boston: Little, Brown, 1995.

Gubert, Betty Kaplan, Mirian Sawyer, and Caroline M. Fannin. *Distinguished African Americans in Aviation and Space Science*. Westport, CT: Oryx, 2002.

Hacker, Barton C. "Where Have All the Women Gone? The Pre-Twentieth Century Sexual Division of Labor in Armies." *Minerva* 3, no. 1 (Spring 1985): 107–48.

Hampf, Michaela. *Release a Man for Combat: The Women's Army Corps during World War II*. Köln: Böhlau Verlag Köln, 2010.

Hankins, Michael W. *Flying Camelot: The F-15, the F-16, and the Weaponization of Fighter Pilot Nostalgia*. Ithaca, NY: Cornell University Press, 2021.

Hartmann, Susan. *The Home Front and Beyond: American Women in the 1940s*. New York: Twayne, 1995.

Haynesworth, Leslie, and David Toomey. *Amelia Earhart's Daughters: The Wild And Glorious Story of American Women Aviators from World War II to the Dawn of the Space Age*. New York: William Morrow Paperbacks, 2000.

Hegarty, Marilyn E. *Victory Girls, Khaki-Wackies, and Patriotutes: The Regulation of Female Sexuality during World War II*. New York: New York University Press, 2008.

Herbert, Melissa S. *Camouflage Isn't Only for Combat: Gender, Sexuality, and Women in the Military*. New York: New York University Press, 1998.

Higonnet, Margaret Randolph, Jane Jensen, Sonya Michel, and Margaret Collins Weitz, eds. *Behind the Lines: Gender and the Two World Wars*. New Haven, CT: Yale University Press, 1987.

Higonnet Margaret R., and Patrice L.-R. Higonnet. "The Double Helix." In *Behind the Lines: Gender and the Two World Wars*, edited by Margaret Randolph Higonnet, Jane Jensen, Sonya Michel, and Margaret Collins Weitz, 31–48. New Haven, CT: Yale University Press, 1987.

Honey, Maureen. *Bitter Fruit: African American Women in World War II*. Columbia: University of Missouri, 1999.

———. *Creating Rosie the Riveter: Class, Gender, and Propaganda during World War II*. Amherst: University of Massachusetts Press, 1984.

Hopkins, W. Wat. "Pearson." In *Biographical Dictionary of American Journalism*, edited by Joseph P. McKerns. Westport, CT: Greenwood, 1989.

Huebner, Andrew. "Gee! I Wish I Were a Man: Gender and the Great War." In *The Routledge History of Gender, War, and the U.S. Military*, edited by Kara Dixon Vuic, 68–86. New York: Routledge, 2017.

Hunter, Lawrence. *The Flying Prostitute*. Lincoln, NE: Writers Club Press, 2000.

Hurley, Alfred. *Billy Mitchell: Crusader for Air Power*. Bloomington: Indiana University Press, 2006.

Johnson, M. Houston. *Taking Flight: The Foundations of American Commercial Aviation, 1918–1938*. College Station: Texas A&M University Press, 2019.

Kasson, John. *Houdini, Tarzan, and the Perfect Man: The White Male Body and the Challenge of Modernity in America*. New York: Hill and Wang, 2002.

Keegan, John. *The Second World War*. New York: Viking, 1990.

Keil, Sally Van Wagenen. *Those Wonderful Women in Their Flying Machines*. New York: Rawson, Wade, 1979.

Kelley, Robin D. G. *Race Rebels: Culture, Politics, and the Black Working Class*. New York: Free Press, 1994.

Kerber, Linda K. *No Constitutional Right to Be Ladies: Women and the Obligations of Citizenship*. New York: Hill and Wang, 1998.

Kieran, David, and Edwin A. Martini, eds. *At War: The Military and American Culture in the Twentieth Century and Beyond*. New Brunswick, NJ: Rutgers University Press, 2018.

Kiernan, Denise. *The Girls of Atomic City: The Untold Story of the Women Who Helped Win World War II*. New York: Touchstone Books, 2013.

Kinder, John. "The Embodiment of War: Bodies for, in, and after War." In *At War: The Military and American Culture in the Twentieth Century and Beyond*, edited by David Kieran and Edwin A. Martini, 217–39. New Brunswick, NJ: Rutgers University Press, 2018.

———. *Paying with Their Bodies: American War and the Problem of the Disabled Veteran*. Chicago: University of Chicago Press, 2015.

Kindsvatter, Peter. *American Soldiers: Ground Combat in the World Wars, Korea, and Vietnam*. Lawrence: University Press of Kansas, 2003.

Knaff, Donna. *Beyond Rosie the Riveter: Women of World War II in American Popular Graphic Art*. Lawrence: University Press of Kansas, 2012.

Kohn, Richard H. "The Danger of Militarization in an Endless 'War' on Terrorism." *Journal of Military History* 73, no. 1 (January 2009): 177–208.

Ladevich, Laurel, dir. *Fly Girls*. Boston, MA: Silverlining Productions and WGBH Boston, 1999.

Landdeck, Katherine Sharp. *The Women with Silver Wings: The Inspiring True Story of the Women Airforce Service Pilots of World War II*. New York: Crown, 2020.

Larson, Mary A. "Research Design and Strategies." In *History of Oral History: Foundations and Methodology*, edited by Thomas Lee Charlton, Lois E. Myers, and Rebecca Sharpless, 98–99. Lanham, MD: Rowman and Littlefield, 2007.

Lemay, Kate Clarke, ed. *Votes for Women: A Portrait of Persistence*. Princeton, NJ: Princeton University Press, 2019.

Lentz-Smith, Adriane. *Freedom Struggles: African Americans and World War I*. Cambridge, MA: Harvard University Press, 2009.

Light, Jennifer. "Programming." In *Gender and Technology: A Reader*, edited by Nina E. Lehrman, Ruth Oldenziel, and Arwen P. Mohun, 295–328. Baltimore: John Hopkins University Press, 2003.

Little, Ann M. *Abraham in Arms: War and Gender in Colonial New England*. Philadelphia: University of Pennsylvania Press, 2007.

Lutz, Catherine. "Making War at Home in the United States: Militarization and the Current Crisis." *American Anthropologist* 104, no. 3 (2002): 723–35.

MacKenzie, S. P. *Flying against Fate: Superstition and Allied Aircrews in World War II*. Lawrence: University Press of Kansas, 2017.

Mackin, Elton E. *Suddenly We Didn't Want to Die: Memoirs of a World War I Marine*. Novato, CA: Presidio Press, 1993.

MacLean, Nancy. "The Hidden History of Affirmative Action: Working Women's Struggles in the 1970s and the Gender of Class." In *No Permanent Waves:*

Recasting Histories of U.S. Feminism, edited by Nancy Hewitt, 356–78. New Brunswick, NJ: Rutgers University Press, 2010.

Magid, Ken, dir. *Women of Courage of World War II*. Lakewood, CO: Km Productions, 1993.

Marshall, S. L. A. *Men against Fire: The Problem of Battle Command*. Norman: University of Oklahoma Press, 1947.

Marten, James. *America's Corporal: James Tanner in War and Peace*. Athens: University of Georgia Press, 2014.

Mathers, Jennifer G. "Women and State Military Forces." In *Women and Wars*, edited by Carol Cohn, 124–45. Malden, MA: Polity Press, 2013.

Matthews, Mark. *Smoke Jumping on the Western Fire Line: Conscientious Objectors during World War II*. Norman: University of Oklahoma Press, 2006.

May, Elaine Tyler. *Homeward Bound: American Families in the Cold War Era*. New York: Basic Books, 1988.

McEuen, Melissa A. *Making War, Making Women: Femininity and Duty on the American Home Front, 1941–1945*. Athens: University of Georgia Press, 2011.

McManus, John C. *Deadly Sky: The American Combat Airman in World War II*. New York: Penguin, 2016.

McPherson, James M. *For Cause and Comrades: Why Men Fought in the Civil War*. New York: Oxford University Press, 1997.

Melosh, Barbara. *"The Physician's Hand": Work Culture and Conflict in American Nursing*. Philadelphia: Temple University Press, 1982.

Merryman, Molly. *Clipped Wings: The Rise and Fall of the Women Airforce Service Pilots (WASP) of World War II*. New York: New York University Press, 1998.

Meyer, Alan. *Weekend Pilots: Technology, Masculinity, and Private Aviation in Postwar America*. Baltimore: Johns Hopkins University Press, 2015.

Meyer, Leisa. *Creating GI Jane: Sexuality and Power in the Women's Army Corps during World War II*. New York: Columbia University Press, 1996.

Milam, Ron. *Not a Gentleman's War: An Inside View of Junior Officers in the Vietnam War*. Chapel Hill: University of North Carolina Press, 2009.

Milkman, Ruth. *Gender at Work: The Dynamics of Job Segregation by Sex during World War II*. Urbana: University of Illinois Press, 1987.

Miller, Erin. *Final Flight, Final Fight: My Grandmother, the WASP, and Arlington National Cemetery*. Silver Spring, MD: 4336 Press, 2019.

Mittelstadt, Jennifer. *The Rise of the Military Welfare State*. Cambridge, MA: Harvard University Press, 2015.

Moore, Brenda. *Serving Our Country: Japanese American Women in the Military during World War II*. New Brunswick, NJ: Rutgers University Press, 2003.

———. *To Serve My Country, to Serve My Race: The Story of the Only African-American WACS Stationed Overseas during World War II*. New York: New York University Press, 1997.

Morrissey, Charles T. "The Two-Sentence Format as an Interviewing Technique in Oral History Fieldwork." *Oral History Review* 15 (Spring 1987): 43–53.

Moye, J. Todd. *Freedom Flyers: The Tuskegee Airmen of World War II*. Oxford: Oxford University Press, 2010.

Mundy, Liza. *Code Girls: The Untold Story of the American Women Code Breakers of World War II.* New York: Hachette Books, 2017.

Myers, Sarah Parry. "Women Airforce Service Pilots (WASP)." In *An Encyclopedia of American Women at War: From the Home Front to the Battlefields*, edited by Lisa Tendrich Frank, 610–13. Santa Barbara, CA: ABC-CLIO, 2013.

———. "'The Women behind the Men behind the Gun': Gendered Identities and Militarization in the Second World War." In *The Routledge History of Gender, War, and the U.S. Military*, edited by Kara Dixon Vuic, 87–102. New York: Routledge, 2017.

Noakes, Lucy. *Dying for the Nation: Death, Grief and Bereavement in Second World War Britain.* Manchester: Manchester University Press, 2020.

Noakes, Lucy, Claire Langhamer, and Claudia Siebrecht, eds. *Total War: An Emotional History.* Oxford: Oxford University Press, 2020.

Norman, Elizabeth M. *We Band of Angels: The Untold Story of American Nurses Trapped on Bataan by the Japanese.* New York: Pocket Books, 1999.

O'Connell, Aaron B. *Underdogs: The Making of the Modern Marine Corps.* Cambridge, MA: Harvard University Press, 2012.

Oldenziel, Ruth. *Making Technology Masculine: Men, Women, and Modern Machines in America, 1870–1945.* Amsterdam: Amsterdam University Press, 1999.

Oliver, Kelly. *Women as Weapons of War: Iraq, Sex, and the Media.* New York: Columbia University Press, 2007.

Ortiz, Stephen R. *Beyond the Bonus March and G.I. Bill: How Veteran Politics Shaped the New Deal Era.* New York: New York University Press, 2010.

———. *Veterans' Policies, Veterans' Politics: New Perspectives on Veterans in the Modern United States.* Gainesville: University Press of Florida, 2012.

Peiss, Kathy. *Zoot Suit: The Enigmatic Career of an Extreme Style.* Philadelphia: University of Pennsylvania Press, 2011.

Peniston-Bird, Corinna, and Emma Vickers, eds. *Gender and the Second World War: Lessons of War.* Houndsmills, UK: Palgrave Macmillan, 2017.

Pennington, Reina. *Wings, Women, and War: Soviet Airwomen in World War II Combat.* Lawrence: University Press of Kansas, 2001.

Pfau, Ann Elizabeth. *Miss Yourlovin: GIs, Gender, and Domesticity during World War II.* New York: Columbia University Press, 2008. http://www.gutenberg-e.org/pfau/.

Phillips, Kimberley L. "'All I Wanted Was a Steady Job': The State and African American Workers." In *New Working-Class Studies*, edited by John Russo and Sherry Lee Linkon, 42–54. Ithaca, NY: Cornell University Press, 2005.

———. *War! What Is It Good For? Freedom Struggles and the U.S. Military from World War II to Iraq.* Chapel Hill: University of North Carolina Press, 2012.

Piehler, G. Kurt. *Remembering War the American Way.* Washington, DC: Smithsonian Institution Press, 2014.

Pisano, Dominick. *To Fill the Skies with Pilots: The Civilian Pilot Training Program, 1939–1946.* Washington, DC: Smithsonian Institution Press, 2001.

Pitt, Jorden. "'Ceasing to Be of Value': Flying Fatigue and Social Deviancy in the Second World War." Presentation, Eighty-Seventh Society for Military History Annual Meeting, Norfolk, VA, May 21, 2021.

Planck, Charles E. *Women with Wings*. New York: Harper and Brothers, 1942.

Purcell, Sarah. *Sealed with Blood: War, Sacrifice, and Memory in Revolutionary America*. Philadelphia: University of Pennsylvania Press, 2002.

Rich, Doris L. *Jackie Cochran: Pilot in the Fastest Lane*. Gainesville: University Press of Florida, 2007.

Rickman, Sarah Byrn. *Nancy Love and the WASP Ferry Pilots of World War II*. Denton: University of North Texas Press, 2008.

Roberts, Mary Louise. *Sheer Misery: Soldiers in Battle in WWII*. Chicago: University of Chicago Press, 2021.

Roediger, David R. *Wages of Whiteness: Race and the Making of the American Working Class*. New York: Verso, 1991.

Rosenberg, Alan. H., dir. *"A Brief Flight": Hazel Ying Lee and the Women Who Flew Pursuit*. Pacific Palisades, CA: LAWAS Films Productions, 2003.

Roth, Tanya. "'An Attractive Career for Women': Opportunities, Limitations, and Women's Integration in the Cold War Military." In *Integrating the US Military: Race, Gender, and Sexual Orientation since World War II*, edited by Douglas Walter Bristol Jr. and Heather Marie Stur, 74–95. Baltimore: Johns Hopkins University Press, 2017.

———. *Her Cold War: Women in the U.S. Military, 1945–1980*. Chapel Hill: University of North Carolina Press, 2021.

Rupp, Leila. *Mobilizing Women for War: German and American Propaganda, 1939–1945*. Princeton, NJ: Princeton University Press, 1978.

Rutenberg, Amy J. *Rough Draft: Cold War Military Manpower Policy and the Origins of Vietnam-Era Draft Resistance*. Ithaca, NY: Cornell University Press, 2019.

Sambaluk, Nicholas Michael. *The Other Space Race: Eisenhower and the Quest for Aerospace Security*. Annapolis, MD: Naval Institute Press, 2015.

Saylor, Thomas. "Lee, Hazel Ying (1912–1944)." In *An Encyclopedia of American Women at War: From the Home Front to the Battlefields*, edited by Lisa Tendrich Frank, 358–60. . Santa Barbara, CA: ABC-CLIO, 2013.

Scharff, Virginia. *Taking the Wheel: Women and the Coming of the Motor Age*. New York: Free Press, 1991.

Schrader, Helena. *Sisters in Arms: British and American Women Pilots during World War II*. Barnsley, UK: Pen and Sword, 2006.

Scott, Wilbur. "Veterans and Veterans' Issues." In *At War: The Military and American Culture in the Twentieth Century and Beyond*, edited by David Kieran and Edwin A. Martini, 127–46. New Brunswick, NJ: Rutgers University Press, 2018.

Sherry, Michael S. *In the Shadow of War: The United States since the 1930s*. New Haven, CT: Yale University Press, 1995.

———. *The Rise of American Air Power: The Creation of Armageddon*. New Haven, CT: Yale University Press, 1987.

Shopes, Linda. "Oral History and the Study of Communities: Problems, Paradoxes, and Possibilities." *Journal of American History* 89, no. 2 (September 2002): 588–98.

Simbeck, Rob. *Daughter of the Air: The Brief Soaring Life of Cornelia Fort*. New York: Atlantic Monthly Press, 1999.

Sjoberg, Laura. *Gender, War, and Conflict*. Malden, MA: Polity Press, 2014.

Slim, Hugo, and Paul Thompson. "Ways of Listening." In *The Oral History Reader*, edited by Robert Perks and Alistair Thomson, 114–25. London: Routledge, 1998.

Spector, Ronald. *Eagle against the Sun: The American War with Japan*. New York: Free Press, 1985.

Stallman, David A. *Women in the Wild Blue . . . Target-Towing WASP at Camp Davis*. Sugarcreek, OH: Carlisle Printing, 2006.

Stremlow, Mary V. *Free a Marine to Fight: Women Marines in World War II*. Washington, DC: Marine Corps Historical Center, 1994.

Stur, Heather Marie. "Men's and Women's Liberation: Challenging Military Culture after the Vietnam War." In *Integrating the US Military: Race, Gender, and Sexual Orientation since World War II*, edited by Douglas Walter Bristol Jr. and Heather Marie Stur, 142–66. Baltimore: Johns Hopkins University Press, 2017.

Summerfield, Penny. "Oral History as an Autobiographical Practice." *Miranda* 12 (February 2016): 1–14.

Summerfield, Penny, and Corinna Peniston-Bird. *Contesting Home Defense: Men, Women and the Home Guard in the Second World War*. Manchester: Manchester University Press, 2007.

Takaki, Ronald. *Double Victory: A Multicultural History of America in World War II*. New York: Little, Brown, 2000.

Theres, James, dir. *The Hello Girls*. Lincoln Penny Films, 2018.

Thomason, Alistair. "Four Paradigm Transformations in Oral History." *Oral History Review* 34 (2007): 49–70.

Tiemeyer, Phil. *Plane Queer: Labor, Sexuality, and AIDS in the History of Male Flight Attendants*. Berkeley: University of California Press, 2013.

Truxal, Luke. "The Politics of Operational Planning: Ira Eaker and the Combined Bomber Offensive in 1943." *Journal of Military Aviation History* 1 (2017): 1–22.

Van Vleck, Jenifer. *Empire of the Air: Aviation and the American Ascendency*. Cambridge, MA: Harvard University Press, 2013.

Vuic, Kara Dixon. "Gender, the Military, and War." In *At War: The Military and American Culture in the Twentieth Century and Beyond*, edited by David Kieran and Edwin A. Martini, 195–216. New Brunswick, NJ: Rutgers University Press, 2018.

———. *The Girls Next Door: Bringing the Home Front to the Front Lines*. Cambridge, MA: Harvard University Press, 2019.

———. *Officer, Nurse, Woman: The Army Nurse Corps in the Vietnam War*. Baltimore: Johns Hopkins University Press, 2010.

———, ed. *The Routledge History of Gender, War, and the U.S. Military*. New York: Routledge, 2017.

Walck, Pamela E., and Ashley Walter. "Soaring Out of the Private Sphere: How Flyin' Jenny and Comics Helped Pioneer a New Path for Women's Work during World War II." *Journalism History* 44, no. 4 (2019): 195–206.

Walker, Nancy A., ed. *Women's Magazines, 1940–1960: Gender Roles and the Popular Press*. Boston: Bedford St. Martin's, 1998.

Ware, Susan. *Still Missing: Amelia Earhart and the Search for Modern Feminism*. New York: W. W. Norton, 1993.

Weber, Rachel. "Manufacturing Gender in Commercial Military Cockpit Design." *Science, Technology, and Human Values* 22, no. 2 (Spring 1997): 235–53.

Weigley, Russell. *The American Way of War: A History of U.S. Military Strategy and Policy*. New York: MacMillan, 1973.

———. *Eisenhower's Lieutenants: The Campaign of France and Germany, 1944–1945*. Bloomington: Indiana University Press, 1981.

Weinbaum, Alys Eve, Lynn M. Thomas, Priti Ramamurthy, Uta G. Poiger, and Madeleine Yue Dong. *The Modern Girl around the World: Consumption, Modernity, and Globalization*. Durham, NC: Duke University Press, 2008.

Weitekamp, Margaret. A. *Right Stuff, Wrong Sex: America's First Women in Space Program*. Baltimore: Johns Hopkins University Press, 2004.

Westbrook, Robert B. "'I Want a Girl, Just Like the Girl That Married Harry James': American Women and the Problem of Political Obligation in World War II." *American Quarterly* 42, no. 4 (December 1990): 588–611.

Williams, Kayla. *Love My Rifle More Than You: Young and Female in the U.S. Army*. New York: W. W. Norton, 2005.

Wolk, Bruce H. *Jewish Aviators in World War II: Personal Narratives of American Men and Women*. Jefferson, NC: McFarland, 2016.

Young, Alfred. *Masquerade: The Life and Times of Deborah Sampson, Continental Soldier*. New York: Knopf, 2004.

Young, Cheryl J. *Love at First Flight: One Woman's Experience as a WASP in World War II*. St. Cloud, MN: North Star, 1994.

Yow, Valerie. "'Do I Like Them Too Much?' Effects of the Oral History Interview on the Interviewer and Vice-Versa." *Oral History Review* (Summer 1997): 55–79.

Zagarri, Rosemarie. *Revolutionary Backlash: Women and Politics in the Early American Republic*. Philadelphia: University of Pennsylvania Press, 2007.

Zegenhagen, Evelyn. "German Women Pilots at War, 1939 to 1945." *Air Power History* 56 no. 4 (Winter 2009): 12.

———. "'The Holy Desire to Serve the Poor and Tortured Fatherland': German Women Motor Pilots of the Inter-War Era and Their Political Mission." *German Studies Review* 30, no. 3 (2007): 579–96.

Zaretsky, Natasha. *No Direction Home: The American Family and the Fear of National Decline, 1968–1980*. Chapel Hill: University of North Carolina Press, 2007.

Dissertations and Master's Theses

Gibson, Emily K. "The Flag: Gender and the Projection of National Progress through Global Air Travel, 1920–1960." PhD diss., Georgia Institute of Technology, 2017.

Landdeck, Katherine Elizabeth Sharp. "Pushing the Envelope: The Women Airforce Service Pilots and American Society." PhD diss., University of Tennessee, Knoxville, 2003.

Sandy, James. "A War All Our Own: American Rangers and the Emergence of the American Martial Culture." PhD diss., Texas Tech University, 2016.

Stewart-Smith, Natalie Jeanne. "The Women Airforce Service Pilots (WASP) of World War II: Perspectives on the Work of America's First Military Women Aviators." Master's thesis, Washington State University, 1981.

Index

CPTP (Civilian Pilot Training Program).
   See Civilian Pilot Training Program

DACOWITS (Defense Advisory Committee on Women in the Services),
   160–61, 225n35
dating, 76, 80, 105, 108–9
DAV (Disabled American Veterans),
   148, 151
Deaton, Leoti, 77
Defense Advisory Committee on
   Women in the Services (DACOW-
   ITS), 160–61, 225n35
Disabled American Veterans (DAV),
   148, 151
discrimination: gender, 16, 82, 96,
   141–43, 152, 226n41; race, 21, 46–49,
   171n40, 185n181; sexuality, 55,
   173n71
Disney, Gini Alleman, 137, 140, 156
Double V Campaign, 7, 45

Earhart, Amelia, 11, 21–22, 25–26
Eastern Flying Training Command, 95,
   107–8, 208n123
Eaton, Bob, 151
Equal Rights Amendment (ERA), 141–43
ERA (Equal Rights Amendment), 141–43

femininity and military service: femininity as disruption, 13–14, 101–2,
   123, 126–27, 171n39; and morality
   standards, 54; as motivation for
   men's service, 173n69; and physical appearance, 11, 57–58, 61, 125,
   172n54; and public fears, 51; white,
   middle-class conception of, 44, 55;
   women's construction of, 160
feminism: second-wave, 16–17, 135–36,
   140–43, 147–48, 150, 153, 220n81;
   women's views on, 26, 140–43, 148,
   171n41, 178n65
ferrying. *See* assignments
Ferrying Division, 35–36, 100, 104, 106,
   122

Fifinella: as mascot, 65; Order of, 136,
   137–39, 145
Fifinella Gazette, 65, 69, 157
Finley, Ethel, 28, 96
flight instructors
—men: interactions with WASPs, 56,
   76; job loss after CPTP, 4, 15, 121,
   125–27, 134; Link Trainer instructors,
   62; response to female pilots, 1, 77;
   WASP trainees' experiences with,
   69–73, 77–79
—women: as CPTP instructors, 31;
   postwar jobs as instructors, 133, 139;
   WASP assignments as instructors,
   94–96, 131; WASP trainees' experiences with, 69–73, 77; work before
   World War II, 17, 22
flying demonstrations, 93–94, 159
Fort, Cornelia, 17, 39
funerals. *See* benefits

Gee, Maggie, 47–48, 76
gender ideals. *See* femininity and mili-
   tary service
Gillies, Betty, 85, 134
Goldwater, Barry, 141–42, 144–45, 155,
   217n30
Gough, V. Scott Bradley, 28
Granger, Byrd Howell, 146–47
Great Depression, 1, 18, 28, 30–31, 40, 49
grief, 5, 71–72, 130–31
Gunderson, Eleanor "Gundy," 64

Harmon, Elaine Danforth, 31, 41, 56, 134,
   138, 155, 157–58
Haydu, Bernice "Bee" Falk, 28, 48, 136
Heckler, Margaret, 151
heroism: associated with protection,
   7; disrupted by WASPs, 13, 15, 83,
   104, 106–7, 109, 144; perception as
   male, 6, 9, 38, 102; and self-sacrifice
   in women, 101, 172n54, 207n110; and
   type of service, 8, 13, 38, 149; of veteran organization, 16, 137, 153
Hobby, Oveta Culp, 55, 119, 123–25

homosexuality, 55, 173n71. *See also* lesbians
House Resolution 3321, 148
House Resolution 3358, 120
House Resolution 4219, 120–22
House Resolution 6595, 144
House Resolution 15035, 143

international women pilots: Germany, 2–3, 29, 34, 172n65, 177n44, 179n91; Romania, 2–3, 29; Soviet Union, 2, 29, 99

James, Teresa, 17–18, 24, 27, 42, 85, 109, 143
Jensen, Caroline, 157–58
jet aviation: women's experiences, 133, 156, 215n97; women's exclusion from, 16, 119, 131, 135, 171n47
Jewish Americans, 45, 48, 186n198
Jones, Elaine, 132
Judd, Pearl Brummett, 23

Ladies Courageous (film), 129
Lawrence, Kathryn "Kay," 71–72
Lee, Hazel Ying, 48, 132
lesbians: fears of, 55–57; serving in the WASP, 57; stereotype of servicewomen as, 54–55; government regulation of, 55, 173n71
Lewis, Dorothy "Dot" Swain, 158
Life (magazine), 57
Lindbergh, Charles, 25–26
London, Barbara "BJ" Erickson, 40, 178n72
Love, Nancy Harkness: as advocate of women's aviation, 2, 14, 18, 33–35, 84; background, 28, 32–33; experience in the China-Burma-India theater, 99–100; leadership style of, 33; relationship with the media, 36; and WAFS uniform design, 60
Lyngh, Robert, 149–52

makeup, 11, 23, 55–56, 58, 133, 161
Marine Corps Women's Reserve, 4, 40–41, 44, 58, 119, 122
Mau, Christine, 156
McKeown, Dora Dougherty Strother, 94, 133
McIntyre, Dorothy Lane, 46
McSally, Martha, 157
media
—coverage of early female aviators, 25–26
—coverage of the WASP program, 38, 160–61; and AAF censorship, 53, 56–57, 89; emphasis on feminine ideals, 51, 58, 102, 126; and gendered portrayal of military women, 10, 44, 55, 60, 101, 123; during militarization bill debates, 15, 118, 124–29, 141; portrayal of the WASP program as glamorous, 66, 109, 127, 129
memory of war, 4, 8–9, 101, 150, 171n53, 207n108, 221n88
Merchant Marines, 2, 8, 219n57
Mexican Air Force, 95, 204n74, 204n75
militarization. *See* congressional militarization bills
military academies. *See* service academies
military service: as career opportunity, 13, 101, 131, 134, 141, 143; as citizenship obligation (*see* citizenship through military service)
Mink, Patsy, 143–44
Minton, Madge Rutherford, 48
Moorman, Dorothea Johnson, 94
Moses, Beverly Jean, 3
motivations: for military service, 2, 5, 7, 9–10, 14, 38–39, 41, 130; pinups as, 10–11; for veterans' benefits, 137, 144
music. *See* songs

NASA (National Aeronautics and Space Administration), 131–33, 159
National Aeronautics and Space Administration (NASA), 131–33, 159

Teague, Olin "Tiger," 145–48
test piloting, 2–3, 15, 82–83, 87, 90–91, 101, 133
Tibbets, Paul, 94
Tunner, William H., 104–5, 122
Tuskegee Airmen, 45–46, 49, 95

uniforms: as form of identity, 15, 62, 81, 137, 151; regulations, 59–61, 64, 69, 98, 146, 190n63; controversy over, 11, 15, 51, 54–55, 61, 81
United States Coast Guard Women's Reserve (SPARS), 4, 41, 44, 58, 119, 123, 168n8
US Office of War Information, 53

Veterans Administration (VA), 142, 144–46, 148–49, 151, 153–54
Veterans of Foreign Wars, 148–51

WAC (Women's Army Corps), 44, 100, 123; admittance of women of color, 45, 47; and militarization, 4, 119–20, 123; regulation of sexuality, 55; rumors about, 5, 9, 55; uniforms, 60–61
WAFS (Women's Auxiliary Ferrying Squadron), 56, 98, 134; expansion of roles, 83–84; formation of, 2, 35–36, 43; and formation of the WASP program, 4, 18; media coverage of, 36, 53, 129; uniforms, 60; work culture of, 85
War Department Bureau of Public Relations (WDBPR), 37, 51, 53
Watson, Florene Miller, 27, 41
WAVES (Women Accepted for Voluntary Emergency Service), 4, 33, 40–41, 44, 55, 58, 119, 122–23
WDBPR (War Department Bureau of Public Relations), 37, 51, 53
weapons training, 98
Western Flying Training Command, 94, 106–7
WFTD (Women's Flying Training Detachment), 2, 4, 18, 35, 37–38, 43

whiteness: claims to citizenship, 7, 172n53; field of aviation, 21, 23–24; passing as white, 6, 10, 44, 47–49, 190n59; protection of white women, 9, 37, 101. See also discrimination: race; Mexican Air Force
Women Accepted for Voluntary Emergency Service (WAVES), 4, 33, 40–41, 44, 55, 58, 119, 122–23
Women's Armed Services Integration Act, 160
Women's Army Corps. See WAC (Women's Army Corps)
Women's Auxiliary Ferrying Squadron. See WAFS (Women's Auxiliary Ferrying Squadron)
Women's Flying Training Detachment (WFTD), 2, 4, 18, 35, 37–38, 43
women's liberation movement. See feminism
Women Marines, 4, 40–41, 44, 58, 119, 122
women of color: Chicana or Hispanic, 44; Chinese American, 44–46, 47–48; Native American, 23, 41, 44–45, 47–48
women pilots in other countries. See international women pilots
women's work, nontraditional, 11, 39, 41–42, 54, 56, 122–23
work culture: at AAF bases, 15, 81, 83, 85–86, 105; of army wives, 142; of flight attendants, 12, 173n78; of the Marine Corps, 168n13, 174n83; of the military, 6, 9, 156, 160; of military men, 67; of training, 13, 51–53, 65, 67; of women in other professions, 174n81
Wright brothers, 19
Wyall, Mary Anna "Marty" Martin, 42, 137

Yonally, Lillian Lorraine, 50
Yount, Barton K., 66, 69, 95, 193n104

Printed in the USA
CPSIA information can be obtained
at www.ICGtesting.com
LVHW042320301023
762228LV00039B/66